"This book looks at the curious, wonderful vocational work of God through the lenses of the four gospels. Pastors will surely find new meaning in their vocations and new enthusiasm for their work by reading Richard Burridge's wise, encouraging book."

Will Willimon
Duke Divinity School

"In *Four Ministries, One Jesus*, Burridge brings to bear both his academic expertise and his ministerial experience on four aspects of life-in-ministry, namely, teaching, pastoral ministry, suffering, and praying. By exploring these ministerial duties in concert with the Evangelists' variegated, mutually reinforcing portraits of Jesus, Burridge helps all who minister, whether ordained or not, to do so with a clearer vision of and greater fidelity to the One who came teaching and doing good. I warmly and enthusiastically commend this volume to all who would walk in Jesus's steps and minister in his name."

Todd D. Still
Truett Seminary

"There is a bewildering gap between the academic study of the Bible and the sort of patient, practical, and delightful biblical attention we need in our churches, our souls, and our world. I love Richard Burridge's voice because he reads the Bible expecting God to speak, and life and health and grace to erupt. Blessed indeed must have been those preparing for ordination who first heard these addresses. Blessed will they be who read and meditate on them now."

Jason Byassee
Vancouver School of Theology

"Like a suspension bridge with cables rooted on either side of a canyon (an image that Burridge uses), this book links Christian scripture and tradition on the one side with the realities of ministry in the world church on the other. The book carries the reader over the gap in a readable and highly informative way. Burridge uses the four portraits of Jesus in the four gospels to draw out the meaning of the formation criteria of a range of churches from across the world. It is instructive especially for those exploring licensed and ordained ministry and, indeed, for anyone engaged in ministry. I commend this book warmly."

Stephen Spencer
Anglican Communion

Four Ministries, One Jesus

Exploring Your Vocation with the Four Gospels

Richard A. Burridge

WILLIAM B. EERDMANS PUBLISHING COMPANY
GRAND RAPIDS, MICHIGAN

Wm. B. Eerdmans Publishing Co.
4035 Park East Court SE, Grand Rapids, Michigan 49546
www.eerdmans.com

25 24 23 22 21 20 19   1 2 3 4 5 6 7

ISBN 978-0-8028-7673-7

Library of Congress Cataloging-in-Publication Data

Names: Burridge, Richard A., 1955- author.
Title: Four ministries, one Jesus : exploring your vocation with the four
    Gospels / Richard A. Burridge.
Description: Grand Rapids : Eerdmans Publishing Co., 2019. | Includes
    bibliographical references and index.
Identifiers: LCCN 2018033133 | ISBN 9780802876737 (pbk. : alk. paper)
Subjects: LCSH: Bible. Gospels—Criticism, interpretation, etc. | Jesus
    Christ—Person and offices—Biblical teaching. | Pastoral
    theology—Biblical teaching. | Church work—Biblical teaching. | Pastoral
    theology—Church of England.
Classification: LCC BS2555.6.C56 B88 2019 | DDC 226/.06—dc23
    LC record available at https://lccn.loc.gov/2018033133

The grids of competencies of the Theological Education for the Anglican Communion
Priests are used by permission.

Quotations from the Candidacy Manual of the Evangelical Lutheran Church in America
are used by permission.

There is a public Facebook page dedicated to this book where you can post comments and
questions, and join in the discussions. See www.facebook.com/FourMinistriesOneJesus.

Dedicated with thanks to all those who have allowed me to share
their journeys of vocation and ministry over many years,
especially Chaplaincy Assistants
and members of Vocation Groups
at the University of Exeter
and King's College London

This international edition is also dedicated to
all the ordinands and theological students
to whom I have had the privilege
of lecturing and speaking
during my travels around the world
and across the Anglican Communion
over so many years—
thank you for all your encouragement and interest

Contents

Preface and acknowledgments for this international edition

This little book began life as a set of four addresses at a particular ordination retreat for the Diocese of Peterborough in England, but was then expanded into a book for those who are exploring a calling to ministry within the Church of England, or training for ordination, or who have been serving in parishes, chaplaincies, or other forms of ministry, whether over many years or even decades—or just a few weeks. As such, it was closely linked into the selection processes and criteria for ordained ministry in the Church of England, as well as the liturgy used at its ordination services. However, I am very grateful to many church leaders and seminary teachers around the world who have encouraged me to produce this international edition, and I am delighted to offer it to the worldwide church in the hope and prayer that it may be of benefit to anyone considering what the secular world thinks is a crazy idea—that God might be asking them to offer a period of years or even their whole life to his service and the ministry of his church in the life of his world, or who is already undertaking this calling.

Over the last three decades in my ministry as Dean of King's College London, it has been a privilege to be invited to teach and speak at many universities, colleges, churches, and seminaries around the world, from whom I have benefited so much and for which I am very grateful. From this rich experience around the globe and across all the Christian traditions, I have learned something of what †Desmond Tutu, Archbishop Emeritus of Cape Town, calls *ubuntu*, the African idea that "a person is a person through other persons," that our humanity is bound up with that of others. After all, it took at least two people to bring us into the world, and many others to teach us to eat, walk, and talk, and how to live together. We only know what to do because we do it in relationship—and one of the most severe punishments is solitary confinement, to deprive someone forcibly of human company. When Archbishop Tutu connects that African concept with his deep Christian conviction that God loves each and every one of us, regardless of our color, race, nationality, gender, creed—or even, as he is fond of saying, "the size of our nose!"—then it is powerful enough to change not only South Africa, but the whole world. And thus I have learned that despite our many differences, and the sorry history of inter-religious conflict and violence, all human societies have felt the need to set aside people to be chosen and trained to lead them in the worship of the divine and to care for one another—and that is what this little book is all about. Therefore I am delighted to have this opportunity to rewrite and edit it for a wider audience—and I hope that, whatever your church or Christian tradition, you will find something of value here to help you learn about ministry and service, to God and to the world which he created and loves so very much. As part of that international community, we have created a public Facebook page dedicated to this book where you can post comments and questions, and join in the discussions. See www.facebook.com/FourMinistriesOneJesus.

I must express my gratitude to so many people and places: within the *United States*, I have spent time in many Episcopal seminaries, including Virginia Theological Seminary, Alexandria, Virginia; General Theological Seminary, New York; Berkeley Divinity School, New Haven, Connecticut; Seabury-Western Theological Seminary, Evanston, Illinois; the University of the South, Sewanee, Tennessee; Seminary of the Southwest, Austin, Texas; Church Divinity School of the Pacific, Berkeley, California; and the then Anglican Theological Institute at Saint Michael and Saint George, Saint Louis, Missouri. In addition, it has been a pleasure as an Anglican to be invited to lecture and spend time in other leading seminaries train-ing ministers across many denominations, notably Princeton Seminary; Yale Divinity School; Duke Divinity School; Candler School of Theology; Truett Seminary; Southwestern Baptist Theological Seminary; Graduate Theological Union, Berkeley; Fuller Seminary; Regent's College, Vancou-ver—as well as lecturing or teaching in departments of theology or religion in many major American universities.

Having been involved in some of the preparations for the 1998 Lam-beth Conference of Anglican Bishops at Canterbury, I was honored that the Archbishop of Canterbury chose my commentary on *John* for advance reading and use in the daily Bible studies at the 2008 Lambeth Conference. As a result, I have been privileged to be invited to spend time and teach at many colleges and theological schools across the *Anglican Communion*: Saint John's College, Auckland, New Zealand; Trinity Theological School, Trinity College, Melbourne, Australia; Saint Francis College, Brisbane,

Australia; Ming Hua Theological College, Hong Kong; Harare Diocesan Clergy School, Zimbabwe; Honolulu Diocesan Clergy School, Hawaii; Saint Nicholas College, Cape Coast, Ghana; the Anglican Centre in Rome, Italy; Clergy School for the Anglican Province of Mexico, Mexico City; the College of the Transfiguration, Grahamstown, South Africa.

Because of the historic commitment of King's College London to *South Africa*, not least in having †Desmond Tutu study there, together with many other church leaders and politicians during the years of the struggle with apartheid, it has been a joy to spend time and teach at theological colleges and schools across the Anglican Province of Southern Africa, including: clergy schools for Dioceses of Cape Town, Pretoria, Johannesburg, and the High Veld; the College of the Transfiguration, Grahamstown; theology schools and ministry training through faculties at the University of the Western Cape; Stellenbosch University; University of Cape Town; University of Pretoria; North-West University in Potchefstroom; University of KwaZulu-Natal, Pietermaritzburg; and the University of South Africa (UNISA), Pretoria.

While most of this teaching has been at Anglican and Protestant seminaries and universities, I have also been privileged to lecture and participate in conferences and discussions at the *Roman Catholic* Theological Seminary in Barcelona, the Australian Catholic University in Melbourne, the American Catholic University in Washington, DC, the Catholic Seminary in Mexico City, and at the Vatican with the Lateran and Pontifical Gregorian Universities in Rome, and clergy and ordinands schools for the *Russian Orthodox Church* in Moscow at the invitation of the Metropolitan Archbishop.

I wish to give particular individual thanks to Michael Thomson, who has been my editor at Wm. B. Eerdmans Publishing Company for some two decades, for his deep friendship and encouragement, not to mention his endless patience in getting me to complete manuscripts! I am thankful to various friends and colleagues at multidenominational seminaries and theological colleges who worked through the original Anglican version and steered me in the direction of material and resources about selection processes, criteria and competencies, and liturgies and services for ordination in their various traditions, notably: the Reverend Dr. Greg Sterling, Dean of Yale Divinity School, and his colleague William Goettler for their very helpful and informative webpages; the Reverend Dr. Todd Still, Dean of Truett Seminary, Baylor University, and Dr. Greg Garrett of Baylor University; the Reverend Dr. Don Hagner, the Reverend Dr. John Goldingay, and Dr. Tod Bolsinger, all of Fuller Seminary, Pasadena. Chief of all I must thank the Very Reverend Dr. Ian S. Markham, Dean and President of Virginia Theological School (VTS), Alexandria, for all his encouragement over several decades for my research and writing, not least in inviting me to stay at VTS in early 2018 to complete this book; and also for the assistance of the Reverend Dr. Robert Heaney, Director of the Center for the Anglican Communion at VTS, for his assistance with the theological competencies in Anglican churches across the world; the Reverend Dr. Mitzi J. Budde, head librarian and professor at the Bishop Payne Library at VTS for all her assistance with books and resources, not to mention all things Lutheran; and finally to the Reverend David Casey, a third-year seminarian at VTS who researched many of the criteria and selection processes and ordination services included herein.

Finally, I am more grateful than words can say to my wife, Dr. Meg Warner, herself formerly Assistant to the Archbishop of Brisbane and Primate of Australia and a lecturer at Trinity Theological School, Melbourne, whom I met during my travels in the Anglican Communion, for her extraordinary gift of moving to live—and travel!—with me, for all her reading and rereading of my writings, for her encouragement and correction in my research and teaching, and for changing my life with her love, thus making all of this possible.

RICHARD A. BURRIDGE
Easter, 2018

Preface and acknowledgments for the original UK edition

I am grateful to the Right Reverend Donald Allister, Bishop of Peterborough, for inviting me to lead the retreat and preach at the ordinations in Peterborough Cathedral, to the Reverend Steve Benoy, Peterborough Diocesan Director of Ordinands, and the men and women preparing to be ordained as deacons and priests who originally shared these reflections at Launde Abbey in Petertide 2015—and for their enthusiasm and encouragement to turn them into this book.

I am glad to dedicate this book with thanks to all those who have allowed me to share the journey of their calling and discernment of their vocation, whether to ordained ministry or work as a lay person, over many decades, especially students and staff at the University of Exeter and King's College London. In the midst of all my administrative and other duties as Dean, I look forward each month to the meetings of the Vocation Group where we share each other's stories of the ordinary, and extraordinary, ways in which God guides and calls us. I have also relished the privilege of all the years of pastoral conversations with individuals—and I am delighted, and proud, of so many instances of faithful ministry, lay and ordained, in the church and around the world.

I am grateful to all those who first encouraged and fostered my vocation at Oxford and Sevenoaks and those who oversaw my training at Nottingham and Bromley. I have enjoyed working in various aspects of theological education and ordination training, including serving on the Council of St. John's College, Nottingham, and the Academic Boards of Studies at the North Thames Ministry Training Course and St. Mellitus College, London. It has been a privilege to work within the Advisory Board of Ministry and subsequently the Ministry Division, chairing the Education Validation Panel for a decade and participating in more committees and working parties than I can bear to remember! I am also honored to have been an Educational Selector and now Adviser for the Bishop of London, and grateful to all who have shared in various selection conferences and Bishops' Advisory Panels.

In addition, I would like to thank all the churches, dioceses, theological colleges, seminaries, and universities which have invited me to teach or lead study days and conferences within the UK, across the Anglican Communion and around the world, and all those who participated for all their encouragement and support.

Finally, I am particularly grateful to all those who read and commented on various drafts of this book in manuscript, especially to the Reverend Hilary Ison, Selection Secretary, and Ian McIntosh, Head of Formation, at the Ministry Division of the Archbishops' Council, Church House, for their help about the criteria and processes for selection, and to Professor Russell Goulbourne, Dr. Christopher Southgate, Canon Gordon Oliver, and Dr. Clare Dowding for all their annotations, comments, and eagle-eyed corrections which helped enormously to make this a better book. The errors which remain are proof that I am still a work in progress—and God has not finished with me yet!

RICHARD A. BURRIDGE

Easter, 2017

Four Portraits of Jesus's Mission and Ministry

"Proceed with caution," warned the sign on the gate across the narrow road leading into the grounds of Launde Abbey on the borders of Rutland and Leicestershire. It was wise advice: cows and sheep were wandering freely across lush meadow grass, or sprawled on the warm tarmac, apparently asleep in the summer sunshine. The taxi bringing me from the railway station would have come off worse in any chance encounter. Meanwhile, animal droppings suggested that "proceeding with caution" would be even more sensible if you cut across the fields toward the large country house in the middle distance, dating from the mid-1500s.

By its door a large modern sculpture of the risen Jesus stretched his arms out wide to welcome people who were unloading cars before squeezing luggage up twisting staircases and down narrow corridors. It was Petertide 2015, and the place was full to bursting with expectant men and women who would be ordained as new priests and deacons that coming weekend in Peterborough and Leicester cathedrals. Launde now serves as a retreat house and spirituality center, especially for its two neighboring dioceses. With its medieval chapel going back to the twelfth century and extensive grounds, it was an ideal setting for these ordinands to spend several days in silence and contemplation.

It is the custom for those about to be ordained in the Church of England to leave behind their homes, families, and friends and go away together for three or four days' silent retreat to prepare for the momentous change they will undergo at the laying on of the bishop's hands in the ordination service. They then appear on Sunday morning, usually on Saint Peter's Day at the end of June or Michaelmas in September, processing into a cathedral, resplendent in new robes and awkwardly fingering unfamiliar clerical collars. It can be the most stressful time: I vividly remember moving from my theological college in Nottingham to our curate's house in Bromley, Kent, in the baking hot summer of 1985 when Live Aid was going on at Wembley Stadium. The proposed renovations to the kitchen were only half finished, so the packing cases of our belongings were dumped in the garage—and I had to leave my poor wife to prepare a special lunch after my ordination as a deacon for our families, friends, and the new parish congregation! Twelve months later, we had a new baby and there was the additional terror of being individually examined by the Lord Bishop about the "theological and pastoral reflections on my year as a deacon" which we had submitted to him in advance—and mine, typically, were way over the permitted length! And after he agreed to ordain us as priests on Sunday, there was the awesome responsibility of presiding over the "holy mysteries" for our first eucharist. Perhaps it is hardly surprising that three decades later, I don't remember much that happened on my ordination retreats.

Therefore, to help ordinands prepare, pray, and reflect, a bishop usually invites an older priest to lead their retreat, giving three or four addresses and being available for personal conversation with the candidates, finishing with preaching at the actual ordinations in the cathedral. It was a particular honor to be invited by the Bishop of Peterborough to do this for those he would ordain as deacons and priests in June 2015, since we had first met some forty years previously, when he was a curate and I had just been licensed as what the Church of England calls a "lay reader" (a lay minister or preacher, who is licensed by the bishop to teach, preach, and take Services of the Word, but nothing sacramental) alongside my first job as a schoolmaster.

A long, long time ago . . .

Perhaps it was not surprising that as I began my initial preparations for this ordination retreat, I found myself remembering going to Launde Abbey myself some twenty-five years previously. It was all very different then, in the depths of a harsh winter with the animals huddled together for warmth around a frozen water trough, and most of the main house closed for renovations. I was staying there on my own for a private retreat, having just finished my doctorate, so seeking God's guidance for the next steps. My spiritual director, Gordon, lived close by, and came a couple of evenings for conversation and prayer. One night, warmed by some malt whisky before a roaring log fire, he suggested that it was time I "started to read the gospels." Given that I had just spent the best part of a decade researching their Greek text, I thought at first that the cold must have affected his brain—but respecting his wisdom, I was mulling it over the next day as I "proceeded with caution" across the fields, picking my way carefully between the frozen cowpats and the slippery grass by the lake.

As I pondered what "reading the gospels" might mean, particularly in the light of my research about their biographical literary genre, I suddenly got a picture in my mind of the four traditional symbols of the gospels—the lion, the ox, the eagle, and the human face: could I use those images as a way of explaining the different portraits of the "one Jesus" in the "four gospels"? So I rushed back to my cold and cramped attic room and scribbled it all down in my journal, getting excited about this divine revelation, a vision for a possible book. I could barely contain myself as I tried to explain it to Gordon that evening and thank him; but he just shook his head, buried his face in his hands, and then patiently explained that he believed that I needed "to read the bloomin' things"—not do any more writing, research, or analysis on them!

Therefore, he strongly suggested that I should put the new book aside for a year or two. Wanting to be obedient, I did so, and to my amazement, when I did finally put pen to paper, words and ideas just poured out. The four faces of the cherubim and the four living creatures around the throne of God are found in the visions of Ezekiel and Saint John the Divine (Ezek. 1:4–28; Rev. 4–6). Yet within only a few decades of the gospels being written, these symbols came to be associated with them as the four accounts of Jesus's mission and ministry, life and death were preserved individually but brought together into a "fourfold" collection in a codex, an early form of a bigger "book," longer than the individual scrolls used for each gospel on its own. The symbols often appeared in early frescoes across the ancient Mediterranean and lavish illustrations in Celtic manuscripts like the *Lindisfarne Gospels* and the *Book of Kells*.

While the four symbols are popularly thought to refer to the evangelists themselves, I was struck by the fact that the frescoes and Celtic manuscripts depict the symbolic animal *alongside* each gospel writer, or even hovering above them, inspiring them as they write. Writing in the middle of the second century, Irenaeus of Lyons describes the symbols as "images of the disposition of the Son of God," aspects of the mission or purpose of Jesus—the lion his royal power, the ox his sacrifice, the human his human coming, and the eagle his Spirit (*Against the Heresies* 3.11.8–9). Since these living creatures were visual symbols in an age of low literacy levels, I used them as images to describe the four gospel portraits of Jesus for our increasingly visual (post)modern age, where "icons" populate our computer screens and designer logos provide "visual identity" for everything from clothes to football teams.

Unfortunately, many people, if they can remember the gospels at all, have the four of them all mixed up in their heads: just ask any small group to tell you a familiar story, like the feeding of the five thousand, and separate details from different gospels will quickly emerge all jumbled together. Therefore, in *Four Gospels, One Jesus?*, after an introduction to critical and literary ways of reading the Bible, I undertook four narrative readings of the picture of Jesus in each gospel in turn, using the particular visual aspect of the symbol to interpret each writer's individual portrait. Thus the lion captures Mark's account of Jesus rushing and roaring around Galilee, fighting against evil, until eventually he becomes passive in Jerusalem, where he suffers and dies horribly alone. In contrast, Matthew's human face highlights Jesus's teaching of the people of Israel through five discourses, while Luke's image of the burden-bearing ox reflects his portrayal of Jesus's concern especially for the poor, vulnerable, and marginalized, even to the point of being sacrificed for them. Finally, the high-flying, all-seeing eagle represents John's account of Jesus with God "in the beginning," taking flesh to dwell among us in the incarnation, gathering his disciples under his wings before ascending to his Father in his risen power. In the conclusion, I reflected on how we might preserve this diversity of four portraits of the one Jesus within the New Testament, as well as discussing some questions around history, truth, and interpretation today.

I tried to write the book in an accessible style for a wider audience, but it has been amazing to see it go round the English-speaking world as well as be translated into Russian, Korean, Chinese, and Malay, languages spoken in places where the church is growing. Finally, I was privileged to present a copy to Pope Francis, when he made me the first non–Roman Catholic to receive the Ratzinger Prize for Theology, named after his illustrious predecessor. In his citation, Cardinal Ruini explained to the Pope that the prize was because I had established "the indissoluble connection between Jesus and the Gospels." It certainly seemed a long way from "proceeding with caution" around the fields of Launde Abbey!

Back to the future

It is perhaps not surprising that, returning to Launde Abbey twenty-five years after my previous visit, to help candidates to prepare for ordained ministry, I found myself coming back once again to these four extraordinary gospel portraits of Jesus's life and death. It reminded me of T. S. Eliot's idea of arriving "where we started," and knowing the place "for the first time." Neither I, nor the nervous ordinands whom it was my task to lead into prayer and reflection, could know what lay ahead for each of them in their future ministry.

Being recognized for any form of public ministry, whether as a lay minister or "reader," a deacon, a priest, or even a bishop, has to begin with a sense of "calling," a vocation to join in the mission of God to the world which he loves. It might come through a stray comment like "Have you ever thought of becoming a minister? I think you'd be good at that." When I was a student, several people, including my parish priest and university chaplain, made suggestions like that—and it was enough to make me run in the opposite direction! I even trained as a reader and spent nearly a decade speaking and preaching and leading services as a layperson. I firmly believed, and still believe, that you don't need a "dog collar" to talk about Jesus. And yet that seed continued to grow secretly over many years, niggling at me, an idea which just would not go away, until finally I found myself discussing it with a rather amused bishop, who said simply, "The rest of us have all known this for years, Richard; I'm glad if God has finally got through to you! I'll put you into the selection process straightaway."

But stray comments, vague niggles, or even deeply spiritual experiences are not enough on their own. Therefore it is entirely right that most churches around the world have careful selection procedures to discern whether someone is really being called by both God and the wider church to a life of ordained ministry and mission. In the Church of England this process can take several years, as people work with vocational advisers and Diocesan Directors of Ordinands (DDOs), culminating in a national Bishops' Advisory Panel (BAP), a residential conference over several days where candidates go through exercises and interviews with independent BAP Advisers, who have been nominated by bishops and trained by the church. To guide all this work, there is a set of selection criteria, revised on a regular basis, to assist both the candidates themselves and those who are supporting and ultimately discerning their call. Finally, the ordination liturgies—the actual words used in the services themselves—include not only questions and binding vows to challenge candidates, but descriptions of the ministry of both priests and deacons, which the former Bishop of London liked to refer to as "the Job Spec."

It has been fascinating to work through the various websites and printed material produced by the main Protestant denominations across North America—the Episcopal Church, the United Methodist Church, the African Methodist Episcopal Church, the Presbyterian Church (USA), the Lutheran church, the United Church of Christ, the Disciples of Christ, and the Baptists—to see how they compare with the Church of England system. Of course, the processes in these different churches do vary quite a bit, generally in the light of their distinct traditions: some—like the Episcopal, Methodist, and Lutheran churches—tend to put more emphasis on the corporate and communal call of the church, with clear national or regional structures, while others—like the United Church of Christ, the Disciples of Christ, or the Baptists—are much more local and congregational, with a greater stress on the individual's personal sense of calling. However, despite these differences, there is a remarkable amount of convergence: all the churches take someone's sense of vocation very seriously indeed, with careful examination of each individual's faith, understanding, and personal characteristics, often measured against a list of "criteria" or "competencies," and expect their future ministers to undertake some form of rigorous ministerial training and theological education. I have tried to provide a list of these documents and websites with extracts from the criteria and processes, as well as the services and liturgies, in the appendices at the back of this book.

Since these twin themes of vocation and mission properly dominate both the selection criteria or competencies and the ordination services and liturgies, they seemed the obvious themes for me to focus on during this ordination retreat. However, I quickly noticed that "vocation" and "mission" apply equally to all four gospels, but in different ways, reflecting their different understandings of Jesus's own calling and mission, his life and ministry, his death and resurrection. So the urge to link the four retreat addresses to the four gospels at Launde Abbey, where I had first received this idea about the four symbolic portraits of Jesus, proved irresistible. However, I suspect that the DDO was rather surprised by my request to provide each candidate with a pack containing laminated color reproductions of the evangelists and their symbols from the *Lindisfarne Gospels*, copies of the ordination services, and four highlighter pens!

But I did not want the four sessions to be just me talking at the candidates; I wanted them to be involved, to grapple with the actual texts of the biblical accounts and the ordination services. So each time we met, we looked at a different gospel writer and his symbol, and through that we considered an aspect of Jesus's mission and ministry. We began with the two obvious ministries of preaching and pastoral care. Thus Matthew's portrait of Jesus as the Teacher of Israel enabled us to concentrate upon preaching and teaching, while Luke's depiction of Jesus's concern for the poor and the vulnerable through the burden-bearing ox challenged us to prepare for pastoral ministry. Only then did we turn to Mark, who sets his narrative along the way of the cross, leading to Jesus's suffering in Jerusalem; this provided an opportunity to reflect on the difficulties which inevitably lie ahead for anyone who follows the crucified one. Lastly, John's theological reflection following the flight of the eagle from the heights of the divine to dwell among human beings, whom Jesus then sends as he was sent by his Father, gives us a pattern of prayer to share in the divine life in our mission and ministry today.

In each session, we used the highlighter pens to annotate the ordination liturgies with different colors to represent these four aspects of teaching, pastoring, suffering, and praying, and I encouraged the candidates to use the silent time between the sessions to reflect and prepare for the mission which lay ahead of them in ministry. They could even do that walking around the fields and the lake—though I did warn them to "proceed with caution" and to be careful about what they might be stepping into!

I also wanted to challenge them about how to sustain these four aspects of mission in the future. Preparation for possible decades of ministry is not something which can be done entirely in two or three years at a seminary or by taking a part-time course or through distance learning. In perhaps a silly image, I compared it to a camel filling up once at an oasis, and then heading off across the desert for twenty or thirty years: that way lies madness, and it is likely to end in disaster, with the camel's bones whitened in the sun somewhere behind a sand dune. Therefore, wise ordinands should take steps even before a bishop or senior church representatives lay their hands on their heads to find ways to sustain and develop each of these four aspects of mission and ministry.

It was a delight to see how this simple idea captured their imagination in different ways, and I learned a lot myself through sharing this journey with them. I have to admit that at the actual services in the grandeur of Peterborough Cathedral, I don't think the Precentor was too impressed with the candidates clutching these tatty and dog-eared draft printouts with various phrases all colored in, rather than the beautifully produced official copies on their seats—but we certainly all enjoyed it!

How to read and use this book

And now it is your turn. I was grateful to the Bishop of Peterborough and his DDO, and to the candidates, for their encouragement to turn my notes into this book. And of course, this approach is relevant for a much wider readership than just those about to be ordained: it starts much earlier and further back, and it goes on for a lifetime. I have been fortunate over the last three decades to work with young (and not so young!), enthusiastic students (and not a few members of staff) who are fired up by a sense of God's call—even if they are not sure what they are being called to yet. Taking them through the Church of England's selection criteria has been really helpful in guiding them and helping them to grow and develop. It has been a real joy and fascinating to accompany people along the path of discerning their vocation, even if it sometimes becomes clear that they are being called to other ways of serving God than getting ordained. After all, as a wise old bird once told me, "God only calls those to be ordained whom he does not trust to remain lay"!

You may be like my young students, looking ahead excitedly to life after university, or perhaps a bit older with years of experience behind you and wondering what God wants you to do with the rest of your life. Whatever your context, I hope that these four studies of teaching, pastoring, suffering, and praying might help you work out what God is saying and where he might be leading you. And whether you think offering for ordination is possibly the way forward, or, like me as an undergraduate, you want to be involved in mission and ministry as a lay person, the various selection processes in different churches with their criteria and competencies can be a useful tool, so I have included discussion of them in each chapter, drawing on the material listed in the appendices. They are, of course, particularly important for anyone who is currently exploring their sense of calling with a vocational adviser or a mentor or guide, or preparing for any sort of ministerial interviews or a selection conference.

On the other hand, you may be in the middle of theological training at a seminary or in preparation for some other form of recognized ministry, but I hope that these reflections will also be useful in that process—and it's a good idea to have a careful look at the services used for ministry and ordination in your particular church or tradition, also referenced in the appendices, long before you get to any retreat or preparation for the big event! In addition, I would like to offer these studies to those who already have years or even decades of faithful ministry behind them. At the start of John's vision in Revelation, the risen Jesus complains that some Christians at Ephesus have lost the love which they once had and warns them to recover it, lest they lose the lampstand which stands for their church (Rev. 2:4–5). The irony that there is no longer a living church amid the ruins of that ancient city on the Turkish coast is a challenge to us all today. Sadly, there are people with whom I trained at my theological college (or seminary), or who were selected or ordained at the same time as me, who are no longer active in Christian ministry, and I am painfully aware of the times when I feared that I personally would not be able to keep going myself. So even if some of this material may seem old hat to those readers with years of experience, let me encourage you to find new ways to sustain your preaching and teaching, your pastoral ministry, in the midst of whatever suffering and difficulties you experience, and find again the divine life undergirding all you do and say.

Thus while the overall themes of vocation and mission run throughout this book, each of the four main chapters will begin with a consideration of a different aspect of Jesus's ministry as depicted in each gospel in turn. We will follow this slightly unusual sequence, beginning with preaching and teaching in Matthew and pastoral care in Luke, before going on to consider the challenge of suffering the way of the cross in Mark, which will lead us finally into participating in the divine life through prayer and spirituality in John. I have also included a line drawing of each evangelist and their symbol based on the *Lindisfarne Gospels*; as with those on the original retreat, you may find it stimulating to use it as a visual aid to your prayer and meditation, and your reflection on the gospel texts. You will find it helpful to have a copy of the particular gospel to hand, and perhaps read it right through by yourself first, looking for this aspect of ministry.

Then, second, we will look at the selection processes, the various criteria and competencies used in discerning a call to ministry and the actual words used in different ordination services. If you wish, you could repeat the exercise we did on the retreat, by highlighting the criteria and liturgy reproduced in the appendices, or downloading and printing out the particular texts used in your church tradition and using highlighter pens to mark them up, or underline with a pencil, if coloring in seems too childish or sacrilegious. Finally, we will consider how each aspect of mission might work out in your ministry, reflecting on some of my own personal experiences first as a reader (a lay minister or preacher), then as a parish priest, a university chaplain, and latterly Dean of King's College London, before concluding with some practical suggestions about how you might sustain this through years of faithful service, particularly when the going gets tough.

From time to time, there will be various questions, inviting you to reflect on the gospel accounts, the selection processes, or the ordination services and liturgies and encouraging you to write down something about it all. I have found it a helpful personal discipline myself throughout my ministry to keep a spiritual journal, and I often encourage potential ordinands to get an exercise book or notebook; you might want to have one to hand while you are reading. Every chapter will also conclude with noting that we do not walk this path alone, but that we all need others who accompany us, or with whom we meet from time to time to share, discuss things, or pray together. I hope you have someone like that; think about who helps you in your journey of faith, and ask them to accompany you through these reflections and explorations—and if you don't have someone like that already, try to find one. Whatever stage you are at in your pilgrimage and your sense of ministry, however defined, I pray that you will also know the presence of the risen Lord Jesus, walking with you as he did with the disciples on the road to Emmaus, opening your mind to understand the scriptures (see Luke 24:26–27, 32, 44–45).

PART I

Matthew

Teaching Good News

Figure 1. Saint Matthew, *Lindisfarne Gospels*, Folio 25b

1. Matthew's portrait of Jesus as the supreme teacher

In the *Lindisfarne Gospels'* introductory page illustrating Saint Matthew (Folio 25b; see fig. 1), he is shown seated, writing his book, with his feet up on a stool. Hovering above him is the *imago hominis*, the image of a human being with wings, sounding a trumpet and inspiring Matthew as he writes his gospel. This image makes me think about Matthew's portrait of Jesus as the human face of God: Matthew depicts Jesus supremely as a teacher.

After a couple of introductory chapters about Jesus's birth, his baptism and temptation, and the call of the first disciples, Matthew begins his main narrative by telling us that "when Jesus saw the crowds, he went up the mountain; and after he sat down, his disciples came to him. Then he began to speak, and taught them, saying . . ." (Matt. 5:1–2). What we now call the Sermon on the Mount then follows for the next three chapters, before Matthew concludes, "Now when Jesus had finished saying these things, the crowds were astounded at his teaching, for he taught them as one having authority, and not as their scribes" (7:28–29). As we shall see in this chapter, Jesus's teaching ministry is so central for Matthew that he structures his entire gospel around not just the Sermon on the Mount, but also another four sermons or discourses; he marks out how important this aspect is by ending each one with a similar statement: "and it happened when Jesus had completed these sayings" (7:28; 11:1; 13:53; 19:1; 26:1).

Jesus as the new Moses

One of the other interesting things about the *Lindisfarne Gospels'* picture is that there is another man peering at Saint Matthew from behind the curtain. Some experts in Celtic art suggest that it's Moses, as he is bearded, has a halo to appear holy, and is also clutching a book. We might think that these features do not necessarily narrow it down too much! However, I think it's a pretty good guess: the fact that Jesus goes up onto the mountain to talk to the people and teach them is bound to make Matthew's early Jewish Christian readers think of Moses. In the opening genealogy Matthew links Jesus back to the whole history of Israel, from Abraham through David and the exile in Babylon (1:1–17). Then he moves on to the infancy stories, where Matthew describes an evil king (Herod) who wants to kill all the little boys, while Jesus is miraculously saved by fleeing to a foreign country, Egypt, from which God eventually calls him back to Nazareth after the death of the evil king. This is all very reminiscent of the story of Moses being hidden in the bulrushes when Pharaoh is killing Hebrew boys, after which Moses has to flee and then return to Egypt later to lead God's people to the promised land (compare Matt. 2:16–18 with Exod. 1:15–2:10; Matt. 2:13–14 with Exod. 2:15–22; and Matt. 2:19–20 with Exod. 2:23).

Mountains and pulpits

These similarities between Jesus and Moses echo throughout Matthew's gospel—he's even got this fascination with mountains! For example, the temptation narrative in Matthew finishes with Jesus going up onto a high mountain (Matt. 4:8–10, like Moses surveying Israel from Mount Pisgah in Deut. 34:1–4), whereas in Luke it ends with Jesus going into the temple (Luke 4:9–13). Throughout Matthew's gospel, all the really important things happen on high places: Jesus goes up mountains to pray and to heal; the feeding of the five thousand and the transfiguration both take place on mountains; he teaches from the Mount of Olives in Jerusalem; and finally the whole gospel ends on a high mountain in Galilee where the final commissioning of the disciples takes place, whereas Luke's gospel ends in the temple again (Matt. 14:23; 15:29–31; 15:32–39; 17:1; 24:3; 28:16–20—compare Luke 24:52–53). Matthew's stress on Jesus's teaching ministry and mountains not only sounds very much like Moses; it also reminds us that a very significant part of Christian ministry, for which you are preparing, may not take you up a mountain but it does place you at what is sometimes called "six feet above contradiction"! In many older churches, the pulpit really was placed that high above the people to help them hear what the preacher was saying in the days before microphones and amplification systems. However, even from a lectern or a reading desk today, the preacher is endowed with a certain authority—and does not expect to be interrupted or questioned.

So, meditating upon Matthew's portrait of Jesus as a teacher can help us spend some time thinking about the ministry of teaching and preaching.

Five blocks of Jesus's teaching

Clearly, the Sermon on the Mount is crucial for Christian ministry. It is often referred to as the "quintessence of Jesus's teaching." In your ministry, I'm sure that you will meet, if you haven't already, someone who argues that "you don't have to go to church to be a Christian, you should just have to keep the Sermon on the Mount." That makes me wonder if they've read it recently! I know that I find that I cannot live up to the extraordinary demands of Jesus's teaching in this sermon—which is why I *do* find it necessary to go to church, to ask for God's forgiveness and pray for strength to follow Jesus. But no matter how clever Matthew has been in collecting together sections of Jesus's teaching to form the Sermon on the Mount, it is only the first of *five* sermons or discourses. The fact that there are five blocks of teaching reminds us of the "books of Moses," the first five books in the Bible, often called the Pentateuch (from the Greek *pent-* for "five"). Thus we have another link back to Moses, suggesting that Jesus does not only teach from mountains, but that he brings a new law and teaching from a new Moses.

Closer analysis of the five discourses reveals Matthew's artistry and deliberate organization of his story, as they balance each other throughout the gospel in both length and content (see diagram).

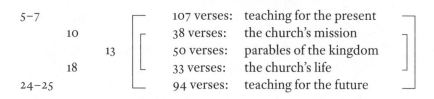

5–7			107 verses:	teaching for the present
	10		38 verses:	the church's mission
		13	50 verses:	parables of the kingdom
	18		33 verses:	the church's life
24–25			94 verses:	teaching for the future

Thus, Matthew's portrayal of Jesus's teaching ministry begins with the Sermon on the Mount, a very long discourse of 107 verses teaching about the present, and it ends with a similarly long discourse of 94 verses which teaches about the future, the coming destruction and final judgment. It's a bit like a double, or even triple, sandwich, where these are the outer

layers of bread. The next layer in comprises two comparatively shorter discourses, 38 verses in chapter 10 focusing on the mission of the disciples and
33 verses in chapter 18 on the life of the church, which once again balance
each other. In the very middle, the nourishing core of the sandwich, we
find 50 verses in chapter 13 about the parables of the kingdom, the heart
of Jesus's teaching.

So, it is worth spending a little time to meditate upon this vital emphasis: how will you make the kingdom of God, better understood as God's
coming "reign" or "rule" than a place or country, the heart of your teaching
and preaching ministry?

Interweaving teaching and ministry

Thus chapter 13 is structurally and theologically central to Matthew's gospel, rather than the Sermon on the Mount; however, it is also significant
that this collection of parables ends with the acceptance or rejection of
Jesus and his teaching (13:51–58). Matthew adroitly weaves the overall
story of Jesus's ministry throughout the main narrative of his gospel around
these five large discourses. After the Sermon on the Mount (chaps. 5–7),
chapters 8–9 give us three sets of miracle stories and healings interspersed
with vignettes of discipleship, including the call of Matthew the tax collector himself. Then, as a good teacher, Jesus not only teaches his disciples about mission in the discourse of chapter 10, but also sends them out
afterward to practice and to follow his example. Unfortunately, this leads
to conflict over the next few chapters (11–13), as some people accept the
good news while others, especially the religious leaders, reject it, or even
accuse Jesus of being controlled by the devil (12:22–45).

Thus it is not surprising that the central collection of parables in chapter 13 ends with the theme of judgment, about the acceptance or rejection
of God's message (13:51–58). We then see an increasing separation developing through Jesus's further ministry in the next sequence of chapters
(14–17), as the Pharisees seek signs or reject Jesus, while a Gentile woman
asks for his help (the crumbs from the table not wanted by God's children,
15:21–28), a story to which we shall return later. So Jesus has to build a
new community of faith, the church based upon Peter as the rock, and
confirmed by the voice of God at the transfiguration (16:13–20; 17:1–8).
This leads us to the discourse in chapter 18 about the life of the church
(including the only occurrences of the Greek word *ecclesia* in the gospels,

16:18; 18:15, 17). Following this discourse on the church, the next couple of chapters (19–22) take us through Jesus's entry into Jerusalem on Palm Sunday, the incident where he turned over the money changers' tables in the temple, and all his subsequent debates with the religious leaders, culminating in his denunciation of the Pharisees in chapter 23, leading into the fifth, and final, long discourse about destruction and judgment in chapters 24 and 25.

In this way, Matthew is beautifully weaving together discourse *and* story, teaching *and* ministry, to show how the two must always go together. Jesus is constantly teaching by story and by explanation, by sermons to crowds and through encounters with individuals. So too for us: what we say in sermons on Sunday must be lived out in our ministry through the rest of the week. No matter how brilliant your rhetoric when you are preaching in the pulpit or wherever, if it is not earthed in the daily life of small groups and personal conversation with the people God brings across your path, no one is going to listen to you!

A task for you

With Matthew's portrait of Jesus as the ultimate teacher who delivers long discourses in between his healing and liberating encounters with people in the forefront of our mind, it is time to see how this aspect of teaching and preaching plays out in the ministry God is setting before you. Now it is time, therefore, to put this chapter down for a moment and turn to the appendices at the back of the book. As I explained in the introduction, when I first used this material at a retreat for ordinands, the candidates had all been given highlighter pens and draft copies of their ordination services, so I asked them to go through the liturgies and highlight in one particular color phrases or sentences which seemed to be about the ministry of teaching and preaching. Normally, I do not like people writing in books or underlining passages, and it upsets me when I find that students have done this in a library book! But since this is more of a practical study, I would like to encourage you to get out a pencil, or even colored highlighters, and note all the relevant phrases which you can find in the criteria and competencies listed for the Anglican Communion across the world, or the United Methodist Church, the Evangelical Lutheran Church in America, or the Disciples of Christ, which you will find reproduced in appendix 2 at the back of this book. Other churches, particularly those which emphasize more "congregationalist" polities or tendencies since the Reformation, tend not to have such national or ecclesiastical guidelines, but prefer more local systems and individual arrangements to discern a person's calling within their own particular church or congregation. You could use the various websites and resources listed in the appendices to download similar lists of criteria and competencies from your own church or tradition—and then work through that, highlighting relevant phrases and passages. Similarly, you can work through one or two examples of ordination services, either those noted in the appendices or again downloading a liturgy or service from your own church tradition. After you have done that, you might want to spend a little time in prayer and contemplation (perhaps in front of the illustration from the *Lindisfarne Gospels*), meditating upon the passages you have highlighted, and perhaps write down your thoughts and reflections in your journal, before picking up reading the rest of this part.

2. The teaching ministry in selection for ministry

All the mainline denominations look for the ability to teach and preach—or the capacity to learn and develop these skills—as a key prerequisite for those who are offering themselves for the ministry. Several criteria used in Theological Education for the Anglican Communion (TEAC) are particularly relevant for this topic of teaching and preaching, especially those relating to spirituality and faith (C), biblical and theological competence (H), and mission and evangelism (J). Similar criteria and competencies are also listed by other churches, notably the United Methodist Church (UMC), the Evangelical Lutheran Church in America (ELCA), and the Disciples of Christ (DoC), so we have reproduced these lists in appendix 2 at the back of this book. In the Church of England's residential conferences where candidates' vocations are examined and discerned, the Bishops' Advisory Panel, these criteria are the particular responsibility of an Educational Adviser, who uses them as the basis of his or her discernment and assessment of each individual candidate's vocation, through the various elements of the interviews and exercises. I have been delighted to act in this capacity for many years myself, and I never tire of discussing these important issues with those who are offering themselves for the ordained ministry.

Understanding your Christian faith

It is humbling to discover the gifts and talents which men and women already have at the start of their journey—and their desire to go further. The TEAC criteria require that candidates should "show an understanding of the Christian faith" and "have a broad understanding of the scope of the Bible and understand the importance of biblical interpretation" (H), which is fed by "reading the Bible . . . systematically," among other spiritual practices (C). Furthermore, this can never be something static and fixed: candidates should have "a desire to deepen their understanding" (H). Similarly the Lutheran church "acknowledges that a rostered minister's adaptive leadership skills, reflecting the cited competencies, will not be fully formed during the candidacy process. A well-prepared missional candidate understands that the candidacy process is the beginning of a lifelong process of learning and formation for leadership" (2.1.4). So this does not mean that you have to have all your theology sorted out before you can offer yourself for ministry! In fact, those who think that they have already managed this, or are overconfident that they know all about what the gospel means for us today, often cause vocation advisers like me some anxiety. On the other hand, I do expect candidates to have read some basic books about the Christian faith and to be able to talk about them sensibly. Above all, however, we are looking for those who are thirsty for the waters of life, who want to read, study, and learn more.

Therefore, it might be a good idea for you to reflect about your "understanding of the Christian faith." How did your journey of faith start? How has your understanding of it developed, grown, or even changed over the years? Perhaps sketch out the story of your pilgrimage in your journal—can you discern how God has been guiding you through it? Do you read books, or use interactive media, to help you take your understanding and faith deeper? Look at the various resources listed in the appendices for some ideas. Perhaps ask an older or more experienced Christian, your vicar or minister, someone you respect and look up to, to give you some guidance—or lend you one or two of their books!

Connecting your faith with daily life

Second, although academic theology is very important, it can never be merely an academic exercise in a so-called ivory tower. In fact, Plato's Academy in ancient Athens was close to the Agora (the marketplace), the temples in the Acropolis, and the place where the democratic Assembly met—all the places where people met to debate and argue about public life, to conduct business, buying and selling, and to worship. Socrates used to make such a nuisance of himself questioning and debating with the political leaders, religious authorities, and businessmen that they all eventually condemned him to death through drinking hemlock! The TEAC criteria seek evidence that candidates are able to "show an awareness of and sensitivity to their own social, and cultural contexts and have the ability to make wise observations about the world around them," and to "have some awareness of world issues and of the differing response of the church to diverse contexts" (G). Similarly, the criterion on mission requires that "Candidates understand the key issues and opportunities for Christian mission within the contemporary culture" (J), though hopefully doing this is a way to life, rather than death, like Socrates! Similarly, a Lutheran "rostered minister understands and interprets context and culture through the lens of Christian faith and leads a community to opportunities where the gospel can be understood and shared by people in specific cultural contexts" (ELCA 2.1.4.2). This need to connect the Christian gospel and faith with the realities of human experience as part of our ministry and mission may be tested not only through individual interviews with candidates, but also through things like presentations, group discussions, and written exercises. It is no good understanding the higher realms of theology if you cannot relate all of this to daily life and the needs and concerns of those among whom you will minister—to be so "heavenly minded" that you are no "earthly use"!

Again, take some time to reflect about whether and how you relate your faith to daily life. When you are engaging with social media, reading the news, or looking at things online, do you find yourself wondering what relevance your faith has to what is happening, or is it kept separate, vacuum-sealed in a safe little box? Are there any novels, plays, or films which have moved you or excited you, and made you think again about the gospel and its implications for us today?

Communicating the good news

This leads us into an important third requirement, the ability to communicate all this to all sorts and conditions of people. Thus the TEAC criterion about spirituality and faith (C) requires not only that candidates "should demonstrate personal commitment to Christ" but also that they possess a "capacity to communicate the gospel" and "can talk comfortably of their faith with a wide range of people and demonstrate the love of God in their lives." Similarly, one practical competence sought is that "Candidates have gifts for and a desire to proclaim the word, communicate the gospel and teach the faith" (I). Equally, the United Methodist Church expects candidates to "communicate persuasively the Christian faith in both oral and written form" (para. 304.e), while a Lutheran "rostered minister actively believes and carries out Christ's command to go out and share the gospel with neighbors" (ELCA 2.1.4.1).

Again this may be discerned through both references and papers in advance, as well as in conversations and exercises at selection interviews or conferences, where candidates are often asked to relate their understanding of the good news to specific situations, real and imagined. Furthermore, the church is not looking for the superstar TV evangelist on their own or the "one-man band." It is about inspiring and teaching others also to communicate the gospel: candidates should "enable others to develop their callings as witnesses and advocates of the gospel by word and action" (TEAC J). Similarly, "a rostered minister prepares disciples to discern the leading of the Spirit as they share the gospel with neighbors in word and deed" (ELCA 2.1.4.3).

To help you consider this aspect, think about occasions when you have tried to explain your faith to others. If you are just starting out on the journey of vocation, ask your pastor, chaplain, or minister if there are any opportunities when they could help you try to communicate something, perhaps to an individual or small group—and where they could perhaps observe you and give you some feedback and encouragement. If you are already studying for the ministry, then practical experience of teaching and preaching—with supervision and feedback—will certainly form part of your training. And if you already have years of ministry behind you, perhaps you could reflect about how long it has been since you last tried something new, or perhaps ask some of your lay people whom you trust and respect to comment about or respond to your teaching and preaching, or invite them to discuss a sermon or talk with you afterwards.

Do I need to be an "intellectual," or an academic theologian?

Overall, therefore, the preaching and teaching ministry requires you to "have the necessary intellectual capacity and quality of mind to undertake a course of theological study and preparation and to cope with the intellectual demands of ministry" (H). Without this, a preacher could do a lot of damage and a teacher might lead people into misunderstanding and error. However, this does not mean that you have to be a "superbrain" or an "egghead" to offer yourself for this ministry. In fact, on a couple of occasions I have regretfully found that I could not recommend candidates with excellent degrees or even a doctorate, because they were unfortunately so fixed in their ways and habits of thinking that I shuddered to think of them being let loose on unsuspecting congregations! Therefore it is right that the TEAC criteria require candidates to "have an enquiring faith" (C) and to be "willing to learn and modify their opinions" (D)—for without this, it is impossible for people to grow and develop. Equally, candidates for the United Methodist Church must "accept that Scripture contains all things necessary for salvation through faith in God through Jesus Christ; be competent in the disciplines of Scripture, theology, church history, and Church polity; possess the skills essential to the practice of ordained ministry; and lead in making disciples for Jesus Christ" (UMC 304.1 *i*). Similarly, Lutheran candidates must be able to "understand the Word as law and gospel; teach Scripture; share the faith with others; provide Christian education for all ages and cultures; articulate theological wisdom, and live a disciplined spiritual life" (ELCA 2.1.2.2), while the Disciples of Christ must have the "capacity to engage in theological reflection" (DoC A.2.d).

This means that the preacher and teacher must provide a model for their congregation and people: candidates must "have potential to guide and shape the life of the church community and God's mission in the world" (TEAC F), so that they can "enable others to develop their callings as witnesses and advocates of the gospel by word and action" (J). If the minister is not himself or herself engaged in a process of learning and discovering yet more riches contained within the good news of Jesus Christ, then there is no chance for the poor people who have to listen to them to grow in their faith themselves!

It is interesting to note that all of these aspects—some basic knowledge of the gospel and a desire to learn more and increase it, the capacity to relate it to daily life, and the ability to communicate it to others in a clear and accessible way—are desired by the four church traditions listed here, and I have no doubt that they are also common to the other mainstream churches. They need to be recognized and affirmed in candidates who are offering themselves for ministry so that they can be developed and increased through theological education, ordination training, and preparation for ministry. Then after two or three years of such training, you will be ready for the great day when you are licensed for a public ministry of preaching and teaching. But it is crucial to recognize that this is not the end of the process: it is only the start, and it is vital that you continue to grow in your understanding of your faith and develop your ability to communicate it—and we will return to that shortly after we have looked at the services of ordination.

3. The teaching ministry in the ordination services

Having seen this important stress on developing your understanding of your faith, and learning to relate it to daily life and to communicate it to others in the criteria and processes for selection for training, we turn now to see how these aspects of the ministry of preaching and teaching also feature in ordination services. Sometimes it is easy to underestimate liturgies; they can seem like just a long list of words on a page which we have to go through, repeating them parrot-fashion. Some people think that liturgical prayers and the written words of services are somehow less "spiritual" than *extempore* talking to God, even though that way of praying can sometimes sound rather incoherent or repetitive.

Actually, words are very important, for they have tremendous power to bring new things about, so they are worth taking time with, both to create them and to use them properly. At the beginning of creation, God only had to say, "let there be light"—and there was light! (Gen. 1:3); and so on, through the rest of the creation story, God speaks the words, and things come into being. In a wedding service, it is the very *words* spoken by the couple, in their vows and promises to each other, which in fact create the marriage, and change their real status from being two separate individuals into one couple, legally for society and sacramentally in the eyes of God. So too, in the liturgies for ordination, there are lots of words which are said before and at the actual laying on of hands which change your status from lay into ordained, a minister or a pastor, a deacon or an elder. Once again, the words and actions have a legal effect with regard to your status as "a minister of religion" and you are now to be called "the Reverend"—and those from a more sacramental or catholic tradition also believe that the words and laying on of hands effect an "ontological change," turning a lay person into a priest. It is a huge occasion, which is why many churches send their candidates away for several days' silent retreat, to pray and prepare for it—so that when you hear these words being said to you, or over you, or about you, you will have thought and prayed about them and walked with God in preparation for your ordination.

In appendix 3 at the back of this book, I have sketched out the overall shape of a service of ordination, which seems to be shared by most Christian churches. However, the actual words of the different denominations' liturgies are full of rich resources for our understanding of the calling to teach, preach, and be ministers of the word. I have provided links to resources and orders of service for most of the mainline churches, so if you have not done this exercise yet, stop reading and have a go at discovering phrases which seem to refer to this ministry in an example taken from your own church or denomination—and then compare it with one from a completely different tradition. Look carefully at the passages you have noted or highlighted from these examples, as we go through the service section by section.

The gathering, welcome, or call to worship

Ordination services are usually conducted by one or several senior church leaders or bishops, beautifully adorned in gorgeous robes, representing the wider authority of the church beyond that of just the local congregation—and often the service will take place in a major church or cathedral. The bishop or senior leader will welcome everybody and set the tone of celebration for the service which lies ahead, which is likely to include a reminder about the importance of preaching and teaching: thus the bishop's introduction to a Church of England ordination service begins with the statement that "God calls his people to follow Christ . . . to declare the wonderful deeds of him who has called us out of darkness into his marvellous light." This reminder that the ministry of proclaiming the gospel belongs to all Christians through our baptism is also noted by the Presbyterian Church of the USA (PCUSA), where the moderator introduces the ordination of deacons and elders thus: "in baptism, N. and N. *were* clothed with Christ, and *are* now called by God through the voice of the church to enter into ministries of service and governance, announcing in word and deed the good news of Jesus Christ," while ordination to both Word and Sacrament commences: "in *his/her* baptism, N. was clothed with Christ, and is now called by God through the voice of the church to enter upon ministry of Word and Sacrament."

The presentation of the candidates

Most ordination services then move quickly to the presentation of the candidates, where the bishop or senior minister will want to be assured that these people have been properly called and examined, and that they accept and believe the Christian faith. In the liturgy of the Episcopal Church (TEC), the bishop first asks those presenting the candidates, "Has *he* been selected in accordance with the canons of this Church? And do you believe *his* manner of life to be suitable to the exercise of this ministry?" Having been assured of this by the presenters, the bishop turns their attention to the ordinand: "Will you be loyal to the doctrine, discipline, and worship of Christ as this Church has received them? And will you, in accordance with the canons of this Church, obey your bishop and other ministers who may have authority over you and your work?" The candidate must then declare, as required by Article VIII of the Episcopal Church's Constitutions and Canons: "I am willing and ready to do so; and I solemnly declare that I do believe the Holy Scriptures of the Old and New Testaments to be the Word of God, and to contain all things necessary to salvation; and I do solemnly engage to conform to the doctrine, discipline, and worship of The Episcopal Church." Similarly, in the United Church of Christ (UCC), a representative of the association must read the Constitution and By-laws regarding ordination, and challenge the ordinand, "do you, with the church throughout the world, hear the word of God in the scriptures of the Old and New Testaments, and do you accept the word of God as the rule of Christian faith and practice?" The ordination services of the Lutheran Church (ELCA) and the Methodists similarly require candidates to confess their acceptance of the Christian faith and their willingness to teach according to the holy scriptures, within the particular confessions and disciplines of their respective church traditions.

This is important in order to ensure that new ministers are not about to start teaching something which is against the scriptures, the creeds of the worldwide church, and the traditions of your denomination. If you have never thought about this, or even read this service, now might be a good time to spend a while praying through the questions in your church's liturgy, meditating upon each section, and writing down your thoughts in your journal. And if you do have a problem with any part of it, or if you are not sure whether you would be able to make these declarations, then it would be a good idea to discuss it soon with your minister or spiritual director.

The declarations or statement of ministry

The senior minister, leader, or bishop will usually then deliver a substantial statement, declaring or describing the office, work, or ministry to which these candidates will be ordained. The former Bishop of London used to call this part the "Job Spec," since it comprises a list of tasks or functions which a deacon, priest, elder, or minister will be expected to perform—and preaching and teaching will inevitably feature importantly in this list. Thus, in the United Methodist Church (UMC), elders are "to preach and teach the Word of God" and "to lead people to faith in Jesus Christ," while elders and deacons of the Presbyterian Church (PCUSA) are similarly charged to be "ministers of the word." A sample Baptist ordination service includes the declaration "preach and teach the Word of God." For the Episcopal Church, the bishop tells priests that "it will be your task to proclaim by word and deed the Gospel of Jesus Christ, and to fashion your life in accordance with its precepts. . . . You are to preach," while deacons are to "study the Holy Scriptures, to seek nourishment from them, and to model your life upon them. You are to make Christ and his redemptive love known, by your word and example, to those among whom you live, and work, and worship." If this is the "job description," then this aspect is rather demanding, so again, spend some time praying and thinking about it. Of course, you are likely to feel daunted by the challenge—if you thought you were up to it, I'd be worried! But at the very least, does it excite you? Do you find yourself thinking, "Yes, that's what I really want to do"?

Questions, vows, and promises

In order to know if the candidates are ready to undertake all these things in their ministry, most churches require that they must be questioned directly and make solemn promises—and once again, the ministry of preaching and teaching dominates the liturgy. Lutheran candidates are asked, "Will you be diligent in your study of the holy scriptures and faithful in your use of the means of grace?" to which they reply, "I will, and I ask God to help me." Similarly, Methodists are asked, "Will you be faithful in prayer, in the study of the Holy Scriptures?" and "Will you, in the exercise of your ministry, lead the people of God to faith in Jesus Christ?" prompting the response, "I will, with the help of God." The UCC Association Representative asks, "do you promise to be diligent . . . in reading the scriptures," "zealous in maintaining the truth of the gospel," and "faithful in preaching and teaching the gospel?" to which a simple "I do" will suffice. Presbyterians are asked, "Will you be a faithful minister, proclaiming the good news in Word and Sacrament, teaching faith," and respond, "I will." After such solemn vows and promises, it is not surprising that the Anglican bishops in both Australia and the Episcopal Church pray for their ordinands, "may the Lord who has given you the will to do these things give you the grace and power to perform them" (TEC; APBA), a phrase which is echoed by the Disciples of Christ, "may God who has given you the will to do these things give you grace to perform them; N, the God who called you is faithful and will not fail you" (DoC).

As with the previous sections, let me encourage you to meditate and reflect upon these promises, for they, like wedding vows, are not to be made lightly or thoughtlessly—and they will take you a lifetime to fulfill in practice. And, once again, if you have any difficulties with any of these promises, do discuss them soon with your minister or spiritual director.

The invocation of the Holy Spirit and prayers

After such solemn promises and vows, which no human being can possibly keep in their own strength, it is not surprising that most services now turn to prayer. Sometimes the bishop or senior ministers will leave their seats facing the candidates and all kneel together with them, looking towards the altar or holy table, or some other symbol of facing God. It is right that the particular help and guidance of the Holy Spirit is invoked to provide the candidates with the strength, courage, and wisdom they will need, especially if they are to teach and preach the word of God: "Gracious God, pour out your Spirit upon your servant N., whom you called by baptism as your own. Grant *him/her* the same mind that was in Christ Jesus. Give *him/her* a spirit of truthfulness rightly to proclaim your Word in Christ from pulpit, table, and font, and in the words and actions of daily living. Give *him/her* the gifts of your Holy Spirit" (PCUSA); "Bless and sanctify by your Holy Spirit your servant, N, . . . bestow on N the power of your Holy Spirit" (UCC). Further prayer may include singing the *Veni Creator Spiritus*, a canticle and custom dating back to earliest days of the church, as an invocation of the Holy Spirit to "our souls inspire, and lighten with celestial fire," to give us his "sevenfold gifts," and to "teach us to know the Father, Son, and thee, of both, to be but one" (TEC, AME, ELCA). Other prayers may take the form of a litany, prayed together with responses from the people answering each request (TEC, ELCA).

The ordination or laying on of hands

Finally, we come to the actual moment of ordination itself. If water is the sign of baptism, and rings for marriage, the symbolic or sacramental act which brings about the reality of ordination is laying on of hands. This goes right back to the days of the earliest church in Antioch: "while they were worshipping the Lord and fasting, the Holy Spirit said, 'Set apart for me Barnabas and Saul for the work to which I have called them.' Then after fasting and praying, they laid their hands on them and sent them off" (Acts 13:2–3; see also Paul's comments about laying hands on Timothy in 1 Tim. 4:14 and 2 Tim. 1:6).

Sometimes there may be a longer prayer prayed by the bishop or senior minister(s) perhaps stretching their hands out over the whole group, but the climax is when each candidate kneels before those officiating, who lay their hands upon the ordinand's head and pray for them by name to receive the gift of the Holy Spirit for their ministry. This may be done by the bishop or leader alone, symbolizing their authority (as in the Anglican tradition for deacons, TEC, CofE), or by several senior ministers together, symbolizing the corporate nature of leadership (AME)—or indeed by all the ministers present, symbolizing the collegiality of ministry, which is never mine alone (ELCA, UMC, PCUSA, ABC and in the Anglican tradition for priests, TEC, CofE).

The ordination prayer may include specific words about preaching and teaching: "Eternal God, through your Son, Jesus Christ, pour out your Holy Spirit upon *name* and fill *her/him* with the gifts of grace for the ministry of word and sacrament. Bless *her/his* proclamation of your word. . . . Make *her/him* a . . . patient teacher" (ELCA); "Take now authority as elders in Christ's holy Church to proclaim the word of God" (UMC); "We thank you, gracious God, for calling your servant N. into your church by baptism and to this ministry of Word and Sacrament. By your Holy Spirit, give N. all gifts and graces needed to proclaim the truth of the gospel in love" (PCUSA); "You are to be a faithful dispenser of the Word of God" (AME). So once again, take some time to look carefully at the words and actions used in your church tradition, reflect and meditate upon them— and ask God to grant you the gift of his Holy Spirit for this ministry of preaching and teaching.

Giving of the Bible and the welcome

Finally, in many traditions the candidates are reminded again of the importance of the scriptures for this ministry as they are given a copy of the New Testament or the whole Bible: thus the Episcopal bishop says, "Receive this Bible as a sign of the authority given you to preach the Word of God and to administer his holy Sacraments. Do not forget the trust committed to you as a priest of the Church of God" (TEC), while for the UCC, this is done by the Association Representative: "Receive at our hands this Bible of which you are appointed as an interpreter. Be diligent in the study of its message that you may speak with the authority of truth and be a faithful minister of the word and sacraments." In the Presbyterian church, "symbols appropriate to the ministry of deacons and elders may be presented," which may well include a Bible (PCUSA, DoC), while other traditions will present or vest the newly ordained minister with a stole (ELCA), worn diagonally over the left shoulder for deacons and straight around the neck for priests within the Anglican tradition (TEC).

In some churches (e.g., UCC, ABC, DoC, UMC), a certificate may be presented, denoting the newly ordained person's authority to teach and preach on behalf of the church: "I present you with this certificate of ordination. May it be a sign of your apostolic authority," to which the Disciples of Christ model order of service suggests that "the newly ordained may say a brief word of thanksgiving to the congregation and to those who have challenged and sustained her/him in her/his faith journey"—though it does warn, "**This is not an 'academy-awards' type of thank you!"** (asterisks and bold in the DoC original!). Most churches then welcome the newly ordained to their new ministry with words from various representatives, while Lutherans are introduced to the assembly by the presiding minister: "Will you, assembled as the people of God and speaking for the whole church, receive _name/s_ as _a messenger_ of Jesus Christ, sent by God to serve all people with the gospel of hope and salvation?" (ELCA). This is often followed by the opportunity for everyone, proud families and expectant congregations alike, to applaud their new ministers. In a service set within the context of a communion or eucharist, this naturally leads into greeting each other with the sharing of the peace.

The commissioning and sending out

Like the ministry of the word with its appropriate hymns, readings, and sermon which probably preceded the ordination ceremony, if there is a Eucharistic Prayer over bread and wine, it is likely once again to include some reference to the ministry of teaching and preaching. However, eventually what is often a long service reaches its conclusion as the new ministers are lined up with the bishop or senior leaders and given a final prayer of blessing and commissioning, before being sent out from the church or cathedral into their new ministry in the church and the world, including preaching and teaching.

We have spent quite a long time on this close study of the words of the liturgies of the ordination services, but I hope that it has revealed how central this ministry of teaching and preaching is for those who are being ordained as ministers in the different churches. It may have also been reinforced of course by the hymns and readings chosen for any particular service, and in the sermon, which in the Anglican tradition is usually given by the same person who led and directed the candidates on their ordination retreat. This is why this emphasis on preaching and teaching features so prominently in the processes, criteria, and competencies for selection, and why so much time and energy are devoted to this during the years of theological training and preparation before you finally come to be ordained. Whatever stage you may be at personally, reflecting upon these extraordinary words will pay dividends—whether this is something you are just beginning to feel your way towards, or whether you are preparing for ordination soon, or perhaps, like me, you can look back over several decades of active ministry: whichever it may be, I hope that spending time in studying the liturgy of your own church and other traditions will challenge you afresh, and renew you in your desire to teach and preach the gospel.

4. Teaching and preaching in your ministry

So far we have seen how Matthew portrays Jesus as the supreme teacher throughout his gospel, and how this ministry of teaching and preaching is highlighted in the criteria and processes for selection for theological training as well as in the actual liturgies of the ordination services themselves. Now therefore it is time to turn to how these aspects of teaching and preaching might be put into practice in your ministry, and to consider how you might sustain this ministry through the years ahead. And if you have already been doing it for years, perhaps together we can rekindle something of the first love and excitement for your preaching and teaching. In the introduction we noted the warning which the risen Jesus gave to the church in Ephesus, where today there is practically no Christian witness (Rev. 2:4). How can we avoid that happening in our churches and ministry today?

Teaching and preaching in the New Testament

While this ministry of teaching and preaching is absolutely central in Matthew's picture of Jesus as the Rabbi or Teacher, it is by no means confined to it; rather, throughout the rest of the New Testament, there is a constant stress on the significance of teaching as a gift of the Holy Spirit and a ministry expected of the early Christian leaders. Thus, Paul even describes it as a gift of the Spirit: "those who have different charismatic gifts (*charismata*) must exercise them according to the grace (*charis*) given to us ... the one who teaches, in teaching" (Rom. 12:6–7). Over recent decades there have been debates, arguments, and even schisms over the charismatic gifts of the Spirit, with a lot of attention given to the more spectacular or supernatural gifts, like speaking in tongues. But the list in 1 Corinthians 12:4–11 is not the only enumeration of the different charismatic gifts distributed by God through his Holy Spirit to enable his church to grow. Perhaps more consideration of the gifts listed in Romans 12, especially with regard to this ministry of teaching, might prove more helpful for the growth of the church in the longer term!

Similarly, Ephesians reminds us that "each of us was given grace according to the measure of Christ's gift." There are particular gifts which relate to Christian ministry and the leadership of the church: "the gifts he gave were that some would be apostles, some prophets, some evangelists, some pastors and teachers." But it is clear that these gifts are not to make the clergy into superstars or TV personalities; God's gifts are not given to us for *our* benefit, but for the sake of others, to enable them to grow and flourish and serve others in their turn. It can never be about "*my* ministry." Ephesians goes on to stress that such gifts and ministries enable the important task:

> to equip the saints for the work of ministry, for building up the body of Christ, until all of us come to the unity of the faith and of the knowledge of the Son of God, to maturity, to the measure of the full stature of Christ. We must no longer be children, tossed to and fro and blown about by every wind of doctrine, by people's trickery, by their craftiness in deceitful scheming. But speaking the truth in love, we must grow up in every way into him who is the head, into Christ. . . . (see Eph. 4:7–16)

No matter how eloquent a preacher may be, no matter how gifted a teacher, if they attract attention to themselves, this is a misuse of God's gifts, which are given for the church to grow into maturity, not hero worship.

One of the earliest examples of "criteria for ministry" lists the qualities for deacons and those who aspire to "oversight," *episcopē*; while this is translated as "bishop" and gives us the word "episcopal," this is written before the church has formalized the threefold order of bishops, priests, and deacons (let alone bishops wearing purple shirts like the Roman emperor!). A key ability is that they must be an "an apt teacher," literally *didactic* in Greek (1 Tim. 3:1–2). Those who perform this task well, "laboring in preaching and teaching," even deserve to be paid double (1 Tim. 5:17–18)! Meanwhile, Titus is told that such a minister "must have a firm grasp of the word that is trustworthy in accordance with the teaching, so that he may be able both to preach with sound doctrine and to refute those who contradict it" (Titus 1:9). I remember when I was a young schoolteacher, our new curate was preaching against going to see a new film which he thought was mistaken in its depiction of Jesus. Personally, I disagreed with him, but I understood how our vicar defended him for trying to carry out his ordination charge to proclaim truth and refute error.

And finally, before we all rush into this ministry of the word, we should heed the somber words in James 3:1–2: "not many of you should become teachers, my brothers and sisters, for you know that we who teach will be judged with greater strictness. For all of us make many mistakes." I love the combination of the solemn warning in the first verse with the realism of the second. Yes, we will all make "many mistakes." That's why we need each other, and preachers and teachers themselves need wise mentors to help them along the way. That young curate with whom I disagreed is a diocesan bishop now, and we still work together and respect each other greatly. It's a very precious ministry, teaching and preaching, and not one to be undertaken lightly—and the rest of the New Testament underlines Matthew's portrait of Jesus's own preaching and teaching.

"This was to fulfill"; "it was said . . . but I say to you"

Throughout Matthew's gospel, there are repeated references to the prophets, as he seeks to relate the story of Jesus back to the Hebrew scriptures. Matthew saw in what was happening with Jesus the fulfillment of what had been said centuries earlier, and so this becomes a kind of refrain for him: "this was to fulfill"; "then was fulfilled what was spoken" (see Matt. 1:22; 2:15, 17, 23; 4:14; 8:17; 12:17; 13:35; 21:4; 27:9). Similarly he depicts Jesus himself as consciously wanting to fulfill the prophecies: "Do not think that I have come to abolish the law or the prophets; I have come not to abolish but to fulfill" (Matt. 5:17; see also 13:14; 26:54, 56). But this is no mindless following of a predetermined path. After that verse at the start of the Sermon on the Mount, Jesus interprets several of the commandments—those about murder, adultery, divorce, swearing oaths and retribution, loving neighbors and hating enemies—with the phrase "you have heard that it was said . . . but I say to you." For Jesus, it is not enough simply to fulfill the letter of the commandments and avoid murder, adultery, or whatever: we have to go on further, to get rid of hatred, lust, and the desire for revenge, if we are truly to follow him; we must take the scriptures and live them out even more fully today as we seek to proclaim the loving rule or reign of God.

Too much preaching and teaching misses out on this important balance of old and new, and ends up either churning out what sound like impossible or irrelevant scriptural instructions, taking no account of their original context or intention, or, at the other extreme, just repeating whatever is the latest trendy fad or idea with no regard for the teaching of scripture and the tradition at all! If you are to develop a ministry of preaching and teaching for people today, you need to be like a great suspension bridge, like that over the Clifton Gorge in Bristol, or the one across the Golden Gate at the entrance to San Francisco Bay. They are both held up by enormous, thick cables which are buried deep in the rock on either side. So too for you: to be able to get that capacity to relate what it says in the text to what is going on in your life and in the lives of people today, you must be rooted deeply both in the scriptures at one end and in understanding of our contemporary society and culture at the other. If either end is too shallow, or breaks free, the whole bridge will collapse, and people will plunge into the abyss below. However, if we can enable people to be deeply rooted in both the word of the living God and the world we live in, then they will flourish and help to build a better society for all God's children.

Different levels and contexts

Matthew presents Jesus teaching in at least three different levels or contexts. First, there are his discourses or sermons to crowds of people, the general population, where he tends to talk in stories and parables. This is a way of teaching that isn't forced and that allows his various hearers to react differently. I am sure that there were some local subsistence farmers who heard the parable of the sower, and went off saying things like: "That there lad, now, 'e unnerstands what 'tis like for us poor farmers; I got a field just like that, full of thistles 'n' weeds 'n' rocks!" They may have missed the spiritual lesson of the parable entirely—but at least they got the point that Jesus cared about them and understood their problems. And maybe, just maybe, one of them might have turned to the others and said, "You know what? I reckon 'e's on to something, something even more important, you know, God 'n' stuff." Find ways of using stories in your preaching—and try to resist the urge constantly to have to explain *everything*. Leave something to your hearers' imagination. After all, explaining a joke usually takes all the humor away. And Jesus was nothing if not a master of humor—just think of camels going through the eyes of needles, or people with logs in their eyes trying to help someone with a speck of dust in theirs!

Second, there are the times when the disciples finally get to be alone with Jesus, often after one of the longer discourses, and want to ask him: "Now, hang on a minute; what on earth was *that* all about?" In Matthew's central chapter of the parables of the kingdom, it is precisely after the parable of the sower that the disciples ask him why he speaks to the people in parables, and again after the story of the field with wheat and weeds growing together (Matt. 13:10, 34–36). It is in this more intimate context that Jesus spells out the meaning of his parables for the disciples, preferring to leave his enigmatic, riddling stories for the general population to puzzle about and think through. Significantly, many biblical critics think that some of the more allegorical explanations are more likely to have been developed in the early church rather than derive from Jesus himself; at their basic level, parables in their original form usually have only one main point. Too much allegorizing can lead to some serious theological problems: is God really begrudging like a miserable old judge, or who is he in bed with when the friend wants bread at midnight? (Luke 18:2–6; 11:5–7).

Individual encounters

Third, some of the most significant instances of Jesus's teaching emerge through his conversation with individuals, particularly those who come to him asking for help. Perhaps the most pivotal story in Matthew's account of Jesus's ministry takes place not even in Israel, but up north in the district of Tyre and Sidon, near Beirut in modern Lebanon, where a Canaanite woman seeks his help for her daughter (Matt. 15:21–28). Up to this point, Jesus has told his disciples to go only to "the lost sheep of the house of Israel," and he repeats this phrase to her now (Matt. 10:6; 15:24). He even uses the Jewish derogative word for Gentiles, "dogs," as his reason for not giving her "the children's food" (15:26). Yet her persistence, her love for her daughter, and her clever answer that the "dogs" can eat the crumbs that fall from the table lead Jesus not only to praise her, but also to heal her daughter instantly (15:27–28).

Interpreters of this passage are divided: the more traditional explanation shies away from the implication that Jesus might have used such offensive language and rejected her so rudely, suggesting instead that he always intended to heal the girl but merely wanted to elicit her mother's declaration of faith. Others prefer to take the story more at face value where the mother seems actually to change Jesus's mind through her feisty refusal to be ignored. Whichever you think is correct, it remains true that this story changes the whole direction of Jesus's ministry in Matthew's account, as he begins to realize that the "lost sheep of the house of Israel," especially the religious leaders, are not going to accept his teaching, and so he begins to build a new community, the *ecclesia*, or church, founded upon the rock of Peter, and to whom his teaching is now directed (Matt. 16:18; 18:15, 17). There is a lesson here for all of us who are preachers and teachers, who can easily fall into just regurgitating the same old stuff without growing and developing new ideas or directions. We need to have similar individual encounters with people in deep pain or need, to take the gospel to where life really hurts—and to be prepared to have to do some serious rethinking when we are challenged by others!

The pulpit and beyond

If there are these three levels or contexts for Jesus's ministry in Matthew's gospel—sermons to crowds and the general public, group teaching to disciples, and individual encounters—this is a good reminder that the ministry of teaching and preaching must go on in lots of places and times other than Sunday morning's appearance in the pulpit, or short ten-minute talks. Yes, of course, sermons are important and it is crucial that they have a good theological undergirding, but they are not the place to teach too much theology: our sermons should also inspire people and exhort them to live out the gospel; yes, you want to get the brain thinking, but perhaps even more to enable the heart to respond, and people's lives to change as a result of your words.

There are so many other opportunities beyond the pulpit to teach the faith. Like the disciples asking Jesus for further explanation of his public discourses, small groups are better for instruction and discussion, through house groups, Bible-study circles, Lent groups, and short courses on certain books of the Bible or different aspects of the faith. Your ministry will include classes such as those for people who are searching for faith, sometimes called "Agnostics Anonymous," or those preparing for baptism or confirmation. The Occasional Offices of baptism, marriage, and funerals—sometimes called "hatching, matching, and dispatching"—provide wonderful opportunities to explain our faith, often to people who do not know what they think or believe, but who turn to the church in their great joy at the arrival of a child, or in committing themselves to a new life of loving another, or in their sadness from death or tragedy. The latter will most likely involve the opportunity for personal conversation with the individuals and family affected, but groups or short courses for those preparing for christenings or baptisms and weddings should be part of every church's ministry.

Finally, most parishes have a school in their area, and many a newly ordained minister has found out the hard way that taking assemblies for seven-year-olds does not necessarily guarantee an easy audience. Certainly, several occasions from those early days are still burned in my memory, but I was grateful for the experience and I learned a lot from some very patient primary schoolteachers! Religious education is increasingly under pressure in our educational system today, so here is a phenomenal privilege, joy, and responsibility which anyone who seeks a ministry of teaching the Christian faith should embrace.

We saw above that ordination liturgies include instructions like "tell the story of God's love" and "unfold the Scriptures, to preach the word in season and out of season, and to declare the mighty acts of God." Sermons, groups, and classes provide opportunities for teaching "in season," but Jesus's example in Matthew also encourages us to be on the lookout for unusual opportunities, "out of season," or when we are least expecting them, which means we need to keep ourselves fresh and find ways of sustaining this ministry over the years.

5. Sustaining teaching and preaching in your ministry

So, finally, after all this study of Matthew's portrait of Jesus the teacher, and how this is worked out in selection and training for ministry, we come to the vital question: how will you sustain your passion for preaching the gospel and teaching the faith throughout your ministry? In the introduction, I warned you against approaching ordination and ministerial preparation like a camel, filling up for three years at the oasis of theological training and then plodding across the desert for the next couple of decades. Such an approach simply will not do; not only will you not be able to sustain it through years of ministry, but it is also dangerous—both for you and for the people entrusted to your care. You have got to find a way of nourishing yourself, deepening and developing your understanding of your faith over the years as you seek to teach it to others.

It has been a great privilege over the years to spend time with Archbishop Desmond Tutu, who studied for both his BA and his master's degrees in theology at King's College London in the middle of the 1960s, in preparation for his ministry in the beautiful but troubled land of South Africa. The first visit that I hosted for him was nearly thirty years ago at the University of Exeter where I was then Lazenby Chaplain. I showed the packed program planned for two days to his accompanying assistant on the train from Heathrow as we raced across Salisbury Plain at 125 mph, who sighed, took out a red pen, and knocked out about half the events: "If he's going to do *this*, he won't be able to do *that*; if he is going to speak *here*, he needs to be quiet beforehand *there*."

"Come aside," pray, read, and reflect

Over many years, Archbishop Desmond had learned that he needs to take in before giving out; if he is going to talk *about* God, he has to have quiet time to listen *to* God first. In fact, Matthew shows this same rhythm in the ministry of Jesus: after his baptism and before he starts his teaching ministry with the Sermon on the Mount, he goes to spend time in the desert, where he is tempted by the devil and has to decide about his priorities to serve God alone (Matt. 4:1). Equally, after delivering the central collection of parables and hearing the news about the death of John the Baptist, Jesus again withdraws "to a deserted place by himself"—even if the crowd quickly discover where he has gone and hasten to follow him, which leads to the feeding of the multitude (Matt. 14:13–15).

Now, if that's true for Jesus and Desmond Tutu, it's even more necessary for you and me. You will need to set aside time for study, prayer, and reflection without which your teaching and preaching ministry will simply run out of gas, and you will be a noisy gong or clanging cymbal (1 Cor. 13:1), not to mention a thirsty camel. These times can be of different lengths and frequency, with occasional longer periods undergirded by regular and even daily discipline. It's a good idea to try to plan a week's retreat or study every year or so; sometimes that might be for prayer at a religious community— and we shall return to this later—but also you will benefit from times spent back at seminary, college, or university, where you can do some reading in the library and catch up on scholarship for a period. More regularly, many ministers have found that they need at least a day or two a month, or a morning a week, to keep their theological studies developing.

Underpinning it all must be a daily discipline of prayer and reading the Bible. Anglican clergy are supposed to say the Daily Offices, morning and evening prayer, liturgies which are themselves steeped in scripture, as well as the psalms, canticles, and the daily readings. Other people find some form of daily Bible-reading notes helpful, and there are many booklets and schemes available from publishers and organizations like the Bible Reading Fellowship, the Bible Society, or Scripture Union. If you are following one of these or reading through a particular book of the Bible, try to get a good commentary or two which have both a scholarly basis and a practical application so you can use them to accompany your daily devotions.

What about next Sunday?

The problem with Sunday is that it comes round every week, and many clergy in parochial ministry will find themselves preaching at least once. The temptation, of course, is to leave preparation until the end of the week, especially if you are exhausted by a spectacular performance this Sunday! But it's a good idea to look ahead to next Sunday or to the next time you will preach as soon as you can; look through the readings which are set by the lectionary or the themes which have been planned for the service, and at the very least start to get some ideas regarding what they are about, and what you might be wanting to say. If you can, look at a commentary or two, or even go to a library, or look at some of the resources available online these days, and get the creative juices flowing. It can be as though you set part of your brain to go off like a "working party" and let it all marinade over several days before you ever get round to actually starting to write the sermon. You'll be surprised how often you might find yourself thinking about it in the bath, or while just walking around—and then when you do start to write, there will probably be a good idea or two waiting for you.

Recently, I was intrigued to find an elderly but highly respected priest, not known particularly as a "Bible-thumper," in the section of our library at King's College devoted to biblical studies and commentaries, on several Friday mornings, just sitting there reading, or getting up to go to the shelves painfully to pull down yet another heavy volume. When I summoned the courage to ask him about this, he explained that this had been his discipline for some fifty years, to try to spend every Friday morning reading the lessons set for Sunday, and, if possible, looking at some commentaries upon them. He did this whether he was preaching or not, but obviously this practice informed his preaching and teaching ministry. I felt humbled, yet also encouraged, by his example. In fact, King's provides a reduced or even free library membership to London clergy through a local association to assist them in doing this—but sadly, the pressures of parish ministry are such that far too few take up this offer.

"He died to take away your sins, not your mind"

I have a picture of Jesus hanging in my office, originally produced by the Episcopal Church in the USA, which simply says, "He died to take away your sins, not your mind." It's been there for over a couple of decades, having moved with me several times. I am amazed by how many people comment upon it: on one occasion, Rowan Williams, then Archbishop of Canterbury, must have noticed it while robing for a service in our chapel, since he quoted it, with emphatic approval, in his subsequent sermon and emphasized the importance of continuing to keep our intellectual and theological studies alive.

There's an old adage that you can always tell when a vicar got ordained by checking their shelves for the date of the most recent book that they bought! You cannot simply fill up at the oasis and set off through the desert: you need to keep up your reading—and that means buying, borrowing, or downloading things to study. I don't say this because I'm an author—although religious publishers are struggling these days with increasingly little profit in this market. And yet, it is vital for the growth of the church and for the continuing education of clergy and lay people alike that we find a way of acquiring books or making time to read; trying to have something always "on the go" will help feed you and prevent you going stale.

Of course, this is not easy, especially for stipendiary clergy on a hard-earned modest stipend. I was surprised, but delighted, during my first lectures in the USA when busy clergy kept asking me to recommend a good commentary on Matthew. Since English clergy didn't tend to have similar requests, I asked them why the interest in Matthew, only to receive the mystifying reply, "Well, it's Year A." That was my first introduction to the Revised Common Lectionary (RCL), in which the readings for most Sundays work their way through Matthew in Year A, Mark in B, and Luke in C. I was disappointed that there wasn't a fourth year for John, and tried to argue for that when, like many churches around the world, the Church of England also later adopted the RCL. But at least it does mean that it is worth your investing in a good commentary on one of the synoptic gospels each year—since you are going to be preaching from it most Sundays!

Otherwise, make a point of reading some book reviews in publications like church newspapers or monthly magazines, or subscribe to journals like *Theology* or *Expository Times*, designed for busy ministers. And then, of course, there are so many online resources these days—blogs and discussion boards—where you can get ideas, and websites where you can read extracts of books to check them out; some suggestions are included in the appendices. So whatever stage you are on your journey towards or through ministry, try to develop habits of reading and thinking which will sustain you over the years. And if it is hard to do this on your own, find a couple of friends or colleagues with whom you can read things together—and then discuss it all, maybe over a drink or two, or a meal.

Being a bridge-builder between faith and daily life

And don't confine your reading or thinking solely—or even mainly—to theology or explicitly Christian books. We saw above how both the criteria for selection and the ordination services stress the importance of relating the gospel to the culture and society around us. The well-respected evangelical preacher John Stott had the media and thousands of shoppers literally on his doorstep every day when he was vicar of All Soul's Church in the center of London's Regent Street, next door to BBC Broadcasting House. He cultivated throughout his life the habit of watching films and TV, or going to the theater, or reading popular novels for the explicit purpose of finding out what society was watching and reading, or thinking about. He would often take close friends or trusted advisers with him, and then get them to discuss it with him, so that he could find ways to relate the Bible and Christian theology to what was going on and where ordinary people were itching. He would then illustrate his sermons and teaching with fresh and relevant examples which people could instantly recognize. You could do a lot worse than follow his example—and it's a great excuse to go to the movies!

Finally, it's a big mistake to think that study and theological reflection should finish when you leave college, or after a bishop has laid their hands on your head. I was initially confused by the fact that graduation ceremonies at the end of college or seminary education are often called "commencements" in the United States, just when things were finishing. But of course, it is absolutely right: leaving college is the "commencement" of your real life, and, for ministers, of your ministry. Equally, it is also the end of being spoon-fed or pushed through various curricular activities: rather, it is the commencement of taking responsibility for your own learning and professional development in the ministry of teaching and preaching.

And as well as all these informal ways of learning to deepen our faith and relate it to our life today, the joy is that it is never too late to go back to college or to keep up some formal study alongside your ministry. One of my great joys over many years has been teaching and supervising busy clergy who nonetheless make time to pursue a part-time master's or even study for a doctorate at King's College. I did my own PhD part-time during the early years of my ministry, so I remember how hard it can sometimes be, sitting up late or getting up early, typing at the computer with a grizzling baby on your shoulder! In addition, these days there are lots of distance learning or extension studies courses online, from many different theological or Bible colleges, seminaries, and distinguished universities, like King's.

In the end, perhaps it does not really matter which approach you adopt to enable you to continue learning and growing in your faith and theological understanding—whether it is part-time study or informal reading and discussion—as long as you do *something*! Unless you really want to run the risk of running out of energy and insight under the many and tough pressures of ministry, it is wise to find ways early in your journey to nourish yourself in the scriptures and in your understanding of the Christian faith if you're going to be a "herald," a "messenger," and proclaim "the wonderful deeds" of God, "who has called us out of darkness into his marvelous light," as the various ordination liturgies put it so well.

Conclusion

For many people, Christian ministry often begins with teaching and preaching—and this is certainly not confined to those who are ordained or in full-time ministry. These two aspects are central to Matthew's portrait of Jesus's ministry throughout his gospel, as he arranges Jesus's teaching into five great blocks with the parables of the kingdom right at the center; and yet, we also noted how the narrative of Jesus's ministry to the crowds, his disciples, and various individuals is structured and fitted around these great discourses. This interplay between teaching and preaching and practical ministry to people and groups is vital for any attempt to follow Jesus's example today.

Careful attention to the processes, competencies, and criteria for selection for training and the liturgies of ordination used in the different churches reveals how these aspects of teaching and preaching are still considered to be absolutely central to Christian ministry today right across all our traditions. Therefore, we have also considered briefly a wide range of possible opportunities for preaching and teaching in ministry today beyond the obvious pulpit, through encounters with individuals and groups, in schools and wider society. Finally, we have discussed various possible ways of sustaining a lifelong habit of learning and growing in your own understanding of faith and its relation to our daily life together in society. Wherever you happen to be on your own personal journey of faith and ministry, I hope that some of these ideas will help and inspire you along the way—and will help you to find ways of nourishing yourself so that you can minister to others in turn.

For prayer and further reflection

You might want to consider these questions taken from the various ordination services, or look again at your own church's liturgy:

- Do you accept the Scriptures of the Old and New Testaments to be, by the Holy Spirit, the unique and authoritative witness to Jesus Christ in the Church universal, and God's Word to you? Will you fulfill your office in obedience to Jesus Christ, under the authority of Scripture, and be continually guided by our confessions? (PCUSA)
- The church in which you are to be ordained confesses that the holy scriptures are the word of God and are the norm of its faith and life. We accept, teach, and confess the Apostles', the Nicene, and the Athanasian Creed. We also acknowledge the Lutheran confessions as true witnesses and faithful expositions of the holy scriptures. Will you therefore preach and teach in accordance with the holy scriptures and these creeds and confessions? (ELCA)
- Are you persuaded that the Scriptures of the Old and New Testaments contain all things necessary for salvation through faith in Jesus Christ and are the unique and authoritative standard for the church's faith and life? (UMC)
- Are you persuaded that the Holy Scriptures contain sufficiently all doctrines required of necessity for eternal salvation through faith in Jesus Christ? Are you determined out of the said Scriptures to instruct the people committed to your charge, and to teach nothing as required of necessity to salvation, but that which you shall be persuaded may be concluded and proved by Scriptures? Will you be ready with all faithful diligence always to banish and drive away all erroneous and strange doctrines contrary to God's Word, and to use both public and private monitions and exhortation as well to the sick as to the whole within your charge as need shall require and occasion shall be given? (AME)

You will be required to assent to such statements and vow to keep these promises whatever your church, and Episcopalians must "**solemnly declare that I do believe the Holy Scriptures of the Old and New Testaments to be the Word of God, and to contain all things necessary to salvation**" (TEC Article VIII).

Therefore, think and pray about them now. Perhaps write down some reflections about them in your journal, or discuss them with your spiritual director or vocational advisers. Take them into your prayers, and ask God for the ability, the courage, and the strength to be able to make these responses—and to keep them. You may also find it helpful to post comments and questions (in general terms, of course!) on the Facebook page for this book: www.facebook.com/FourMinistriesOneJesus.

PART II

Luke

Pastoral Care

Figure 2. Saint Luke, *Lindisfarne Gospels*, Folio 137b

1. Luke's portrait of Jesus's pastoral ministry

If we look at the depiction of Saint Luke in the *Lindisfarne Gospels*, Folio 137b (see fig. 2), we see Luke seated as he writes with what looks like a flying cow jumping over him. The Latin inscription, *imago vituli*, tells us that the image is that of a "bull calf," reflecting the Greek *moschos*, used in Revelation 4:7 and the Septuagint version of Ezekiel 1:10; on the other hand, Ezekiel's Hebrew, *shōr*, is actually an ox—and many of the early frescoes and Celtic manuscripts depict a large horned beast. While the corresponding pictures of Matthew and Mark show them looking intently at what they are writing, Luke appears to be slightly cocking his head, as though listening to his animal. Why might a *bull* or an *ox*, of all creatures, be inspiring Luke? you might well ask. I have to admit, as a biblical scholar, that there are some gospel commentators that think Luke is "a bit of a plodder"! I think that's rather unfair, so, instead, I would like to invite you to think a little bit about the place of an ox in preindustrial society. The many biblical references to oxen, particularly in the Hebrew scriptures, demonstrate that before machines came along, the ox was one of the most powerful engines that the human race had.

The Bible even likens God to "the horns of a wild ox" (Num. 23:22; 24:8). It was the ox that did all your hard work, pulling the oxcart or plow, dragging heavy burdens, working the threshing floor or treading out the grains (Num. 7:3; Deut. 22:10; 1 Chron. 12:40; 1 Kings 19:19; Deut. 25:4; Hos. 10:11). The ox did it all, and so provided wealth for the poor: "where there is no ox, there is no wealth," says the book of Proverbs (Prov. 14:4). It's not surprising then that the ox was even important enough to feature in the Ten Commandments: "You shall not covet your neighbor's . . . ox" (Exod. 20:17). Finally, the ox was also a sacrificial animal. The priests made hard work of sacrificing six hundred under Hezekiah, so when King Solomon sacrificed twenty-two thousand oxen at the dedication of the temple, that must have kept the butchers going for quite some time (2 Chron. 29:33; 1 Kings 8:63)!

So, it's those images that I want us to bear in mind as we consider Luke's portrait of Jesus and what that might have to say to your pastoral ministry, particularly caring for the vulnerable and the marginalized, if the ox is the bearer of burdens, and ultimately a sacrificial victim.

Origins and steady progress

After the opening stories about the announcement of the conceptions of John the Baptist and Jesus, Luke gives us a brief account of the birth of Jesus in the backyard of a hostelry on the edge of the Roman Empire. His simple sentence that Mary "laid him in a manger, because there was no place for them in the inn" (2:6), has given rise to the whole tradition which we re-create every Christmas time with the "stable" that isn't actually mentioned anywhere in the gospels. Cribs and school nativity plays then populate this stable with the shepherds (who do at least come to a "manger" in Luke 2:16), plus the wise men (who go much later to a "house," according to Matt. 2:11). The inevitable livestock usually includes an ox somewhere at the back, not found in any gospel, but because it says in Isaiah that "the ox knows its master" (Isa. 1:3). Nonetheless, the tradition of the ox and Luke's description of the visit of poor humble shepherds, rather than Matthew's rich and powerful wise men or kings, help to set the atmosphere for Luke's portrait of Jesus's pastoral ministry among the poor as the bearer of burdens.

If the ox is an animal that puts one foot in front of another rather sedately, then this is rather a good image for the way in which Luke goes about writing his gospel, which he himself describes as "an orderly account" (Luke 1:3). Unlike the dizzying pace and rush which we will find in Mark's gospel next, Luke's account is very steady, being carefully written and organized. Luke is the one gospel writer who usually gives indications of time and place, mentioning who was the emperor, who was the high priest, who was the tetrarch, and where it was all going on (see Luke 1:5; 2:1–2; 3:1–2). He likes to introduce stories with the traditional Hebrew phrase "and it came to pass," using it fifty times in his gospel alone, while the other three evangelists use it only thirteen times combined.

This gives us a steady rhythm, and, after the opening stories of the infancy and baptism and temptation, Luke structures his gospel very deliberately into three parts: he begins with Jesus's ministry in Galilee for the first third of the gospel (4:14–9:50), which concludes with Jesus's determination to "set his face to go to Jerusalem" (9:51). Actually, the long journey down the Jordan valley from the Sea of Galilee to Jericho skirting around Samaria (what we call the West Bank today) occupies the gospel's middle part, its longest section (9:51–19:27); Jesus meets all sorts of people along the way, spreading the good news, healing and meeting their needs. If Matthew structures his gospel around the five discourses to highlight Jesus's teaching, then Luke's account reveals his pastoral care and ministry, which then continue even after the entry into Jerusalem, into the gospel's third part (19:28–24:53).

Caring for the poor and the vulnerable

Throughout Luke's gospel, we find extraordinary stories of Jesus's ministry among the poor and outcasts, the vulnerable and marginalized, and those who were not Jews. Matthew begins with Jesus giving his sermon from the mount, up high, like Moses. Luke, however, depicts him coming down to teach at the people's level—literally, "on a level place"—where his first reaction is to touch and heal them (Luke 6:17–19). Only then do we get Luke's version of the Beatitudes; Matthew has eight blessings which are quite spiritual: "Blessed are the poor in spirit. . . . Blessed are those who hunger and thirst for righteousness' sake" (Matt. 5:3, 6). On the other hand, Luke has just three, and they are much more practical: "Blessed are you who are poor. . . . Blessed are you who are hungry now. . . . Blessed are you who weep now." They are matched by equally practical, corresponding woes: "Woe to you who are rich. . . . Woe to you who are full now. . . . Woe to you who are laughing now" (Luke 6:20–26). As befits his symbol of the ox, this interest in the rich and the poor runs throughout Luke's gospel, with lots of references to money—gold, silver, copper, and so on—but always with a particular interest in and concern for the humble poor. This is an extraordinary attitude when you think of the great tradition in the Hebrew scriptures that wealth is a blessing from God. When staying in the United States, I often see evangelists preaching this message on TV and inviting people to send them some money, in return for which they will "miraculously"—or magically?—get Jesus to go into people's bank accounts and sort out all their problems. Unfortunately, this so-called prosperity gospel has now spread from America across Africa, and, increasingly, around our poorer communities in London. If it has any scriptural justification, which I doubt, it certainly does not come from Luke!

Furthermore, this pastoral care for the poor is also extended to the vulnerable and the marginalized, including sinners, lepers, the crippled, the blind, and even people like tax collectors, who were often not accepted by wider society, especially the religious leaders. It is only in Luke's gospel that we find Jesus telling those who seek seats of higher honor to "go and sit at the lowest place"; uniquely to Luke, he continues, "when you give a luncheon or a dinner, do not invite your friends or your brothers or your relatives or rich neighbors, in case they may invite you in return, and you would be repaid. But when you give a banquet, invite the poor, the crippled, the lame, and the blind" (see Luke 14:7–13). Luke then follows this with the parable of the great dinner, the messianic banquet of the kingdom, which is also in Matthew (Luke 14:15–24; Matt. 22:1–10). However, when the invited guests begin to make excuses about having bought some land or got married, it is only in Luke's version that the master admonishes the slave to "Go out at once into the streets and lanes of the town and bring in the poor, the crippled, the blind, and the lame" (Luke 14:21). Jesus does not just talk about inviting these poor people, he "walks the talk" himself, consorting with lepers (5:12–16; 7:22; 17:11–19), the crippled (5:17–26; 7:22), the blind (7:21–22; 18:35–43), and tax collectors (5:27–30; 15:1–2; 19:1–10).

If we are also to live out our "teaching and preaching of the good news for the poor" which we saw in Matthew, we will also need to examine our pastoral ministry—and who it is focused upon, and those with whom we spend our time. And even if, as ministers, we do not go looking for the poor and the vulnerable, they will find you. Wearing a clerical "dog collar" down the streets, or on the bus or tube, is an open invitation to be asked for money, and any home marked as a vicarage or clergy house will have a steady stream of callers at the door, each with their own, often convoluted, story about their needy situation. We will return to this later on and discuss how you might respond, but for the moment, it would be good to spend a little time reflecting on Luke's portrait of Jesus's pastoral care of the poor and the vulnerable in his ministry.

Women

Another marginalized group which features throughout Luke's account of Jesus's ministry embraces those which the old Chinese proverb, immortalized by Mao Tse-tung and John Lennon, termed "the other side of the sky"—women. Remember that adult, free, male Jews (and Greeks) thanked God daily that he had made them that way, and not as slaves, bar-barians, or women! Yet Luke constantly gives us the women's perspective, beginning his gospel not with Matthew's men like Joseph and Herod, but with the story of Elizabeth, who is unable to bear children, of Mary her-self, and of Anna the Prophetess with Simeon in the temple (Luke 1–2). In his account of Jesus's pastoral ministry, Luke includes many encoun-ters involving women which occur only in this gospel: the widow of Nain (7:11–17); the woman with the ointment (7:36–50); a woman in the crowd (11:27); the woman healed on the Sabbath (13:10–17). Women also appear regularly in Jesus's parables in Luke, often paired with a man: the woman with leaven follows the man with a mustard seed (13:18–21); a woman's lost coin pairs the man's lost sheep (15:3–10); the two women grinding, one taken at the End and one left, balance the two men in bed, one taken and one left (17:34–35).

Above all, Luke is the only gospel to depict women among Jesus's disciples, including wealthy women who help to pay for and support their mission: "Joanna, the wife of Herod's steward Chuza, and Susanna, and many others, who provided for them out of their resources" (Luke 8:2–3). Luke alone gives us the story of the sisters Martha and Mary, where Martha is busy in the kitchen preparing food for Jesus and the disciples; Mary, however, is "sitting at Jesus's feet, listening to him." When Martha tells Jesus to tell Mary off and send her back to the women's work in the kitchen, Jesus responds that "Mary has chosen the better part" (Luke 10:38–42). The significance of this is that rabbis were the equivalent of the tertiary ed-ucation system in ancient Israel; after checking out several of them teach-ing, male students would choose one and "sit at his feet and listen" as the mark of a disciple. So Mary is sitting where only men were supposed to sit—yet Jesus affirms her right to be a disciple. Two thousand years later, it seems extraordinary how long and difficult the churches have made the path to full inclusion of women within the ordained ministry as priests and bishops—something more for you to reflect upon, perhaps, whatever your views or your gender.

Non-Jews

In addition to the poor and marginalized, and women, Luke's narrative includes positive examples of people who are not Jewish. It is in Luke that we find Jesus giving the example of the Good Samaritan, from the mixed race descended from Israelites and Assyrians who were shunned by other Jews for five centuries after their return from the exile, who cares for the wounded man when the Jewish priest and Levite "passed by on the other side" (Luke 10:29–37). Only a chapter earlier, Jesus had to stop James and John wanting to rain fire down on the Samaritans (Luke 9:51–56). And there are even Romans, like the centurion who has faith like "none in Israel" (Luke 7:9), who appear through the gospel and continue into the book of Acts.

Thus throughout Luke's gospel, he shows Jesus's pastoral ministry reaching out to people and places which would have been unexpected in terms of the social conventions of the day, to those who are poor and vulnerable and marginalized, those who are outcasts, those who are of the wrong gender or a despised race, all of those, in fact, whom respectable people wouldn't expect to matter. As nationalism or tribalism seems to be reasserting itself in many countries around the world at present, and governments are making it harder for refugees and immigrants to enter into safety, Luke's portrait of Jesus's pastoral ministry should make us pause for thought, and challenges our prejudices.

Sacrificial cost

Jesus does not just live out his pastoral care for others in his ministry, but he ends up laying down that life for them, like the ox being offered as a sacrifice in the temple. Luke's account of the crucifixion focuses upon different details from those highlighted by Matthew and Mark, which enable Luke's wonderful themes through his gospel to come to a climax here at the cross. Thus on the way to the cross, Luke alone tells us that the accompanying crowd included "women who were beating their breasts and wailing for him." Even in his painful progress along the Via Dolorosa to his own death, Jesus stops and turns to care for them: "Daughters of Jerusalem, do not weep for me, but weep for yourselves and for your children. For the days are surely coming when they will say, 'Blessed are the barren, and the wombs that never bore, and the breasts that never nursed.' Then they will begin to say to the mountains, 'Fall on us'; and to the hills, 'Cover us.' For if they do this when the wood is green, what will happen when it is dry?" (Luke 23:26–31). We see on our television screens all the time that when the men fight, so often it is the women and children that get hurt and killed. Within a few decades of Jesus's death, the

Roman siege engines would surround Jerusalem while the different Jewish factions were all fighting each other inside the city—and, of course, the women and children trapped within the walls would pay the price in terrible suffering.

When we get to the place of crucifixion, only Luke has the extraordinary story where a Roman auxiliary carpenter has to nail another carpenter to a cross of rough, splintered wood. Instead of invoking the equivalent of woodworkers' guild regulations or trade union rules, Jesus prays for those who have to do such terrible things under orders: "Father, forgive them; for they do not know what they are doing" (Luke 23:34). A short while later, once again it is only in Luke that we hear one of the criminals crucified alongside Jesus rebuking the other's taunting of Jesus, admitting his guilt and asking Jesus to "remember me when you come into your kingdom." And so the bearer of our burdens, the one who has lived his entire life opening the kingdom of God to those who are usually kept out by religious authorities, ends up dying as he lived, caring for others until the very end and, like an ox, sacrificing himself for them: "truly I tell you, today you will be with me in Paradise" (Luke 23:39–43).

Time to get your pens out again

Therefore, although this image of an ox might have seemed rather curious at first, this brief consideration has shown how apt it is for Luke's portrait of Jesus, especially his steady account of Jesus's pastoral ministry among the poor and vulnerable, his care for the marginalized, regardless of wealth or poverty, gender or race. This is also, of course, the counterbalance to Matthew's stress on teaching and preaching. So now it is time to repeat the exercise you did last time to explore how this aspect of pastoral care is set out in the ministry before you. Once again, I suggest that you put this chapter down, and turn to the appendices at the back of the book. If you have used a highlighter, take a contrasting color this time, and mark all the phrases or sentences which concern pastoral ministry and caring for others in both the selection criteria and competencies, as well as in the liturgies from the ordination services in the various churches. And as before, spend a while in prayer and contemplation, meditating upon the passages you have highlighted this time—and perhaps take some time to write about your thoughts and reflections in your journal or notebook before we come to my observations in the next two chapters.

2. The pastoral ministry in selection for ministry

In our study of Matthew, we saw that several of the criteria for selection for ordination training in the Anglican Communion and other churches were especially relevant for teaching and preaching: in the Church of England, this area is the particular responsibility of the educational adviser at the conference discerning candidates' vocations. Similarly, other criteria apply especially to the pastoral ministry: personality, character and integrity (TEAC D), relationships (E), leadership and collaboration (F), and practical competencies (I). Once again, at an English Bishops' Advisory Panel, one person concentrates on these criteria, namely, the Pastoral Adviser, who will assess the candidate's vocation through them, using the various elements of the interviews and exercises. Similar criteria and competencies are also looked for in our other lists, reproduced in appendix 2. But long before final selection, vocation advisers, local clergy and ministers, and diocesan or regional experts should be helping possible candidates to grow in pastoral gifts and skills and to develop into the sort of person who can exercise "the care of souls"; thus, evidence is sought about how candidates can demonstrate that they fulfill the criteria or possess the competencies—which include many of the qualities we have just seen in Luke's portrait of Jesus's pastoral ministry.

The demanding role of an ordained minister

These sorts of criteria do not make for comfortable reading. For the Anglican Communion, the criterion about "personality, character and integrity" requires candidates to be "mature, stable and show that they are able to sustain the demanding role of a minister, and are able to face change and pressure in a flexible and balanced way" (TEAC D). Lutherans look for a "demonstration of skills for leading a community of faith through change while addressing conflicts that might emerge" (ELCA 2.1.1.4.b), as well as a "willingness to serve, risk and sacrifice for the sake of God's mission, including an ability to identify and lead in exposing the principalities and powers operative in a given context, and responding to life crises as opportunities for experiencing new life" (ELCA 2.1.2.1.c and d). Methodists want their candidates to "be persons in whom the community can place trust and confidence" (UMC 304.*h*).

It's amazing that anyone would want to take on the job! Except, of course, that ordained ministry is not a "job"—it is a calling, a way of life, which makes extraordinary demands on the priest, pastor, or minister, as well as on their family and loved ones. There are no set hours of 9 to 5, since conversations, meetings, and groups have to take place whenever other people are free, especially evenings and weekends—and the knock on the door or the phone call when someone is dying in the middle of the night is all too common. Clergy are often the only caring professionals who actually live among and alongside their people—who are certainly not "clients" or "patients." You will sometimes have to go from a tragic situation of being with someone suffering or dying, to meet a couple who want you to celebrate their wedding or new baby's christening. Sharing other people's joys and sorrows, delights and hurts is an extraordinary privilege—but it can also be emotionally draining! The wise priest who supervised my pastoral training used to describe rushing between birth and death via marriage preparation all on one day as "playing a full set"—and just as tiring, if not more so.

Caring for others

Luke depicts Jesus as almost constantly available, meeting people on the roadside or by the lakeshore, in houses or synagogues—and always having time to give them, asking them what they want, and trying to meet their needs or heal their sufferings. The United Methodist Church wants their candidates to "make a commitment to lead the whole Church in loving service to humankind" (UMC 304.*f*). Anglicans are bluntly told that they should "have an approachable and caring attitude" (TEAC I), while Lutherans must ensure that "a ministry of care encompasses both congregational and community care. Some key aspects of this competency include: a. visitation, b. counseling, c. equipping the baptized to provide ministries of care, both within the congregation and in the wider community," and "e. sensitivity to people in major life and cultural transitions" (ELCA 2.1.3.3).

These criteria about relationships require candidates to "demonstrate self-awareness and self-acceptance as a basis for developing open and healthy professional, personal and pastoral relationships as ministers" (TEAC E). Similarly, Lutheran candidates must demonstrate "a maintenance of clear and healthy boundaries in all relationships" (ELCA 2.1.3.4.c). But maintaining "appropriate boundaries" can be extremely difficult when someone grabs you for "a quick word, Pastor" in the middle of a supermarket aisle when you have just popped out for a pint of milk for your coffee. We noted Luke's particular portrayal of Jesus's care for the poor and the vulnerable, the despised and the marginalized—and there are still plenty like this today. Clergy who display "care and compassion for all people with appropriate relational skills," as the Disciples of Christ put it (DoC A.2.g), will find all sorts and conditions of human beings wanting to talk to them or beating a path to their door, all too often on occasions like family mealtimes.

Working with others

From the call of the first disciples (Luke 5:1–11), Luke shows how Jesus shares his ministry with other people, rather than doing it all himself. He chooses twelve, out of a larger group of followers, to be "apostles," a Greek word which just means "those sent out"—and after a couple of chapters where they accompany him on the road, he soon proceeds to "send them out to preach the kingdom of God and to heal the sick" (6:12–16; 9:1–6). But he does not confine the ministry to these special leaders: not much later, he appoints seventy-two others and sends them on ahead in pairs (10:1–17).

Most churches also seek this collaborative attitude from those offering themselves for the ministry. Thus the Anglican Communion seeks candidates who "are recognised as leaders who have the respect of the congregation and of the wider community," and who "are able to establish good relationships with many types of people" (TEAC E). They must therefore "collaborate effectively with others" (F). Similarly, for Lutherans, this comes out of the fact that "we are church," and therefore candidates must demonstrate a "facility for encouraging collegial decision-making processes" (ELCA 2.1.1.4.d). Furthermore, "we are church together," so the competencies sought in potential ministers include "a. gifts for forming partnerships and networks; b. the practice of reconciliation and mutual empowerment among diverse groups; c. convening and empowering teams for mission; d. a sense of stewardship in cultivating gifts manifest in a community of believers and delegating and sharing tasks tailored to those gifts" (2.1.3.2.a–d). Therefore, it is worth thinking about your own approach to collaboration and experience of working with others, and perhaps noting some examples in your journal.

Of course, none of these pastoral gifts are confined to the clergy, and the wise minister will encourage and support lay people who demonstrate their care for others. As a young curate, I learned huge amounts from several key lay members of our ministry team, including a former headmistress who helped me face primary schoolchildren and a retired doctor who had a particular ministry among the bereaved, backing up our taking of funerals. The days of the "one-man band" (and it often was) and "Father knows best" (and "he," at least, thought he did!) are long gone, thank God—for the lone superstar individual is never a sensible or safe pattern for ministry. Those who are exploring a possible call to ministry need to learn how to work with others and to demonstrate a team spirit long before they ever get to a selection panel or discernment interview—or they are likely to become a nightmare if ever let loose on a church.

Living it out personally

The gospels are written in the genre of ancient biography, which would usually place a person's teachings and speeches in the context of their deeds and actions. Thus Luke includes Jesus's preaching within a narrative of his ministry and life. Like Jesus, ministers need to "walk the talk"; if you are saying one thing but doing something totally different, don't be surprised if no one listens to you for very long. This has to start with our own awareness of ourselves long before we can come to that of others: thus TEAC criterion D requires that "candidates are people of proven integrity" who "have no unresolved personal, spiritual or psychological problems"—a tall order indeed!

Of course, no one is born like this, nor does it happen overnight, so you will also need what the Disciples of Christ term a "commitment to spiritual, physical and emotional wellness sufficient for healthy ministry" (DoC A.2.f). The sense of being called to ministry usually grows over many years, and those involved in encouraging and discerning vocations are looking for evidence of personal growth, often over many years of cultivating habits and practices; for Lutherans, these include "a. a vibrant and resilient faith; b. a balance of work, play and self-care; . . . d. an attention to diet, exercise and mental/physical health, and e. a nurturing of healthy family relationships" (ELCA 2.1.3.4.a, b, d, e). It is crucial, therefore, that anyone who is exploring a possible call to ministry or considering ordination should ensure that they have one or more older and wiser friends or mentors who can help them grow and develop these personal qualities, long before they get anywhere near offering for discernment or the selection processes.

Help—I cannot live up to that!

Panic might seem a perfectly reasonable and natural reaction to the last few paragraphs with all the demands these selection criteria and competencies make for those considering pastoral ministry. It just seems an impossibly high standard. It is also extraordinary how people will treat you differently just because you have a small piece of white plastic tucked into your shirt collar as a priest or some other badge of being a "reverend." Of course, there may be occasional abuse, or more often, apologies if they swear in front of you: "Pardon my French, sorry, Pastor!" But I also remember how humbling it was as a newly ordained curate to find people immediately admitting clergy like me, whom they had never met before, into their homes and the very center of their lives, especially at those moments when the universe seems turned upside down—the birth of a child, the joy of falling in love, the pain of losing a loved one—and expecting us to help them make sense of it. I still find it an amazing privilege after all these years, and one I treasure as a priest. And of course, we all know the tragic consequences of when this trust is abused, or the "naughty vicar" or "fallen TV evangelist" stories so beloved in the tabloid newspapers and social media. Therefore, it is absolutely right that the various churches have clear selection criteria and processes with strict standards before anyone can claim to speak for them—let alone be seen like "God's representative here on earth"! So take some time again now to reflect on these criteria, to pray about them, write something in your journal or notebook—and don't be afraid to discuss your anxieties about fulfilling these expectations with a close friend or spiritual adviser.

However, we saw in our previous discussion of the criteria for the teaching ministry that it did not mean you had to be an "egghead" or super-intellectual—but rather, you need to display evidence of growth and potential for further development. The same is even more true here, which is why exploring a call usually takes years. I have already suggested that you need to be accompanied by others who can help you develop and grow. Often that happens naturally over time as the rough edges get knocked off, but sometimes getting some personal development or counseling can help as well. And remember, however long a church's processes can take, selection is usually only a recommendation for training—another two or three years at a seminary, where you do not just learn facts and ideas for your future ministry, but in which you should be challenged and stretched, and in some cases, it will even feel like being taken apart and rebuilt. Certainly, I found my years at theological college some of the most personally demanding of my whole life.

If all goes well, the seminary, college, or training course will recommend you to the church authorities, like a bishop or other senior leaders, for ordination; in many traditions, like my own Anglican Church, this only leads in turn to several years as a curate or assistant minister under an experienced priest or minister who will guide your further development in pastoral care, especially over things like baptisms, weddings, and funerals. As we shall see later in this study of the pastoral ministry through Luke's portrait of Jesus, this is also a time to develop a "knowledge of community resources for appropriate referrals and participation" (ELCA 2.1.3.3.d). But then, no one becomes perfect overnight. Just be patient: we are all a "work in progress"—and mercifully, God hasn't finished with us yet!

3. The pastoral ministry in the ordination services

G iven all these references in the criteria, competencies, and processes for selection for training, we turn now to see how the pastoral ministry is also featured in the actual ordination services of the various different churches. In the equivalent section of Part I, we considered the power of words, particularly in bringing something into being, like a marriage, or making someone into a deacon or priest, a minister or elder. As with teaching and preaching, it is good to consider what will be said about pastoral care in the ordination liturgies, so that when you hear these words being said to you, or over you, or about you, at your service, you will have thought and prayed about them and walked with God in preparation for your ordination. Once again, stop reading, look at the service outline in appendix 3, and have a go at discovering phrases which seem to refer to this ministry in an example taken from your own church or denomination—and perhaps compare it with one from a completely different tradition. Look carefully at the passages you have noted or highlighted from them, as we go through the service section by section

The gathering, welcome, or call to worship

As we saw in the previous study of ordination services, the service usually begins with a welcome from the bishop, senior minister, or others who are responsible for leading it—and they will often set the tone for the rest of the service. The note of pastoral ministry may particularly be struck if the service includes the ordination of deacons or those whose ministry has a particular focus on service. The opening of the service of ordination of deacons and elders in the Presbyterian church invites everyone to say together **"We remember with joy our common calling to serve Christ"** (PCUSA). Similarly, in a sample Baptist service, the leader welcomes everyone, "As servants of Jesus Christ, we are all called to be ministers, but in addition to this general calling some are called to the church's special ministries. We are gathered today to acknowledge the call of N. to the pastoral ministry of the church" (ABC). Equally, the presiding Lutheran minister reminds the candidates and the congregation that "All baptized Christians are called to share in Christ's ministry of love and service in the world, to the glory of God and for the sake of the human family and the whole creation" (ELCA), while the antiphonal call to worship in the ordination liturgy of the Disciples of Christ includes this exchange: "Leader: There are different ways of serving God, **People: but it is the same God who is served**," after which the leader prays that God will "be present with us, we pray, as we ordain our *sister/brother* to your service" (DoC).

We have already seen how Luke particularly portrays the example of Jesus's pastoral ministry, although of course it is also there in the other gospels. In the same way that Christ gave himself for us, so we are all called to be servants of God in Christ by virtue of being baptized into his life, death, and resurrection. The very words "minister" and "ministry" come from a Latin root meaning "serve/service." Similarly, in Greek, the word for "deacon," *diakonos*, denotes a "servant," and its related verb, *diakoneō*, means "to serve." Its constituent parts, *dia-*, "through," and *konē*, "dust," suggest that being a deacon or a servant involves getting "down and dirty," literally groveling in the dust. Such etymological explanations are not always the best guide to a word's meaning today, but this is a vivid picture of Jesus at the Last Supper, washing his disciples' dusty and dirty feet, which he explains as giving "an example" to all his followers, whether ordained deacon or not (John 13:1–15). And as the old saying goes, "once a deacon, always a deacon." Those in the more catholic traditions who keep the "threefold order" of bishops, priests, and deacons are often reminded that those who are about to be ordained priest never stop being deacons, and even archdeacons and bishops still remain deacons, with service to others taking priority over everything, regardless of their leadership responsibilities. All "ministry" is first and foremost "minister-ing," or serving. To follow the example and pattern of Jesus's ministry is to be committed to a life of service, seeking out the poor, the weak, the sick, the lonely, the oppressed, the powerless, wherever they are to be found—and yes, down in the dust if necessary.

The presentation of the candidates

This stress on the pastoral ministry of service may also be noted as candidates are presented to the bishop or senior leaders. Thus the Association Representative of the UCC tells the congregation that "we have prayerfully examined N. concerning her/his fitness for ministry in Christ's church. We are pleased, on behalf of the United Church of Christ, to authorize the ordination of N. into the Christian ministry," after which they address the ordinand directly: "servant of God, we invite you to come forward" (UCC). Similarly, the Methodist bishop reminds candidates, "You are called to serve rather than to be served" (UMC), reflecting the example of Jesus, who "came not to be served but to serve" (Mark 10:45). Thus, right at the start of the ordination service, we are reminded of the clear connection between teaching and pastoral care, for both aspects require us to follow the example of Jesus. Therefore, if you have not done so recently, spend a little time meditating upon the story of Jesus washing the disciples' feet, or some of the stories of his pastoral care and concern we just noted in Luke's gospel, and write some thoughts about it in your journal or pray about it all.

The declarations or statement of ministry

In our previous study, we saw how at the start of the act of ordination, the bishop or senior minister(s) may declare the various functions and activities which those about to be ordained should perform, like a kind of "job description." In addition to material about teaching and preaching, it is not surprising that these lists also stress pastoral care. Thus, an Episcopal bishop will address candidates to be ordained deacon, "every Christian is called to follow Jesus Christ, serving God the Father, through the power of the Holy Spirit. God now calls you to a special ministry of servanthood directly under your bishop. In the name of Jesus Christ, you are to serve all people, particularly the poor, the weak, the sick, and the lonely," while priests "are to love and serve the people among whom you work, caring alike for young and old, strong and weak, rich and poor" (TEC). Similarly, the African Methodist bishop tells a deacon candidate that "it is his or her office to search for the sick, poor and impotent, that they may be visited and relieved," while elders have "to feed and to provide for the Lord's family, to seek for Christ's sheep that are dispersed abroad and for His children who are in the midst of this evil world" (AME). Presbyterian deacons and elders are reminded that they are the means of "providing for ministries of care and compassion in the world" (PCUSA), while Methodist deacons are "called to share in Christ's ministry of servanthood, to interpret to the church the world's hurts and hopes, to serve all people, particularly the poor, the sick, and the oppressed, and to lead Christ's people in ministries of compassion and justice, liberation and reconciliation, especially in the face of hardship and personal sacrifice" (UMC). Ordinands in the Anglican Church of New Zealand are told directly: "you are marked as a person who proclaims that among the truly blessed are the poor, the troubled, the powerless, the persecuted. You must be prepared to be what you proclaim. Serve Christ simply and willingly, and let your joy in Christ overcome all discouragement. Have no fear; be humble and full of hope" (ANZPB). Finally, a Roman Catholic bishop concludes his declaration (in the form of a homily) to the candidates for the priesthood with this instruction: "keep always before your eyes the example of the Good Shepherd who came not to be served but to serve, and who came to seek out and save what was lost" (RC). These images of love and service, seeking and searching for those in need and dispersed, not only reflect Jesus's parables about shepherds and lost sheep but also remind us again of his own example of care and compassion. It's a tall order!

Questions, vows, and promises

After these challenging descriptions, the bishop or senior minister(s) questions the candidates directly to be sure that they are ready to undertake all these activities in their ministry. Thus, Presbyterian deacons are asked, "will you be a faithful deacon, teaching charity, urging concern, and directing the people's help to the friendless and those in need? In your ministry will you try to show the love and justice of Jesus Christ?" (PCUSA). Similarly, UCC candidates are charged, "will you seek to regard all people with equal concern and undertake to minister impartially to the needs of all?" (UCC). The bishop questions Episcopal deacons, "will you look for Christ in all others, being ready to help and serve those in need?" while a priest must "undertake to be a faithful pastor to all whom you are called to serve, laboring together with them and with your fellow ministers to build up the family of God" (TEC). A sample Baptist ordination service includes the question, "Will you have a loving concern for all people and give your self to minister impartially to them without regard to race, creed, gender, or lifestyle?" (ABC).

These questions use beautiful images of pastoral care, but they are extremely demanding and the promises are daunting. To pledge a positive response, even "with the help of God," is literally a life-changing decision, so once again, spend some time praying and reflecting upon it all now.

The invocation of the Holy Spirit and prayers

After such a challenge, it is right that the bishop or senior minister(s) should kneel with the candidates for prayer including singing the *Veni Creator Spiritus* as an invocation for the strength of the Holy Spirit, followed by further prayers, perhaps in a litany. This may include prayer for all those in need of pastoral care and ministry, such as "for the poor, the persecuted, the sick, the lonely, the forgotten, and all who suffer; for refugees, prisoners, and all who are in danger; that they may be relieved and protected" (ELCA), and "for the poor, the persecuted, the sick, and all who suffer; for refugees, prisoners, and all who are in danger; that they may be relieved and protected" (TEC)—again a very daunting list indeed, but another reminder of the central place of those in need whom we are particularly called to serve in our ministry.

The ordination or laying on of hands

Having been presented, questioned, challenged, and prayed for and with, the candidates now kneel before the bishop or senior minister(s) for the act of the laying on of hands with prayer for the Holy Spirit to ordain each person in turn. Often the actual prayers used at this point will once again feature the pastoral ministry following the example of Jesus, especially for those being ordained as deacons: "O God, most merciful Father, we praise you for sending your Son Jesus Christ, who took on himself the form of a servant, and humbled himself, becoming obedient even to death on the cross. We praise you that you have highly exalted him, and made him Lord of all; and that, through him, we know that whoever would be great must be servant of all. We praise you for the many ministries in your Church, and for calling this your servant to the order of deacons. . . . As your Son came not to be served but to serve, may this deacon share in Christ's service" (TEC Ordination of Deacons). "God of grace, pour out your Holy Spirit on N. and N., that *they* may be faithful deacons in the church. Give *them* openness to the Holy Spirit's leading that *they* may see and serve wherever there is need. Train *them* in the school of prayer that *they* may express the compassion of Christ for the poor and the friendless, the sick, the grieving, and the troubled. Equip *them* with courage to bear the gospel into the halls of power, and to communicate your presence and might among those who are powerless. In everything, give *them* the mind of Christ, who did not grasp at greatness but emptied himself, to become a servant of your reign" (PCUSA Ordination of Deacons).

Giving of the Bible and other symbols; the welcome

We noted in the last study how the importance of the scriptures is stressed once more as the newly ordained are given a Bible as a sign of their authority to preach and teach the gospel. However, pastoral care is indissolubly connected with the ministry of teaching and preaching, so in addition to a Bible, "symbols appropriate to the ministry of deacons and elders may be presented" (PCUSA), or "signs of office" (DoC), or "other insignia of the office of priest or deacon" (TEC). The link of a deacon's servant ministry to Jesus's example of foot washing is made explicit in a red rubric in the UMC liturgy: "*Each deacon is immediately clothed with the shoulder stole, and may receive a Bible and a Book of Worship, a pitcher and basin and/or a plumb line as seems appropriate to the nature of their appointed ministry.*" This is repeated when a pastor or deacon is being appointed to a UMC congregation for the first time:

> *Presenter to deacon*:
> *Name*, accept this Bible,
>   and be among us as one who proclaims the Word. **Amen.**
> *Name*, take this towel and basin,
>   and lead us to be servants of all. **Amen.**
> *Name*, take this plumbline,
>   and faithfully call us toward ministries of compassion and justice.
>   **Amen.**

This exchange helpfully clarifies how the pitcher, basin, and towel remind us of Jesus's foot washing as a servant, while the plumb line echoes God showing Amos a plumb line as a symbol of his ministry to make things straight in Israel (Amos 7:7–8). Similarly, the bishop prays for deacons in

New Zealand: "may [your hands] witness to Christ your Master; he took a towel and a basin; he came among us as one who serves" (ANZPB). Finally, newly ordained Lutheran deacons are charged with scripture at this point:

> Tend the flock of God that is in your charge, not under compulsion but willingly, not for sordid gain but eagerly. Do not lord it over those in your charge, but be examples to the flock. And when the chief shepherd appears, you will win the crown of glory that never fades away. *(1 Peter 5:2–4)*. Think of us in this way, as servants of Christ and stewards of God's mysteries. Moreover, it is required of stewards that they be found trustworthy. *(1 Corinthians 4:1–2)*. (ELCA)

Newly ordained Australians are given a Bible not only for preaching and pastoral care, but also for the ministry of confession and absolution of sins: "take authority to preach the word of God, and to minister the holy sacraments in the congregation where you are appointed. Whose sins you forgive, they are forgiven; whose sins you retain, they are retained" (APBA). Once again everyone, proud families and expectant congregations alike, will want to applaud their new ministers and to greet each other during the sharing of the peace. And if, as in most cases, the ordination is taking place within the context of a eucharist or communion service, it is again likely that the Eucharistic Prayer will include some reference to pastoral ministry and the self-giving example of Christ.

The commissioning and sending out

Equally, the final commissioning and blessing will also make reference to the importance of the pastoral ministry. Thus a newly ordained Presbyterian deacon is expected to give this dismissal before the final blessing:

> Go out into the world in peace;
> have courage;
> hold on to what is good;
> return no one evil for evil;
> strengthen the fainthearted;
> support the weak, and help the suffering;
> honor all people;

love and serve the Lord,
rejoicing in the power of the Holy Spirit. (PCUSA)

Therefore, paying close attention to the words of the liturgies and ordination services helps us to see clearly the vital importance of pastoral
ministry alongside teaching and preaching for those being ordained, especially as deacons. References to this ministry will also appear in the hymns
and readings chosen for a particular service, and in the sermon, perhaps
from the person who led the ordination retreat. Initial discernment of a
vocation through the criteria, competencies, and processes for selection
and years of training and preparation can never be just about theological
education and learning to preach and teach, important though that all is.
It must also include not only developing practical pastoral skills but even
more importantly forming each candidate's character and very life after
the pattern of Jesus, who came not to be served, but to serve, and give his
life for us all.

Wherever you are on your journey, take some time now to reflect upon
these extraordinary images and challenging words from these ordination
liturgies, or look again at the biblical passages about the example of Jesus,
who emptied himself to share our human existence and to die for us, or
read again Luke's portrait of Jesus's pastoral ministry among the poor, the
marginalized, and the vulnerable. We can respond with nothing less than
our complete selves as we seek to serve and care for others.

4. Pastoral care in your ministry

A ll the gospels, of course, do include stories of Jesus's pastoral ministry taking place, as with his teaching and preaching, with individuals and among his community of the disciples—but, as we saw earlier in this study, Luke in particular emphasizes Jesus's broader concern, especially for those who are marginalized or ignored in wider society. This is then reflected in the rest of the New Testament, especially in Paul's appeal to the example of Jesus, who emptied himself and "took the form of a servant" (Phil. 2:5–11), which has so influenced the liturgy for ordination services of deacons, as we have just seen. Therefore, Paul instructs his readers to "welcome one another . . . just as Christ has welcomed you" (Rom. 15:7). Given that wider New Testament context, in this chapter we will look at various aspects of Luke's portrait of Jesus's pastoral care which may have particular relevance for our ministry today, before going on to consider how we can sustain this in the longer term in the final chapter.

Chance encounters along the way

At my own retreat before being ordained deacon, the bishop instructed me, together with the other fresh-faced and nervous candidates, that we had to wear our clerical collar at all times when walking around the parish, traveling on public transport, or even driving the car—and my training vicar made sure it happened, much to my embarrassment. The only problem was that the five-minute stroll between the curate's house and taking prayers in the church could sometimes takes hours, depending on who I bumped into, as well as the strangers who saw the "dog collar" and stopped me! Luke is the only evangelist to include the story of Jesus meeting ten lepers on the road and stopping to heal them; typically he also notes that only the Samaritan came back to thank Jesus (Luke 17:11–19). As well as chance encounters in the street, I would often be invited for meals at kind people's houses, but you never knew who else was going to be there to "meet the new curate." Again, it is only Luke who includes the story of Jesus being invited for dinner at the house of Simon the Pharisee, whose hospitality was rather lacking, with no welcome or washing; on the other hand, a woman scorned by Simon for her dubious morality gate-crashed the party and bathed Jesus's feet with her tears, drying them with her hair and anointing them. Boldly, Jesus took the opportunity to explain to his outraged hosts that those who may indeed have much that needs to be forgiven are more likely to be grateful than "good folk" like Simon who take God's grace for granted (Luke 7:36–50).

Healing and visiting the sick

Like Jesus, we are also invited to visit people in their homes. The ordination services often tell ministers, and especially deacons, to reach out and visit people, especially those who may be lonely, sick, and housebound. I have to confess that this was something I did not particularly relish as a curate, but once again my experienced training incumbent would frequently give me names and addresses to visit, and he expected a full report back! Of course, society is changing, and parish visiting is more difficult today with so many people commuting and out at work, but it remains a staple part of pastoral ministry, especially taking communion to those who are housebound.

Here, too, Luke shows Jesus visiting the homes of people on the margins. Only Luke tells us that the equivalent of the local clergy asked Jesus to visit the Roman centurion who had a sick slave; although his house was somewhere so-called good Jews might not normally visit, they explained to Jesus that this pagan was "worthy" because he had paid for building their synagogue! But the centurion himself disagreed, sending friends to tell Jesus he was "not worthy to have you come under my roof" and expressing his faith that Jesus could heal his slave remotely—which he did, but not before commenting that the Roman's faith outclassed anything in Israel (7:1–10). On another occasion, Luke describes Jesus wanting to visit Zacchaeus's home, a despised tax collector in Jericho, much to the disapproval of the grumbling locals—but as a result of going there for tea, Jesus proclaimed, "today salvation has come to this house" (19:1–10)! I wish I could say that this was the outcome of many of my home visits as a curate, but they were often an important opportunity as well as an expression of love and pastoral concern.

Jesus would also go to the areas where the sick and suffering would be gathered (Luke 4:40–41; 6:18–19). If you have a hospital in your local area, it's well worth getting to know the chaplains. In these days of data protection, clergy cannot simply walk into a hospital and demand a list of names of their parishioners in the way it used to be done. So I would encourage you to build links with the chaplaincy team and ask people to let you know if any members of your congregation, or your local people, are in hospital. Even if you aren't able to cure them instantly as Jesus could, it's amazing what a friendly face, an encouraging word or prayer, the touch of a hand, or the sharing of a bedside communion can do to help the healing process.

In addition to visiting the sick in homes and hospitals, another possible location is in church. Luke includes several stories of Jesus healing people in the context of synagogue worship on the Sabbath which also appear in other gospels (cp. Luke 4:33–37 with Mark 1:23–28). Other similar stories appear only in Luke and reflect his concern for women and the marginalized, such as Jesus healing a woman who had been "bent over" and crippled for eighteen years, again in the synagogue on a Sabbath, much to the consternation of the religious authorities (Luke 13:10–17; see also the healing of a man with dropsy in the home of a ruler of the Pharisees on the Sabbath, unique to Luke 14:1–6). A good routine expression of pastoral care for those who are sick is through the liturgy by providing prayer and the laying on of hands during the regular eucharist, or organizing special healing services, perhaps including the possibility of anointing. My experience is that such services are often greatly appreciated, and they also provide good opportunities to develop the gifts of lay people who feel called to this ministry.

Hatching, matching, and dispatching

We saw in the previous study that the ministry of the so-called Occasional Offices—baptism, weddings, and funerals—provides great opportunities for explaining the Christian faith, especially to those outside the church but who are reaching out for something greater than everyday life, which they have glimpsed in the joy of a birth, the wonder of a new love, or the terrible loss of a loved one. Important though these occasions can be for sharing the gospel, we need to be careful about (ab)using them to "preach at" people, especially when they are vulnerable. At their heart, these events are supremely pastoral occasions—although you may be surprised when those whom you have helped at such times turn up at the back of church sometime later!

Such times are fantastic opportunities when those who do not normally darken our doors actually come and ask for help. Even in these days of "naming ceremonies" and civil weddings, any church seeking to follow the example of Jesus, who came not to be served but to give himself for others, should not be putting too many hurdles in people's way when they are seeking God's grace—even if they don't understand that's what they want, not yet at any rate. They may just feel the need to say "thank you" or "help!" to Something or Someone bigger than themselves. It is significant that in England, everyone resident in the parish still has the legal right to ask for these services from their local Church of England vicar, although I recognize that this may not be true elsewhere in the world. Baptisms and weddings usually take time to organize, and will provide opportunities for pastoral conversations and home visits, as well as perhaps encouraging people to join with others to undertake short preparation courses before the actual great event.

However, funerals often crop up with little warning other than the desperate phone call in the middle of the night, or the undertaker's inquiry about the minister's diary next Wednesday. After a whirlwind introductory week or two of following my training vicar around the parish after my ordination, he went off on his summer holidays (he had been coping on his own for some months, so he deserved it)—but he left me in charge with instructions to "try not to mess it up too badly . . ."! Sure enough, the phone was soon ringing, and I faced several long walks on my own up a garden path to visit grieving and bereaved families. Despite my nerves and the sense of deep inadequacy, I remember being struck by the sheer privilege of sitting alongside people, weeping with those who wept, or having a drink with those who were drinking(!), hearing stories and looking at old photos of those they "loved, but see no longer," as the funeral prayers put it.

Luke gives us a wonderful picture of Jesus approaching the gates of the town of Nain, just as the funeral bier of a young man was being carried out, followed by his grieving mother. In those days, as a widow, she would have no means of support, having lost her only son—and Jesus was filled with compassion for her pain and loss, and went immediately to her side. Though I must admit that I don't know what our parish funeral directors would have done if I had been able to follow Jesus's example of bringing the dead person back to life (7:11–17)! On the other hand, we can at least make sure that the bereaved person is not left to grieve and cope on their own.

Accidents and tragic suffering

It is striking, even in these more secular days, how often news reporters visiting local communities which have been devastated by an accident or tragedy seem to end up interviewing the local pastor or minister, who becomes some kind of spokesperson as well as trying to deal with the grief or coordinate a response. Most of my ministry has been in university settings, where we have less experience of the regular funerals of the old and infirm. However, when death or tragedy strikes, it is felt very keenly, particularly if we have lost a popular student or respected lecturer. We are always ready to help with a funeral if requested, but usually this is better done by the immediate family at home—especially if it has involved an accident or, even worse, a suicide. In such circumstances, it is important to help bereaved families and friends by putting them in touch with local clergy in their area who can also provide longer-term support and care.

However, we do get a lot of requests for some form of memorial service or event, which can range from a formal Choral Evensong according to the 1662 Book of Common Prayer with our renowned Chapel Choir, often including a former colleague giving a tribute to an internationally respected scholar in Chapel, to convening a simple gathering for a silent vigil in their department, or the blessing of a tree or bench in someone's memory. Often what is needed is something to mark what has happened, to help people recognize it and express their grief and shock, and to enable them to move through it into the next stage of life. We are also glad to be able to work with our Student Counselling, Health and Welfare services in providing a listening ear or more professional expertise when needed. While things are different in parish settings, learning to cooperate with such trained colleagues was something which I was glad to discover as a curate, as we shall see in the next chapter shortly.

But perhaps the most common issue around the sudden or tragic death, especially of a young person, is to help with the anger and incomprehension which usually follow. Even those who do not believe in God, or think that the universe is a random set of coincidences, somehow need to be able to shake their fist at the sky, or shout out a question like, why this was "allowed to happen." What did they do to "deserve" this? Significantly, it is Luke who includes the story of Jesus being asked about some Galileans who were slaughtered by Roman troops while at a sacrifice, or the eighteen people killed when the tower of Siloam collapsed upon them. Jesus makes it clear that those to whom such sudden tragedies happen are not "worse offenders" than anyone else, nor is it right to blame God for their suffering (Luke 13:1–5). And yet, I have also known times when people have needed to take out their understandable anger on me as a representative of the church—or even perhaps of God himself—and all we can do at such times is to give them permission or the opportunity to rage and get it out of their system.

Even Jesus could only weep profoundly when coming over the ridge of the Mount of Olives and seeing all of Jerusalem spread out below him, oblivious to the coming destruction. You did not need to be a prophet or have psychic powers to tell the future to realize that if the people carried on behaving towards the Romans as they were doing, the consequences would inevitably lead to siege ramparts, the crushing of children, and the destruction of not leaving "one stone on another"—yet it all too sadly happened only a few decades later in AD 70 (Luke 19:41–44). If you visit that peaceful spot on the hillside today, there is the beautiful church with a teardrop-shaped roof and a window outlined with a cup of suffering through which you can look and pray for the peace of Jerusalem today. It is called *Dominus Flevit*, "the Lord wept"—and pastoral ministry that follows Jesus's example is always likely to include sharing in the tears and griefs of those we are called to serve, as well as their joys.

Give to everyone who asks?

Throughout this study, we have seen how Luke portrays Jesus's particular concern for the outsiders, the poor, and those who are ignored or marginalized. It is illustrated by the three "parables of the lost," the lost sheep (also in Matt. 18:12–14), the lost coin, and the lost or "prodigal" son, the latter two being unique to Luke (15:1–32). This is deliberately referenced in the statements or "job description" in the ordination liturgies, telling us to search for God's children "in the wilderness of this world's temptations"—and the pastoral ministry can never be fully exercised just among our congregations and churches. Of course, we are all tempted to be like the lawyer, again unique to Luke's account, who wanted Jesus to define exactly what "love your neighbor" meant, and who qualified as "neighbor." I don't think he was expecting to get the parable of the Good Samaritan back in reply—and the instruction, "go and do likewise" (10:29–37). But it is so difficult to do this: I still blush to remember rushing to a service, just like the priest and the Levite, through the crowds to get into Saint Paul's Cathedral to preach on that very passage and having to step over a couple of homeless people sleeping on the entrance steps in an attempt not to be late!

Jesus's instruction "give to everyone who asks you" from the Sermon on the Plain (Luke 6:30; also in the Sermon on the Mount, Matt. 5:42) is unambiguous, and almost impossible to obey in every major city on this planet. Simply walking past "on the other side" is difficult enough for everyone, but try doing it in a clerical collar—and don't be surprised at the reactions you get! Some people will try to give something to everyone who asks, as Jesus says—while others are reasonably concerned about whether the money is actually going to help these unfortunates, or simply feed some addiction. One possible solution is to be involved in supporting an agency from a local church or organization working with the poor and homeless, like the work of the famous Connection at Saint Martin-in-the-Fields in the center of London, and trying to refer those begging on the street to somewhere they can get food, shelter, and some care.

Meanwhile, another pressure facing anyone who lives in a clergy house or minister's home is the caller at the door. Most of the time it is obvious that they do have a real need, but it is very difficult to find out what it is because there will often be some long and rambling sob story about needing money to go and visit their "poor sick old mum" or whatever. One solution is to try to provide what is actually being asked for—although on one occasion, I spent an entire evening trying to help someone find their "lost car," ending up buying them a rail ticket and putting them on a train to where they claimed they wanted to go, even though I suspect they got straight off at the next station! Some clergy try to have some sandwiches made up ready in the kitchen or provide vouchers for a local deli or snack shop to be given out instead of cash—but it is never easy, especially for the rest of the family who have to deal with the person at the door when the minister or pastor is out doing pastoral ministry elsewhere.

All of this, of course, reflects only the local context of meeting the poor and marginalized on our doorstep or local streets. Now that we live in a global village, TV and modern communications also make us painfully aware of the vast inequalities in our world, where half the world's resources are owned by a sufficiently small group of wealthy billionaires who could all fit into a small bus—not that they would ever share a bus, or perhaps anything, with anyone else! I cannot read the parable of the rich man, often known by the Latin word *Dives*, and Lazarus, the poor beggar at his gate, which also only occurs in Luke's gospel (16:19–31), without feeling somehow responsible or even guilty; perhaps it would be even more worrying if we stopped feeling like this?

The "pattern and example of Christ"

Finally, let us return to the stress in the ordination liturgies on the "pattern and example of Christ." We have suggested that Jesus's pastoral ministry, although present in all the gospels of course, is particularly emphasized in Luke's portrait, and this is especially so in his account of the Last Supper and the cross. Matthew and Mark both record an earlier dispute among the disciples about being the greatest and getting the best seats in heaven, which Jesus answers by talking about being a servant, but they locate this on the road to Jerusalem (Matt. 20:24–28; Mark 10:41–45). Luke highlights it by suggesting that a similar argument happened even at the table during the Last Supper; again, Jesus says that this is how Gentiles like to "lord" their authority. But then we get this saying, which appears only in Luke: "for who is greater, the one who is at the table or the one who serves? Is it not the one at the table? But I am among you as one who serves" (Luke 22:24–27). In this way, Luke gives us the verbal expression of what John demonstrates by his story of the foot washing (John 13:1–15). This is the ultimate definition of the pastoral ministry of the deacon, "the one who serves," whether they go on to be subsequently ordained as a priest or bishop, or remain a deacon for life.

Luke then illustrates it further in his particular account of the crucifixion, as we saw above, where Jesus demonstrates his care and concern for the women and children on his way to be crucified, his forgiveness for the soldiers carrying out his execution, and his saving love for the dying penitent thief: "truly I tell you, today you will be with me in Paradise" (Luke 23:26–31, 34, 39–43). The ordination liturgies tell candidates that they are to search for God's children "in the wilderness of this world's temptations"—which is why Jesus emptied himself, took upon himself the human form of a servant and humbled himself even to death on a cross, not just to search for God's children, but to bring us home to be with him in paradise. In undertaking pastoral care, we are simply trying to follow him, and join in, not just today, or even over three years—but for the rest of our lives if we can find a way to sustain this ministry.

5. Sustaining a pastoral ministry

Throughout this study, we have concentrated on Luke's particular portrait of Jesus's pastoral ministry, and it has been a challenging experience. This is made even more daunting by the demands of the criteria and processes for selection, as well as the ordination liturgies themselves. Just now, in the previous chapter, we tried to earth this pastoral ministry in some practical illustrations drawn from daily experience of caring for others and following the example and pattern of Jesus the servant. After such a sobering journey, we could be forgiven for wondering how we can ever dare to respond to this calling. And yet, Luke's picture of Jesus does not just provide us with the seemingly impossible challenge, thanks be to God; he also lets us glimpse a couple of hints about how Jesus managed it all, from which we might find ways not just to survive, but even blossom through it.

"And as he was praying"

Previously, I have advised you not to be foolish, filling up at the oasis of theological training, like a camel, and then trying to head off across the desert wastes of decades of ministry without taking more refreshment and resources on board at regular intervals to help you maintain a ministry of teaching and preaching. Chief among those strategies was to follow Jesus's own pattern, which in turn is followed by great examples like Archbishop Desmond Tutu, of taking time out to be quiet, to reflect and pray, and to read and replenish your own understanding before trying to preach to someone else.

This rhythm is the first clue which Luke provides about how Jesus managed to sustain his extraordinary ministry. If you look carefully at all the major events in Jesus's life—at his baptism (3:21), when he was drained after healing or ministry to others (5:12–16), before choosing the apostles (6:12), at Peter's confession (9:18), at his transfiguration (9:29), before teaching the disciples the Lord's Prayer (11:1–4)—in every case, only Luke includes a phrase like "as he was praying," or points out that Jesus had spent the night in prayer beforehand or withdrew to pray afterwards. It is Luke alone who tells us that Jesus prayed especially for Peter, that after his denial and turning again, he might "strengthen" the others (22:31–32). No wonder that watching Jesus at prayer inspired the disciples to ask him, "Lord, teach us to pray," and Luke's version of the Lord's Prayer follows (11:1–4).

This pattern of prayer continues right through to Luke's narrative of the Passion. In Gethsemane, Luke says that Jesus asks his disciples actually to join in praying with him (22:40; compare "sit here while I pray" in Mark 14:32 and Matt. 26:36). As he is being nailed to the cross, he prays for the carpenters and soldiers, ignorantly carrying out their orders: "Father, forgive them, for they know not what they do" (Luke 23:34). Finally, the one who has been constantly praying, throughout his life, dies with a prayer on his lips, still trusting God, like a child saying the Jewish night psalm, "Father, into your hands I commend my spirit" (23:46; see Ps. 31:5).

And if Jesus's own example of prayer was not enough, Luke also includes several parables about prayer which are unique to his gospel. The parables of the friend at midnight (Luke 11:5–8) and the persistent widow (18:1–8) emphasize the need not to give up, but to continue in prayer. Similarly, the parable of the Pharisee and the tax collector in the temple, also only found in Luke, reminds us that prayer must be done in humility and forgiveness, rather than in self-righteous pride (18:9–14).

Here surely is the secret which enabled Jesus to undertake this extraordinary pastoral ministry, that such a self-giving care for others can only be maintained if we are constantly returning to God as the source and ground of our being to be replenished by his grace and love. This is why selection criteria and competencies about faith and spirituality require things like "candidates should show evidence of a commitment to a spiritual discipline, involving individual and corporate prayer and worship, such as to sustain and energise them in every aspect of their lives" (TEAC C).

"Pray earnestly for the gift of the Holy Spirit"

Luke not only reveals Jesus's life of prayer, but in addition he portrays him as the person of the Holy Spirit, the one who is both uniquely filled with the Spirit and also the giver of the Spirit. Luke refers to the Spirit eighteen times in his gospel (the same as in Matthew and Mark combined) while there are an extraordinary fifty-seven occurrences in his Acts of the Apostles, so many that some commentators suggest it should be renamed the "Acts of the Holy Spirit." The Holy Spirit initiates the action at every stage in Luke's gospel, coming upon Mary, Elizabeth, Zechariah, and John at the start (Luke 1:34–35, 41, 67, 80) and descending on Jesus "in bodily form" at his baptism (3:22), and leads him both into and out of the wilderness (4:1, 14); no wonder that Jesus begins his first sermon at Nazareth by proclaiming "the Spirit of the Lord is upon me" (4:18). Similarly, Jesus is not only supremely filled with the Spirit, but also he is the one who baptizes in the Holy Spirit (3:16). The heavenly Father will give "the Holy Spirit to those who ask him" (according to Luke 11:13; compare "good gifts" in Matt. 7:11). The promise of the Holy Spirit is renewed by the risen Jesus (Luke 24:49) and fulfilled throughout the Acts (see 2:1, 33), where Luke makes it clear that the Holy Spirit is the same as the Spirit of Jesus (Acts 16:6–7).

As we have seen, in many ordination services, the charge from the bishop or senior minister(s) to candidates immediately before the moment of laying on of hands warns them that they cannot bear the weight of this calling in their own strength. Instead, they are told to pray earnestly for the gift of the Holy Spirit, and the senior ministers may personally lead them in prayer by singing the *Veni Creator Spiritus* to invoke the inspiration of the Holy Spirit. When I was doing my clinical pastoral training in the local hospital near my theological college, the senior chaplain instructed us to return to the little hospital chapel after every ward visit and before going to see anyone else. She taught us to imagine a large wicker basket before or even on the altar: we were to bring the burdens of the patients we had been visiting on the cancer wards or wherever, and then visualize placing them in the basket, praying for them—and then leaving them there with the Lord. Then, before leaving the chapel, we were to pray for the inspiration of the Holy Spirit to fill the space left in us, like the tide coming in to fill hollows in the sand. Without this spiritual practice, she warned us that we risked taking people's burdens and dumping them on the next patients we visited! The same exercise might help harassed parish clergy during a pressured day or to let go of the cares of their people before going home, especially if they have loved ones or a family waiting for them, who also rightly want some attention.

"Continue in what you have learned"

We saw how vital it is for clergy not only to continue reading and studying the Bible and theology, but also to learn from books, TV, films, and other aspects of popular culture more about the context in which they are undertaking their ministry of teaching and preaching. The instruction, "continue in what you have learned" (2 Tim. 3:14), could become even a lifesaver in the pastoral ministry, so it is even more important here. It is impossible in the limited time and cramped curriculum of theological education and ministerial training to learn what a lifetime of pastoral ministry will require, let alone develop and hone the necessary basic skills—which is why continuing ministerial education is so important, both formally and informally. Doctors and lawyers have to undertake further professional development throughout their careers, and it is just as essential for those in any form of ministry.

As a newly ordained curate, I was very grateful to be immediately linked into a local group of caring and welfare agencies, including the district nurse service, GP health centers, social services, and even the police. I quickly came to admire them as caring professionals and began to learn how to recognize my limits and when it was a good idea to refer a parishioner on to the experts. At both the universities where I have served, such good working relationships with other welfare agencies have been vital. Through meeting together regularly, we can "take the temperature" of the campus, and discover what are the main issues which are presenting themselves in different ways to all our colleagues. This is also vital to establish the mutual trust and respect which allow each of us with our different areas of expertise to refer students to others, and to accept referrals from them.

Furthermore, having some form of pastoral supervisor can be very helpful for many in pastoral ministry. Trained counselors in universities and hospitals are simply not allowed to practice unless they are themselves under supervision and having some form of counseling. It is just too dangerous otherwise, both for themselves and for those in their care. Therefore, in the chaplaincy team which I coordinated in my previous university, we approached the same psychotherapist who was also the supervisor for the student counseling service. She agreed to run a regular group for a number of our chaplains from various Christian denominations, and eventually I took a personal course with her in Jungian analysis over two years to try to understand what was often going on in the pastoral situations facing me, as well as the impact it was having on my own life

85

and family. This proved to be hugely beneficial, and I now make it a basic rule that those serving in my current chaplaincy team must meet regularly with some kind of supervisor, mentor, or counselor—and this is a proper expense which the university needs to reimburse under staff training and continuing professional development.

Therefore, I would strongly recommend something like this to anyone undertaking any form of pastoral ministry, whether lay or ordained. Without such supervision, it is all too easy for those of us undertaking pastoral care of others to start to believe our own propaganda, or to fall under the spell of "transference," where a student or parishioner transfers on to us their feelings about a teacher, parent, or child. If we start to believe that "Father really does know best" or that we can actually "save the universe"— or at least our own "forgotten corner of the world"—by ourselves, then we are on the slippery slope to madness, risking crashing and burning, or even ending up on the "naughty vicar" pages of the tabloid newspapers. During theological education and ordination training, there should be plenty of opportunities for such supervision and personal growth, but it is all too easy to let that slip away under the pressures of parish ministry. Fortunately, many dioceses and wider church organizations not only run regular courses as part of continuing ministerial education (CME), but maintain networks of pastoral supervisors and advisers. If you are in regular pastoral ministry but do not have some form of such supervision, it would be sensible to have a conversation with someone responsible for ministerial development in your church about it all, and seek their recommendations. On the other hand, if you are still exploring what God may be calling you towards, again, why not talk to your spiritual director or vocational adviser about it and see what they suggest?

Conclusion

In this part, we have been considering the pastoral ministry, guided particularly by Luke's portrait of Jesus. We noted that Luke is often represented by the image or symbol of an ox—but, actually, he is far from being a bit of a "plodder"! Instead he presents Jesus as the bearer of burdens, caring especially for the vulnerable and marginalized, women, non-Jews, and social outcasts, and eventually giving his life sacrificially for the sake of those he came to serve. There is therefore no contrast between Jesus's "mission" and his pastoral ministry: teaching and preaching and the practice of pastoral care are both equally central to Jesus's mission of proclaiming the kingdom of God and making his sovereign rule visible in people's lives. They are different sides of the same coin, and belong inextricably together—which is one reason why we have followed this slightly unusual sequence of going straight from Matthew's account to Luke's portrait.

Second, we discovered how the pastoral ministry is rightly at the center of the criteria, competencies, and processes for selection for training, as well as the liturgies of ordination in all our different churches, setting before ordinands the example and pattern of Jesus, who emptied himself and took the form of a servant, humbling himself even to death on the cross, and thereby making his teaching and preaching into a reality among us. Those who wish to follow him in any form of Christian ministry, lay or ordained, will find pastoral care to be a very demanding and costly calling, especially if they try to serve the wider local community as well as their worshiping congregation, some of whom may be found literally on their doorstep or in the street. And yet, there are extraordinary opportunities and privileges to be discovered as we accompany people through the joys and sorrows of life, from birth, through relationships, and ultimately to death.

Finally, we have discovered that while the pastoral vocation is incredibly demanding and challenging, we have also tried to learn from Luke's portrait something of Jesus's habit of prayer and reliance upon the Holy

Spirit in order to sustain ourselves under such pastoral pressures. I have also suggested some possible ways in which clergy can develop their pastoral skills throughout their ministry, especially in association with other caring professionals, and some possible sources of assistance in avoiding burnout or disaster. Wherever you are on your own journey of faith and ministry, whether just setting out to respond nervously to a possible calling, or looking back over many decades of serving God and his people, it is my prayer that you will have found something here to help and inspire you afresh—for it is an extraordinary privilege to follow in the footsteps of Jesus, the bearer of burdens, who sacrificed himself for us and for all to whom we minister.

For prayer and further reflection

You might want to consider these questions taken from some ordination services:

- Will you be a faithful deacon, teaching charity, urging concern, and directing the people's help to the friendless and those in need? In your ministry will you try to show the love and justice of Jesus Christ? (PCUSA)
- Will you look for Christ in all others, being ready to help and serve those in need? (TEC Deacons)
- Will you undertake to be a faithful pastor to all whom you are called to serve, laboring together with them and with your fellow ministers to build up the family of God? (TEC Priests)
- Will you seek to regard all people with equal love and concern and undertake to minister impartially to the needs of all? (UCC)

Even "with the help of God" these are demanding promises to make and difficult vows to keep, so spend some time now reflecting upon these questions and maybe write your thoughts down in your journal or discuss it all with those helping to guide you. Above all, pray for the ability, the courage, and the strength to be able to make this response—and keep it in the years ahead.

As before, you may also find it helpful to post comments and questions or engage in discussion (in general terms, of course!) on the Facebook page for this book: www.facebook.com/FourMinistriesOneJesus.

PART III

Mark

Suffering the Way of the Cross

Figure 3. Saint Mark, *Lindisfarne Gospels*, Folio 93b

1. The way of the cross in Mark's portrait of Jesus's ministry

We went straight from Matthew's picture of Jesus's ministry of teaching and preaching to Luke's account of his pastoral care and concern for others. I concluded the previous study by suggesting that we followed this sequence partly because these two different aspects of Jesus's one mission and ministry go together very well and function a bit like opposite sides of the same coin. However, it was also the case that I did not want to interrupt the flow of the book (or the original retreat addresses at Launde Abbey) at that point with Mark's symbol and portrait, which are both rather less comfortable—but now that time has come.

Actually, in the *Lindisfarne Gospels* (Folio 93b; see fig. 3), Saint Mark is depicted seated with a rather wonderful lion, *imago leonis*, apparently bounding over his head. The lion is holding a copy of a book in its paws as it hovers over the evangelist, who is writing away. Perhaps the artist is suggesting that the lion was dictating the book to Mark or, at the very least, inspiring him. We often call lions the king of beasts, and they regularly feature in royal coats of arms—but it's still a beast, a wild animal, magnificent, yet also terrible. I have been fortunate to participate in several conferences in South Africa which have sometimes included a trip out to see these wonderful animals in the Kruger Park—such are the struggles, or benefits, of being a biblical scholar! But you have to stay in the vehicle; on one occasion, we were allowed out on an early morning walk, but only with armed guides. Otherwise, it is just not safe. So, is Mark "safe"—and why do we find his portrait uncomfortable?

"Not a tame lion"

If you look through the Old Testament, so often the lion is described as a predator, who appears suddenly to attack flocks or human beings (1 Sam.

17:34–37; 1 Kings 13:24–26). Even when the prophets compare God to a lion, it is a symbol of judgment and destruction (Jer. 49:19; 50:44; Hos. 13:7–8). So, the lion is a rather uncomfortable image in the scriptures. When I first explained the ideas of *Four Gospels, One Jesus?* to my editor at SPCK, he welcomed the lion image because we all love Aslan in C. S. Lewis's *Chronicles of Narnia*. On the other hand, we also know that Aslan is "not a tame lion"—even if that exact phrase never actually appears as such anywhere in the books.

If Aslan is not a tame lion, Mark is not a comfortable gospel. When the actor Alec McCowen memorized the whole of Mark, taking both the West End and Broadway by storm decades ago, there was something disconcerting, or even relentless, in the way he just stood there and recited this extraordinary text out loud in the old King James Version. We started this book with Matthew's gospel, which is beloved by catholics, both Roman and more widely understood, as the first gospel in the canonical order with references to the primacy of Peter. Luke is the favorite for those who consider themselves liberals, with all its references to the poor, the vulnerable, marginalized, women, and non-Jews, which we have just studied. Later we will come to John, which is prized by the evangelicals, with all its promises about the personal relationship with Jesus. Perhaps it is not surprising that Mark's stark account has been neglected down through the history of the church—except during times of persecution or suffering, when it really seems to come alive for the church.

Mark's gospel was probably written in the 60s, only thirty years or so after the death of Jesus. Nero was busy burning Christians in the streets of Rome, while various Jewish factions besieged in Jerusalem were killing each other more than the Romans who were waiting patiently for the end behind their fortifications. Sometimes when I'm reading Mark, I can almost peer through his pages and see the flames or feel the heat and destruction which lie just below the surface. The whole narrative is dominated by the shadow of the cross: Mark has a habit of repeating things in threes, and he records Jesus warning the disciples that he was going to Jerusalem to be crucified no fewer than three times (Mark 8:31–34; 9:31–32; 10:32–34). When Jesus invites his hearers to "take up your cross" to follow him, the disciples just do not understand this, which is another of Mark's key themes. As an old saying puts it, when Jesus calls someone to follow him, it is an invitation to suffering and an ignominious death. Mark's message is that anyone who thinks that following the crucified one is a bed of roses has forgotten about thorns and blood.

I like to compare Mark's structure to a symphony in three movements, each of which describes a different phase of the lion's life, as we shall see shortly. As usual, the first movement, chapters 1 to 8, is taken at a fast pace, and introduces the key themes. Like a lion, Jesus jumps on stage fully grown, roars and rushes about throughout the first chapter. Mark uses the phrase "and immediately" ten times in chapter 1 alone and forty times in the whole of his gospel—which is the same as in Matthew, Luke, John, Paul, and the rest of the New Testament all combined. There is an urgency about the gospel from Mark's perspective. There is no time for birth or infancy stories here: Jesus just appears to be baptized by John—and off we go! He is often called "Rabbi" by people, but Mark contains remarkably little teaching beyond a collection of parables in chapter 4. The lion is a beast of action who chases around the whole of Galilee and gets into fights.

The cosmic struggle

This is well illustrated in a carefully constructed passage which begins as "Jesus went home; and the crowd came together again, so that they could not even eat" (Mark 3:19b–35). I mentioned just now that Mark likes to arrange things in threes, and this story of Jesus not having time to eat at home is structured like a triple-decker sandwich. There are three aspects to the struggle that Jesus is facing. The outer level, the beginning and end of the story, the bread if you like, concerns his family, who try "to restrain him" since people think he is "a sandwich short of a picnic," to continue the image (3:21)! The next layer in, or the next level of misunderstanding and struggle, comes with the religious authorities, who suggest that actually he is not "out of his mind," but rather, he is demon-possessed (3:22).

Finally, Jesus takes us to the real meat at the center of the conflict: "How can Satan cast out Satan? If a kingdom is divided against itself, that kingdom cannot stand." At the deepest level, this is not about his family and friends thinking he is crackers or the scribes calling him demonic; it is nothing less than the ultimate cosmic struggle with evil which Jesus has come to defeat (3:23–27). As we continue through the threefold narrative, we return once more to the layer of the religious leaders, as Jesus warns them about "blaspheming against the Holy Spirit," that is, mistaking what God is doing and describing it as evil, because they said, "he has an unclean spirit" (3:28–30). Then we finally reach the outer level of family and friends again, with his mother and brothers and sisters waiting outside and asking for him. A good Jewish boy should immediately respond to his mother's call, but Jesus's reply is extraordinary: "Who are my mother and my brothers?" Looking at those who sat listening, he went on, "Here are my mother and my brothers! Whoever does the will of God is my brother and sister and mother" (3:31–35).

This is a hugely offensive saying, cutting across both the ancient respect for parents and modern ideas of "family values," but it takes us to the heart of Mark's message. Beyond misunderstanding, rejection, persecution, and even blasphemy is actually the cosmic struggle between good and evil, the Holy Spirit of God and Satan. It affects institutional contacts with the authorities and human relationships with family and friends—but the call of God must take priority, even if it leads to suffering and death. No wonder throughout the rest of this first movement, the disciples increasingly fail to understand and Jesus gets more and more frustrated: "Do you still not perceive or understand? Are your hearts hardened? Do you have eyes, and fail to see? Do you have ears, and fail to hear? And do you not remember?" (see 4:13, 40; 6:50–52; 7:18; 8:17–18). This incomprehension is not the most flattering picture of the future leaders of the church or the first bishops! And yet, in the context of pain and suffering, the times in our mission or ministry when we simply do not understand what on earth (literally) God is doing, perhaps we can draw some comfort from Mark's picture of the bewildered and confused disciples.

Learning to see

Most composers make the middle or second movement of their symphony much slower, in order to develop the themes announced at the start. So too, Mark's central section invites us to reflect more deeply on Jesus's identity and mission: what kind of "beast" do we have here, and what has he come to do? Again, it is very carefully constructed, beginning and ending with two healings of blind men, like bookends, the first at Bethsaida and the second being blind Bartimaeus just outside Jericho (8:22–10:52). It is as though Mark is trying to lift the scales from our eyes, so we can see what is really going on around us as we try to follow the lion.

But it does not happen easily or all at once. In fact, the first blind man does not get healed "immediately"; instead, while he can just about make people out, they appear "like trees, walking" (8:24). Everything is a bit blurry, all out of focus. Interestingly, this is one of the very rare stories that neither Matthew nor Luke include in their gospels, almost as though they are embarrassed that Jesus does not get it right the first time and has to do it twice. So why has Mark included this story of apparent difficulty here, right at the start of the middle, slow section of his symphony?

Maybe the clue comes as Mark goes on to Jesus's question to Peter and the disciples about what they can see: "but you, who do *you* say that I am?" (8:29). Peter, as always, is ready with an instant answer: "you are the Messiah." He could be forgiven for being very pleased with his insight, but Jesus rewards him by immediately announcing that he is going up to Jerusalem—not, as the disciples might assume, to defeat the Romans, but to suffer and die. No wonder everything goes blurry and out of focus for Peter, just like the blind man at Bethsaida, and he protests that this must never happen. Jesus has to give him "a second touch," ripping aside the curtain to expose the cosmic conflict again: "get behind me, Satan!" It's just like the earlier triple sandwich, with the same central struggle with evil. So Jesus has to make it completely clear, that for anyone who wants to follow him, they have to "deny themselves and take up their cross and follow me. For those who want to save their life will lose it, and those who lose their life for my sake, and for the sake of the gospel, will save it" (8:29–37).

Like a careful composer, Mark develops this same theme about the disciples not seeing who Jesus is or understanding what he is going to achieve in Jerusalem through the rest of his middle section. At the transfiguration, Peter starts babbling nonsense about building huts for Jesus to settle down with Moses and Elijah—until even God has to tell him to shut up: "This is my Son, the Beloved; listen to him!" (9:2–8). Then there is the man with the epileptic son with an unclean spirit whom the disciples cannot help (9:14–29). After Jesus patiently explains for the *second* time that he is going to Jerusalem to suffer and die (9:30–32), they finally set off, only for the disciples to show that they have not been listening by arguing about "who was the greatest" (9:33–37)! They even want to stop someone dealing with evil in Jesus's name, because they were "not one of us" (9:38–41), or prevent people bringing children to be blessed by Jesus; no wonder Jesus gets "indignant" with them (10:13–16).

After a rich man turns away because he cannot bear to give up his possessions, Peter wants to know what kind of reward he and the disciples are going to get for following Jesus, only to receive no less than the *third* warning that Jesus is going to Jerusalem to suffer and die (10:17–34; it is significant that Matthew and Luke do not repeat all three predictions of the Passion—Mark, however, really drives the point home). Finally, James and John demonstrate just how little they have understood by asking Jesus for a favor: they just want the best seats in heaven, while the other disciples get angry, but only about not thinking of it first themselves! It really is not a flattering picture of the chosen disciples, nor a comfortable account of the early church. Even Matthew and Luke once again seem embarrassed, since Matthew's account says that their *mother* made the request (Matt. 20:20–22), while Luke omits it altogether. In Mark, however, Jesus does promise these two close disciples that they can indeed share his cup and his baptism, but these are images of his death; he has to explain for the umpteenth time that he has come "not to be served but to serve, and to give his life a ransom for many" (Mark 10:35–45).

Finally, we reach the second "bookend" at the end of this middle section, the other blind man, Bartimaeus. He is so convinced that, as "Son of David," Jesus will "have mercy" and let him "see again," that his simple faith and trust come as a great relief. No wonder, unlike the first blind man at Bethsaida, or Peter and the obtuse disciples, Bartimaeus "immediately"— Mark's favorite word reappears—"regained his sight." What is more, after all Jesus's invitations, he responds and "followed him along the way" (10:45–52). So, far from the middle section of Mark's gospel being just a random collection of stories, in fact it is extremely carefully constructed to develop these underlying themes of pain and suffering, showing how even the disciples, the early church leaders and first bishops, simply did not understand it, no matter how many times Jesus explained it. Mark's lion is indeed a royal "son of David," who is the "anointed one," the "Christ," but he is going to Jerusalem not to be crowned king, but to die. For the attentive reader, Mark has been making it increasingly clear, from it all being rather blurred and in outline for the first blind man right through to the second one, Bartimaeus, seeing "immediately" and following him "on the way."

Death in Jerusalem

Except that the Greek word translated as "way," *hodos*, also means "road." Blind Bartimaeus was sitting by the "roadside" on "the way out" of Jericho, and this particular road leads only one way, up through the wilderness to reach Jerusalem itself, the place Jesus has been constantly warning the disciples is where he is going to suffer and die. And so, after the fast first movement of the lion roaring and rushing about, and the slow middle section clarifying his identity and mission, the third section of Mark's symphony depicts a right royal march—but it is going to end with a funeral.

When Jesus enters Jerusalem and the temple, the lion comes to its lair only to find that it is a "den of robbers," full of buying and selling rather than prayer (11:17). The fig tree, which is "sandwiched" either side around the temple incident, bears no fruit and withers away (11:13, 20) while the tenants of the vineyard will not give the owner its fruit, preferring instead to kill his "beloved son" (12:1–12). In the Old Testament, figs and vines are often used as images of Israel, whom the prophets lambast for not bearing fruit for God (see Jer. 8:13; Hos. 9:10, 16; Mic. 7:1). No wonder that after more arguments with the religious leaders, Jesus has no alternative but to emulate the prophets' warnings of the destruction of Jerusalem: "not one stone here will be left on another; all will be thrown down" (13:2). He also suggests that they should "learn the lesson" of the fig tree, and realize that the inevitable judgment will be coming soon; everyone should "keep awake" (13:28–36).

After the prophecy of the coming judgment throughout chapter 13, the strains of the funeral march dominate Mark's last chapters. The hint that the tenants of the vineyard would kill the owner's "beloved son" (12:1–12) is reinforced as Jesus is anointed by a woman at the house of Simon the leper in Bethany; while some grumble about the waste, Jesus makes it clear that "she has anointed my body beforehand for its burial" (14:3–9). The narrative continues through the Last Supper and the arrest in the Garden of Gethsemane, until at his trial the roaring, rushing lion finally becomes quiet and passive: like Aslan before the White Witch in Narnia, "he was silent and did not answer" (14:61).

Finally, Jesus is condemned and has to "take up his cross," quite literally. He dies all alone in darkness with one last cry, "Eloi, Eloi, lema sabachthani?" Even then, after Jesus has been misunderstood throughout this gospel, his hearers get his final words wrong and think he is calling for Elijah. In fact, he is quoting Psalm 22, "My God, my God, why have you forsaken me?" but his despairing question goes unanswered, except that the veil of the temple, separating God from human sight, is suddenly torn in two (Mark 15:34–38). And yet, after all the disciples' failure to see despite the healing of the blind men, now for the first time a human being actually recognizes Jesus as "Son of God." The only voices previously to acknowledge Jesus as the Son of God were those of God himself at Jesus's baptism and transfiguration, and of the demons—and the ultimate irony is that this person is a Roman centurion, not even Jewish.

Therefore, despite Mark's gospel being so often found uncomfortable, a careful reading, which is attentive to the clues, reveals a master storyteller at work—and what a story! If Mark was written in the 60s against the back-drop of Nero's persecutions and the siege and destruction of Jerusalem, his narrative was composed to reassure those who were suffering that maybe God had not "forsaken" them after all. Through his threefold symphonic structure, the evangelist has painstakingly traced the way of the cross, Je-sus's journey from Galilee to Jerusalem, where he entered into human pain and desolation deeper than even the readers' experience. What is more, not even his disciples and the early church leaders really understood what was going on—so it is hardly surprising if Mark's audience in that terrible decade struggled to keep going on the path of discipleship and felt aban-doned by God. But Jesus knew what he was doing and where he was going, and kept trying to warn the disciples, despite their inability to grasp it all. Those who want to be his disciples now have no alternative, says Mark, but to take up their cross, and follow him through pain and suffering on the lion's royal road toward death.

"Then he isn't safe?" said Lucy.

"Safe?" said Mr Beaver. "Who said anything about safe? 'Course he isn't safe. But he's good. He's the King, I tell you."

(C. S. Lewis, *The Lion, the Witch and the Wardrobe*, Puffin/Penguin, 1959, p. 75)

Marking Mark

The collect for Bible Sunday tells us to "read, mark and inwardly digest" the scriptures. "Mark" in this phrase, of course, means to note carefully, but I have also suggested that you might actually "mark" the texts of the different churches' competencies and selection criteria and the ordina-tion liturgies in the appendices at the back of this book. If you have used contrasting highlighter colors for teaching and preaching as opposed to pastoral care, take a third, possibly more somber, color and repeat the ex-ercise looking for references to suffering and the way of the cross—literally, to mark Mark's theme into the text. One word of warning: they are not as immediately obvious as the two previous themes, but prayer and careful reflection will pay dividends, as we shall discover in the next two chapters. And take time to talk to God about it—as well as to your spiritual director or whoever is helping to guide your vocation.

2. Suffering the way of the cross in selection for ministry

After all the emphasis on teaching and pastoring in the competencies, criteria, and processes for selection, it can come as a bit of a shock to discover that there is little—or in some cases, nothing—immediately included which is obviously relevant here about the way of the cross, or suggestions that those considering Christian ministry need to have experienced persecution or suffering for their faith. On the other hand, maybe it is not so surprising: advertising pain and suffering is perhaps not the best thing to put on a recruiting poster! The clearest expression comes from the Evangelical Lutheran Church in America, who include "the way of the cross" as a key competency:

> **2.1.2.1 Engages the way of the cross.**
> Empowered by the resurrected Christ, a rostered minister shows people the crucified Christ through word and deed and enables them to envision what God is doing in the world and in their lives. Some indicators of this competency include:
> a. willingness to confront and engage suffering in the lives of others and in one's own life, especially among marginalized people,
> b. exhibiting qualities of servant leadership,
> c. willingness to serve, risk and sacrifice for the sake of God's mission, including an ability to identify and lead in exposing the principalities and powers operative in a given context, and
> d. responding to life crises as opportunities for experiencing new life.

However, closer inspection of the other lists reveals that there are hints that our mission and ministry might not always be easy, as we saw in the previous study with particular reference to pastoral care. Thus the

Anglican Communion stresses that candidates need to be "mature, stable and show that they are able to sustain the demanding role of a minister, and are able to face change and pressure in a flexible and balanced way" (TEAC D). In collecting evidence for this criterion, vocational advisers are encouraged to consider candidates' capacity to accept the risk of failure or rejection, to assimilate and deal appropriately with negative or difficult life experiences, showing maturity in learning from mistakes, setbacks, and criticism. In fact, some of the most impressive candidates whom I have been privileged to interview for selection have been those who have had deep experience of suffering and difficulties along the way, but who have been able to discern God at work in their lives through times of joy and sorrow. This is surely right, for unless you have learned something about dealing with your own pains and hurts, you are not going to be able to minister to anyone else's.

Furthermore, the Lutheran criterion about what it means to be church says that candidates should display a "demonstration of skills for leading a community of faith through change while addressing conflicts that might emerge" (ELCA 2.1.1.4.b) as well as the "ability to identify and lead in exposing the principalities and powers operative in a given context" (ELCA 2.1.2.1.c)—and we have just seen how Mark's entire story is about conflict and the difficulties Jesus experienced in his relationships with his own family, his friends, and closest followers, not to mention his debates with the religious authorities and, behind it all, the cosmic struggle with evil.

Following Jesus on the way of the cross

Some of the criteria and competencies also suggest two things that might be able to help with this area: first there is your personal walk with Jesus on the way of the cross. Thus, in discerning vocation, the Anglican criterion about spirituality and faith requires candidates to "show evidence of a commitment to a spiritual discipline, involving individual and corporate prayer and worship, such as to sustain and energise them in every aspect of their lives" (TEAC C). Similarly, the United Methodist Church states that candidates must "nurture and cultivate spiritual disciplines and patterns of holiness" (UMC 304.*b*). Only such a spiritual discipline will enable you to accompany Jesus on the way of the cross, whatever might befall you *en route*.

Second, candidates' "sense of vocation should be obedient, realistic and informed" (TEAC A). The person who gives everything up and arrives on my doorstep with their life in two carrier bags, eagerly claiming that they are going to convert the whole of England and then become Archbishop of Canterbury, may be being "obedient" to their particular sense of calling and sacrifice, but not what I would call "realistic and informed"! In fact, I personally relish the opportunity to guide students who come to me in the first flush of great enthusiasm about experiencing a call, and gradually help them with some reading and conversation to become more "informed" and to develop an "obedient" desire to follow Jesus along the way of the cross—and what that might actually mean for them in practice.

Flexibility, change, and challenge

Anglicans must be "able to face change and pressure in a flexible and balanced way" (TEAC D), while Lutherans have to be willing "to confront and engage suffering in the lives of others and in one's own life, especially among marginalized people" (ELCA 2.1.2.1.a). Mark shows how Jesus is extraordinarily patient with his disciples, who also did not have "informed" ideas about what it was all going to involve for them in the future, especially if they expected to throw the Romans out of Jerusalem and claim the best seats in heaven (Mark 10:35–45)! Instead, Jesus has to challenge them time after time to think again more flexibly, even to the extent of suggesting that Peter is actually being inspired by Satan rather than God even when he recognizes Jesus as Messiah at his confession (8:29–37). Mark's picture of the disciples' failure to understand might appear quite embarrassing even to Luke and Matthew, as they seem to tone it down and depict the early church leaders and first bishops in a rather more flattering light. On the other hand, Mark is certainly being honest and realistic, and he also shows us how the disciples were "obedient" in following Jesus—even when they did not understand him or his mission.

Only the sort of person who is willing to respond to the call of God in Jesus, whatever the cost, is able to lead others into and along the way of the cross. Thus candidates should "engage people and lead them toward active participation in God's mission in the world" (ELCA 2.1.1.4.c), which is not only done through their teaching and pastoral care, but also by their personal example. And this does not mean getting it right the first time, or even all the time—just look at Peter's example. Perhaps this is why Mark is not embarrassed to show the first blind man at Bethsaida still seeing everything blurred and out of focus, despite receiving Jesus's healing touch (8:22–26). There is a great danger for the church in being seduced by contemporary society's ideas of "entrepreneurial leadership" and "measurable success," while secular concepts of making a "career" out of "going into the church" will lead to disappointment at best, and can be downright dangerous. Those who use such terms simply have not read Mark's account of Jesus's mission and ministry under the shadow of the cross and his invitation to follow him on that road. As the churches are constantly revising the criteria and refining our processes for selection, perhaps we might want also to consider including how candidates have experienced suffering and persecution, or responded to opposition and resistance in their attempt to follow Jesus's invitation to take up the cross and follow him, even to humiliation and death.

And undergirding it all needs to be a daily personal discipline for health and wellness: Lutheran candidates are to consider:

a. a vibrant and resilient faith;
b. a balance of work, play and self-care;
c. a maintenance of clear and healthy boundaries in all relationships;
d. an attention to diet, exercise and mental/physical health, and
e. a nurturing of healthy family relationships (ELCA 2.1.3.4),

while Disciples of Christ must show a "commitment to spiritual, physical and emotional wellness sufficient for healthy ministry" (DoC A.2.f).

So while this theme of suffering the way of the cross might not be quite so obvious in the selection criteria and competencies as preaching and teaching, or pastoral care, there are enough hints to make us pause in our rush of enthusiasm. Therefore, once again, take some time now to think and reflect, to pray and meditate, perhaps in front of the *Lindisfarne Gospels'* picture of Mark and his lion, about this picture of suffering the way of the cross. Reread the material in appendix 2 about the criteria and selection process—or those of your own church—in this light, and then perhaps write down your reflections in your journal, or discuss them with your vocational adviser or spiritual director.

3. Suffering the way of the cross in the ordination services

We find something similar happening when we turn to the liturgies used in ordination services. They contain a lot of material about preaching and teaching, and the ministry of pastoral care, as we have discovered in Parts I and II on Matthew and Luke. But here also, as with the criteria and competencies, if we look more carefully, we will still also find this theme of suffering and the way of the cross.

The gathering, welcome, or call to worship

Like most services, many ordination liturgies begin with prayers of penitence; for example, the Presbyterian confession includes "We confess that we have not lived up to our calling. We have been timid and frightened disciples, forgetful of your powerful presence and the strength of your Spirit among us. [*Silent prayers of confession may be offered.*] O God, forgive our foolish and sinful ways" (PCUSA). Whichever prayers are used, the bishop or senior minister(s) will proclaim God's forgiveness for all who repent and his mercy upon them, declaring that we are pardoned and delivered from all our sins, so that we can go forward into this service of ordination. Furthermore, the ordinands and "all present" are invited to renew their baptismal promises, including the renunciations: "trusting in the gracious mercy of God, do you turn from the ways of sin and renounce evil and its power in the world?" (PCUSA).

Many of the readings which the different services provide for the ministry of the Word include references to suffering and conflict, and it is likely that the preacher will encourage the candidates to follow Christ in their ministry along the way of the cross—even if this is not spelled out in the text.

The declarations or statement of ministry

We have already noted in the previous study on Luke the way the declarations or statement about ministry, the "job description," at the start of the ordination liturgies emphasizes following the self-giving example of Jesus, and the call to "serve all people, particularly the poor, the weak, the sick, and the lonely" (TEC deacons), "the sick, poor and impotent, that they may be visited and relieved . . . Christ's sheep that are dispersed abroad and His children who are in the midst of this evil world" (AME). Methodist deacons are "called to share in Christ's ministry of servant-hood, to interpret to the church the world's hurts and hopes, to serve all people, particularly the poor, the sick, and the oppressed, and to lead Christ's people in ministries of compassion and justice, liberation and reconciliation, especially in the face of hardship and personal sacrifice" (UMC). Australian ordinands are solemnly warned: "Remember that you will be called to give account before Jesus Christ: if it should come about that the Church, or any of its members, is hurt or hindered as a result of your negligence, you know the greatness of the fault and the judgement that will follow. Therefore apply yourself with diligence and care, and fashion your life and ministry in accordance with Christ's example" (APBA). The New Zealand Anglican liturgy explicitly links servant ministry with the way of the cross: "follow Christ whose servant you are. Share the burden of those whose cross is heavy" (ANZPB). Challenges like these alone should challenge any romantic ideas of ministry as "entrepreneurial success" or even our hopes or expectations of plain sailing.

"Your own life and that of your household"

There are two particular questions in the vows and promises which will repay some further thought and prayerful reflection regarding this area. Most churches make challenging demands on both the candidates and their families. Thus the Episcopal bishop asks their ordinands, "will you do your best to pattern your life [and that of your family, *or* household, *or* community] in accordance with the teachings of Christ, so that you may be a wholesome example to all people?" (TEC); similarly Methodist candidates are challenged, "Will you do your best to pattern your life in accordance with the teachings of Christ?" (UMC). The African Methodist bishop asks candidates, "Will you be diligent to frame and fashion yourself and your family according to the doctrine of Christ and to make both your-self and them, as much as in you lies, wholesome examples and patterns to the flock of Christ?" (AME). For the Disciples of Christ, a regional minister will ask those seeking to be ministers, "with Jesus as your example, will you, *Name*, endeavour to conduct yourself so that your life is shaped by Jesus Christ, who took the form of a servant for our sake?" (DoC).

This means that you are properly going to be a focus of attention and under some scrutiny. However, it is one thing for ordinands themselves to choose to follow Christ on the way of the cross, but it is often our families and loved ones who find themselves not only walking it with us, but also paying the price—especially when we are not even there! It is important for anyone considering a possible call to any form of ministry to discuss it with their nearest and dearest family and loved ones—but this is especially so if you are offering for full-time stipendiary parish ministry, which usu-ally includes living in an identifiable clergy house which is not only the base for your work, but also the focus of much of the activity, both for the con-gregation and also for callers at the door any time of day or night. Thus the Anglican Communion criteria wisely include a final item, "Candidates have fully discussed with spouse (and family, as appropriate) the consequences of possible selection, training, ordination and ministry" (TEAC L). And while a spouse or partner may be fully supportive of your desire to follow Jesus on the way of the cross, this way of life can often be difficult for any children growing up in—or even being born into—a "fish bowl" of public attention, who certainly did not choose it—and may well not want it.

"The discipline of this church"

Also, following the way of the cross entails surrendering control not only to Jesus, whom you may love and trust, but also to the church, which can still be a fallible human institution. We saw in the first part in our study on Matthew that potential ministers must agree to teach and preach the Christian faith within the confines of the tradition or understanding of their denomination. However, some churches require more discipline than that: thus, Presbyterians are asked, "will you be governed by our church's polity, and will you abide by its discipline?" (PCUSA), while the Epis-copal bishop says to their ordinands, "will you be loyal to the doctrine, discipline, and worship of Christ as this Church has received them? And will you, in accordance with the canons of this Church, obey your bishop and other ministers who may have authority over you and your work?" following it up with a second promise, "will you respect and be guided by the pastoral direction and leadership of your bishop?" (TEC). Roman Catholic ordinands must also promise "respect and obedience" to their Ordinary (their bishop) and his successors, as well as to their "legitimate superior" if they are in a religious order (RC).

The days when nervous young Anglican curates had to seek the permission of their bishop as their "father in God" in order to get married might now appear old-fashioned or quaint, but there have still been times in my ministry when I have had to do what I was told by my bishop, whether I liked it or not. Fortunately, I later came to appreciate his wisdom and guidance: for instance, when the Bishop of Rochester suggested that (at the ripe old age of thirty!) I should serve my first curacy in a rather well-to-do civic parish on the edge of London's posh commuter belt with a high choral tradition, both I and the vicar privately thought that "the old boy might have lost it." As the churchwarden put it a couple of years later at my leaving service, "a long-haired, guitar-swinging evangelical wearing high-heeled cowboy boots sticking out from under his cassock" was definitely *not* what they expected or were used to! On the other hand, after some serious consideration neither the vicar nor I could think of a good reason to refuse the bishop's decision to send me there, so we obeyed him—with interesting results! Admittedly, my time there was not always easy, some of my rough edges got knocked off, and there were certainly periods of conflict and some suffering on all sides, but I also learned so much through it all—and I hope that I made some good contributions to the parish through those years, and I am always made very welcome when I return there now; sometimes, they even invite me to preach again! In retrospect, therefore, perhaps "the old boy" *did* get it right in sending me there for my initial training after all. Furthermore, over the years since, I have often had good reason to be grateful for the wisdom and guidance of my various bishops, and even archbishops—although I still may not agree with everything they say!

Suffering for others

The whole point is that ministry is never about or for you yourself, but for others. The corollary is that we are also not expected to do this alone or unsupported, but to share in the wider life of the whole church, with both the resources and accountability that entails. Thus, after the promises, in the Church of England liturgy, the bishop bids candidates "to remember the greatness of the trust" which they are about to receive for they are to be entrusted with "Christ's own flock, bought by the shedding of his blood on the cross" (CofE). The Australian Anglican Church uses a different image to make the same point: "never forget how great a treasure is placed in your care: the Church you must serve is Christ's spouse and body, purchased at the cost of his own life" (APBA). Ordinands are also solemnly warned that they will be called to account for how they conduct their ministry. Therefore, as we have seen several times already, the bishop or senior ministers remind candidates that they cannot bear the weight of this calling in their own strength, and so lead the candidates in prayer for the gift of the Holy Spirit through singing the *Veni Creator Spiritus*, which includes the lines, "keep far our foes, give peace at home, where Thou art guide no ill can come." Similarly, the Episcopalian Litany for Ordinations concludes by asking "for ourselves; for the forgiveness of our sins, and for the grace of the Holy Spirit to amend our lives" (TEC).

These themes of conflict and suffering may also recur during the ordination prayers, where, as we saw in the previous study, we are reminded that Jesus "humbled himself for our sake, and in obedience accepted death, even death on a cross," and that "he gave his life as a ransom for many," and that suffering on the cross is how Christ won the victory over the powers of darkness and reconciled what was divided. Lastly, if there is a communion, the Eucharistic Prayer will recall Jesus's death and his perfect sacrifice, reminding us of the Last Supper on the night when Jesus was betrayed and abandoned by his closest friends, before feeling forsaken by God himself on the cross. As we have just seen, this atmosphere of darkness is the climax and particular emphasis of Mark's narrative of the ministry and Passion of Jesus—and he does not shrink from it. His great insight is that it was through this pain and suffering that "God was in Christ, reconciling the world to himself," as Paul also came to realize (2 Cor. 5:19).

Therefore, while this theme of suffering the way of the cross may not be as immediately obvious in the ordination services as those of teaching and preaching, and the ministry of pastoral care, careful reflection reveals that it is actually the heartbeat of the liturgy, undergirding everything that is said and done to, for, and over the candidates. Of course, such services are always rightly a joyful occasion, and the opportunity for great celebrations by families and friends, as well as the new parishioners, but this underlying dimension of pain and suffering can never be ignored: it is what makes Christian ministry distinctive, and entirely different from secular ideas of "effective leadership," strategic plans, and entrepreneurial activity.

Once again, therefore, this might be a good opportunity to put this book aside for a moment, and spend some time in prayer and reflection on the liturgies of the ordination services, especially any passages you may have noted or highlighted. Write down your thoughts and reactions in your journal, or discuss them with your spiritual director or whoever is helping to guide the development of your vocation.

4. Suffering the way of the cross in your ministry

After the public attention you will receive for your preaching and teaching, and the more private privilege of walking alongside people in their joys and sorrows in pastoral ministry, this third study on Mark has inevitably struck a more somber note. Let me be abundantly clear: ministry is a joy and a privilege—yes. Witnessing the triumph of God's grace and victory is amazing—yes. Sharing in Jesus Christ's extraordinary mission of healing and liberation is both exciting and humbling at the same time—yes. It is all there in Mark's picture of Jesus's ministry, but, make no mistake, the cost of it was—and still is—phenomenal. Mark's narrative warns us that following the way of the cross inevitably leads to exhaustion, rejection, misunderstanding by family, friends, and the religious establishment, culminating in humiliating suffering and death. This chapter on applying it to our ministry today may not have so many anecdotes or stories as in Parts I and II, since everyone's personal walk along the way of the cross is different—and I have no idea what might happen on yours. But since we are following Mark's narrative of Jesus's ministry on the way to Jerusalem to suffer and die, we will look in a bit more detail at what it all cost him.

Draining—the cost of ministry

In another of Mark's structural "sandwiches," he includes the account of Jesus healing a woman right in the middle of the story of his being called to the house of Jairus, a "ruler of the synagogue," whose daughter is dangerously ill (Mark 5:21–43). Like any loving father, Jairus is distraught, throws himself at Jesus's feet and begs him to come as quickly as possible without delay. It is not hard to imagine his feelings of frustration when Jesus stops to care for the woman who has been suffering from a constant flow of blood for twelve years. The Greek words used suggest that she is permanently menstruating, a condition which Jairus, as the elected "president of the synagogue," would know about, and he would have had to warn people to avoid her. Not only would her condition render the woman ritually impure herself, it would impart her impurity to anyone or anything she touched or who touched her (see Lev. 15:19–28; Matthew's version, 9:20, uses the rare technical term *haemorrhousa*, which occurs also in the Greek version of Lev. 15:33). It means that her touch would normally transmit the impurity to others and thus stop Jesus being able to touch anyone else, let alone to heal Jairus's daughter. Yet when she touches Jesus, it works the other way around: instead of it making him impure, his healing power flows out from him into her—something he realizes instantly, and so he stops to comfort her and complete her healing back into being allowed to associate and touch other human beings, even if the delay must have been frustrating for Jairus (Mark 5:25–34). The extraordinary thing is that not only does this "power flowing out of him" heal the woman, it still stays with him, and he is still able to use the same healing power on Jairus's daughter (5:35–43).

We studied Luke's portrait of Jesus's pastoral ministry in the previous study, but Mark's account particularly brings out the cost of such care and concern. There will be many times in ministry when we feel, like Jesus, that "the power has gone out from us." Caring for people, meeting their needs, bringing them comfort and healing, is draining—physically—and leads to exhaustion. It is even worse when, again like Jesus in this story, one pastoral situation immediately runs into another, and you go from pillar to post, bumping into someone in the street who delays or distracts you with their needs when you are actually on your way to visit someone else. However, unlike Jesus, we do not have unlimited resources—and too many experiences like this, especially back to back, will drain our reserves and leave us literally powerless.

In fact, of course, Christian doctrine teaches us that Jesus, for all his identity as the Son of God, was still fully human—which means that he too would get tired and exhausted when "the power had gone out of him." Mark shows this in Jesus's habit of needing to get away on his own: thus, after his absolutely crazy first experience of ministry (which included calling Peter, Andrew, James, and John, teaching and healing in the synagogue service, healing Peter's mother-in-law, and a public session of healing and exorcism at sundown, all on the same day according to Mark's account, 1:16–34), Jesus certainly deserved a "lie-in" the next morning! Instead, he gets up before sunrise and goes to a deserted place to pray, which is where the disciples eventually find him and drag him off to another busy day (1:35–39).

He also tries to teach this same habit to his disciples when they are "drained" by ministry. After he has sent them out in pairs on mission practice and they "report back," he tells them to "come away to a deserted place all by yourselves and rest a while." Mark even notes that there had been a lot of "coming and going, and they had no leisure even to eat" (6:7–13, 30–32). I'm afraid that this is all too common an experience in clergy households, where the minister rushes in from a busy day to try to grab a quick meal with the patiently waiting family before going out again to an evening meeting—only to have it interrupted by a phone call or yet another knock at the door. Of course, there will be times of pastoral emergency when an urgent response is really necessary—but allowing "the power to go out" of you with constant demands and interruptions will be draining, leading to exhaustion and probably also to resentment from your husband, wife, partner, or children. It would be wise to discuss this carefully all together right at the start and try to establish some ground rules for how you might handle the pressure—and try to build in times to review how things are going in due course.

Abandonment—being forsaken by God

If feeling drained and exhausted is a regular result of "the power going out" of us through ministry, Mark also has a sobering picture of where this will end up—nothing less than feeling abandoned not only by one's friends but even by God himself. We saw that Mark's third and final movement is a funeral march which leads to the cross. Churches often have a service of "Seven Words from the Cross," especially on Good Friday and sometimes set to beautiful music, but actually this is an amalgamation of all the gospels put together, in the same way that carol services blend together Luke's shepherds with Matthew's wise men, all topped off by the Johannine Prologue! It does not help that all the Jesus films tend to mix up the gospel accounts in a similar way—but actually while Luke and John both have three (different) sayings from Jesus on the cross, Mark and Matthew share just one, Jesus's cry of dereliction, quoting Psalm 22: "My God, my God, why have you forsaken me?" (Mark 15:34).

What is more, in Matthew's version, the question is answered by all sorts of Old Testament phenomena which accompany what is termed a "theophany," that is, what happens when God is suddenly and dramatically manifested: there is an earthquake, rocks are split asunder, the tombs open spontaneously, and the dead are raised and start walking around. It reminds us of Elijah's experience of the earthquake, wind, and fire before the "still, small voice," or the Psalmist's descriptions of God appearing, or Ezekiel's vision of dry bones coming to life (1 Kings 19:11–12; Pss. 68:8; 77:15–20; Ezek. 37:12–13). No wonder the centurion and everyone else in the surrounding crowd who witness these miraculous events are "filled with awe" and declare Jesus to be the Son of God (Matt. 27:51–54). Quite clearly, says Matthew, God has *not* forsaken or abandoned his Messiah; instead his death is the ultimate revelation of God's power.

Mark, however, is prepared to contemplate the awful reality of desolation, dereliction, and feeling completely abandoned by every living thing. The whole scene of the crucifixion is one of unrelieved darkness, physically as well as metaphorically, as even the sun refuses to look at Jesus on the cross (Mark 15:33). Jesus has gradually been betrayed by Judas, forsaken by his disciples, who ran away, denied by Peter, condemned by the highest religious authorities, rejected by the crowd, and sentenced by Pilate to one of the most humiliating and painful executions ever devised by cruel human ingenuity. Perhaps this might just be bearable if you felt God was still with you, so the ultimate abandonment comes with this cry of dereliction—literally being God-forsaken (15:34).

Ultimately, this is perhaps why Mark makes best sense to those who are suffering or being persecuted. If it was written against the fiery backdrop of Nero's persecutions and the destruction of Jerusalem, this sense of being abandoned and forsaken by God is exactly how his readers and hearers would have felt. And yet, unlike Matthew, Mark does not rush to supply any answers—no miracles, no earthquake, no dead being raised; the heavens remain obdurately closed, and God has nothing to say. There are times in ministry, especially when tragedy strikes us or those in our care and we are asked the inevitable and gut-wrenching questions, "Why did this happen?" or "Where is God when it hurts so much?"—and we are tempted desperately to try to find an answer, to scrabble together any crumb of comfort, anything to avoid that utter, silent despair. Please, please, please, try to resist that temptation: sometimes, all you can do— and, in fact, the *best* you can do—is just to be there, to sit with those who are suffering in the darkness, and weep with them. And then there are the occasions when we are personally attacked, or our family is threatened, and when even God seems to have deserted us.

At such times, all we can do is to return to Mark's sublime theological insight. To most people in the ancient world, to try to find meaning in the death of a crucified criminal would have been completely crazy. It was so humiliating that this method of execution was totally forbidden for Roman citizens, while Greeks believed that God could not suffer or even experience physical humanity and Jews considered anyone hanged on a tree to be cursed by God (Deut. 21:22–23). And yet, Mark has been deliberately directing his entire narrative toward this point, with Jesus's three predictions of his Passion and all the apocalyptic warnings. It had to be this way. Only a God who is willing to enter into the very depths of human experience, to suffer the worst we could possibly do to him, and still not fight back—only such a God is worthy to be worshiped in a world of all this pain and darkness.

No wonder that this is the moment when the penny finally drops, and alone in the darkness the first human being, a Roman soldier, realizes the incredible truth, and mutters, almost under his breath, "This person really is the Son of God" (15:39, in contrast to Matthew's announcement to everyone, Matt. 27:54). Where is God when it hurts? Right there, says Mark, nailed to that cross, bleeding to death and gasping for breath, abandoned, with all comfort gone. No other God can understand, let alone help us.

The cosmic struggle with evil

Another reason why Mark is an uncomfortable gospel which does not really fit into our modern sensibilities is the brooding backdrop to all his narrative, which, as we have seen, is the cosmic struggle with evil. It begins right after his baptism, as Jesus comes up out of the water and "the Spirit immediately drove him out into the wilderness" (1:12). First we note Mark's favorite word "immediately"; there will be no respite: this struggle will start as soon as the bishop's hands leave your head—if not before. What is more, it is the *Holy* Spirit which "drives" Jesus out; Matthew and Luke have the much more prosaic phrase, "Jesus was led by the Spirit" (Matt. 4:1; Luke 4:1)—which sounds lovely; we all want to be "led by the Spirit," don't we? But Mark says the Spirit "drives" him out; the Greek word, *ek-ballō*, means to throw or "cast out," and it is used more than a dozen times in Mark to refer to driving out demons and evil spirits. Its only other usages are when Jesus "throws out" the crowd of mourners in Jairus's house who laugh at him when he says the little girl is asleep, and when he "drives out" the stall-holders selling things in the temple (Mark 5:40; 11:15). Yet here it is the Holy Spirit who is in the "driving seat"—and he is not being gentle.

Before Jesus can embark on his ministry of driving out everything which is getting in the way of God's love and healing power, he has to be driven out first himself, out into the wilderness where he is alone "with the wild beasts" (like the lion?). Here he has to face himself and be tempted by what Mark calls "*the* satan." Rather than the personal name of an entity, this phrase is a function or job description, "the accuser" or "the opponent," who features in Jewish thought such as at the beginning of Job (1:6–12). Unlike Matthew and Luke, Mark does not go into any details beyond the basic fact that Jesus was "tempted," and then he returns to start his ministry, calling the first disciples, and going "immediately" into the synagogue, where a man also appears "immediately" with an "unclean spirit" (Mark 1:21–23). This marks the start of Jesus's struggle with the forces of evil, opposed to God and oppressing his people with unclean spirits and various forms of sickness or illness, which Jesus has to "drive out" (see 1:26, 32–33, 39), a ministry which he also gives to his disciples (3:15).

This is why Mark constructs his careful three-decker sandwich which we studied earlier: beyond the incomprehension of Jesus's family and friends, and behind the opposition of the religious authorities, lies the central, cosmic struggle with the ultimate opposer, the satan (3:23–27). Even Peter can have his (blurred?) insight that Jesus is the Christ one minute, and be rebuked the next, "Get behind me, Satan," for opposing God's plan for Jesus to suffer and die in Jerusalem (8:33). And so it is that, after all the minor skirmishes with evil spirits and opponents along the road, the way of the cross leads inevitably and inexorably to that desolated hillside and Jesus's cry of dereliction and abandonment. Yet even then, like Job, he will not "curse God and die" (Job 2:9–10). In the end, the struggle with evil can never be won by fighting back using its own methods or descending to its level. Jesus takes it upon himself, lets it do its worst, and still proclaims that love will have the last word.

In our "modern" world, of course, referring to Satan or unclean spirits is another reason why Mark seems more remote. People sometimes assume that it might be more relevant perhaps to those facing direct persecution or battling evil spirits somewhere far away, but not us: "we are more enlightened than that." And yet, I have to say that there have been times in my ministry when it really has felt that a cosmic struggle with evil was the only way to make sense of what was happening. Sometimes it can seem minor and relatively easy: in one parish with which I was connected, a building where schoolchildren often complained about "a face at the window," or feeling suddenly "cold and shivery," was transformed by a formal liturgy of blessing and cleansing with a eucharist. In university halls of residence, I have known poltergeist phenomena of books and cases moving around, which have sometimes seemed connected with a student's repressed urges and deep desires but where prayer has also helped. In both cases, the involvement of an older, more experienced priest who held the bishop's formal license for Deliverance Ministry was vital; every English diocese has at least one, and parish priests would be wise not to hesitate to make use of such a person when necessary. It would also be a good idea to investigate how your church or tradition handles this area.

In all such cases, working with colleagues and other professionals is crucial. On one occasion when a student was manifesting the kind of behavior usually only seen in Hollywood horror films, we took her for a consultation with the university psychiatrist, who interviewed her carefully and then declared her to be as sane and well as the rest of us, saying: "I'm sorry, Chaplain, but this one is more your professional area of expertise than mine." After prayer and anointing with the diocesan expert, everything seemed to be healed, the manifestations stopped, and all was well thereafter.

I don't pretend to be able to explain all of this theologically, and those who think that they can do so sometimes worry me even more than those who dismiss it all as merely old superstition. C. S. Lewis sums it up beautifully in the preface to his *Screwtape Letters*, supposedly written from a senior demon, Screwtape, to a "junior tempter," his nephew, Wormwood: "There are two equal and opposite errors into which our race can fall about the devils. One is to disbelieve in their existence. The other is to believe, and to feel an excessive and unhealthy interest in them. They themselves are equally pleased by both errors and hail a materialist or a magician with the same delight." All I know is that my own ministry and that of friends and colleagues have included such experiences from time to time, and it is then that Mark's picture of a cosmic struggle with evil lying behind or underneath our daily pains, hurts, and frustrations suddenly makes a lot more sense—together with his refusal to seek easy answers to the suffering and darkness of crucifixion.

Being overwhelmed

Finally, Mark's portrait of Jesus and his disciples following the way of the cross can be a helpful warning that there will be times, inevitably, when you will feel overwhelmed and about to drown with all the things being thrown at you. Mark has a lovely story of the disciples taking Jesus with them in a boat to cross the lake at the end of another busy day (4:35–41).

It is still a feature of the Sea of Galilee that this is a dangerous time to be on the water: as the sun goes down, the surrounding hills cool down much more quickly than the water which has been absorbing the heat all day, so the wind will suddenly switch round, from the helpful onshore breeze, which blows boats home during the day, to an offshore gale making life very difficult indeed for returning sailors. The boat is about to be swamped and the disciples are overwhelmed, so they turn angrily to wake up Jesus, who is so exhausted from "the power going out from him" all day that he is unconscious on a "cushion in the stern": "Rabbi, don't you care that we are perishing?" Neither the storm nor their complaint seems to bother Jesus, who calms the storm and then asks them, "Have you no faith?"

Matthew's version probably reflects how the story was preached around the early church, as the disciples more properly follow Jesus into the boat, and, instead of shouting a complaint, they pray to him much more respectfully: "Save, O Lord." Instead of asking these disciples—the first "bishops"!—if they have "no faith," Jesus calls them "men of *little* faith" (Matt. 8:23–27). But Mark's account has raw power and energy which may reflect not only the regular experience of fishermen on the Sea of Galilee but also the flames of persecution in the 60s, and our own experience of ministry, when at the end of a busy day, we feel about to be overwhelmed and submerged—and even worse, God is asleep and doesn't seem to care!

So perhaps Mark's lion is more appropriate a symbol for our mission and ministry than it first appeared. Yes, it is a wild beast, "not a tame lion." But if Mr. Beaver admits that Aslan may be anything but "safe," he also reassures the children: "he's good. He's the King, I tell you." Mark similarly tells it as it is: writing against the backdrop of suffering and persecution, he warns us of the blood, sweat, and tears which are inevitable on the way of the cross. And this book would be incomplete, and I would be irresponsible, if we did not put that challenge before you as part of the call to ministry.

Yes, it is true that "where God guides, he also provides." I pray that you will share Paul's experience when God says, "My grace is sufficient for you, for my power is made perfect in weakness" (2 Cor. 12:9). But, to be honest, there will be times when you feel exhausted, forgotten, forsaken by God and by those you love, when it hurts and you suffer, or when your family are hurting and suffering—at those times, it will feel like a cosmic struggle, however you understand that theologically. So take some time to think about it carefully now, to pray, reflect, and maybe write something down in your journal. You never know, it may come back to help you at some point in the years ahead.

5. Sustaining ministry on the way of the cross

At the end of the two previous studies on Matthew and Luke, we have used the image of a desert which a thoughtless camel tries to cross on the basis of filling up at the oasis. If the story of Mark's lion has shown us anything, it is that the desert or the wilderness is precisely where the "wild beasts" are, the place where we are tempted and confronted by the ultimate opponent, "the satan." Toward the end of the third century, various Christians began to withdraw into the deserts of north Africa, especially in Egypt. While the initial context may have been the persecutions of that period, especially under Diocletian (AD 303), this movement accelerated rapidly after Christianity became the official religion of the Roman Empire under Constantine from AD 313, as a kind of "protest movement" against the church's accommodation with society and the state. They are known today as the Desert Fathers and Mothers, inspired by the early examples of Abba (Father) Anthony the Great and Amma (Mother) Syncletica of Alexandria. They took Jesus's call to poverty and renouncing everything seriously and literally, and once martyrdom was no longer an option, they went into the desert looking for a fight "because that's where the demons are." And yet, Mark also shows that the desert is where Jesus went not just to fight against evil, but also to pray and to recuperate.

"Come away to a deserted place all by yourselves and rest a while"

In this area more than any other, there are no easy answers. The old adage "to every difficult and complicated question, there is an easy and simple answer which is usually easily and simply wrong" rings true. It is interesting that the first suggestion in both the previous studies about how to sustain the mission of teaching and preaching and also the pastoral ministry noted how both Matthew and Luke emphasized in different ways Jesus's habit of praying. This may look like the obvious and simple answer to everything in ministry—but it is far from easy. We have already seen how after Mark's account of Jesus's ridiculously busy first day of ministry, instead of having a "lie-in" the next day, "in the morning, while it was still very dark, he got up and went out to a deserted place, and there he prayed." This was clearly not just round the corner; the Greek word here is *erēmos*, which is literally a desert or wilderness, and the disciples had to go "hunting" before they could find Jesus and tell him "everyone is searching for you" (Mark 1:35–37).

If Jesus needed to go and hide somewhere to pray and recover, then this is going to be even more true for us. We will discuss the importance of retreats for prayer in the next study on John, but actually they can also be very tiring. Here we shall concentrate on the fact that when "the power goes out" from something, it has a flat battery—and needs recharging. This is right at the heart of the way God has organized the cosmos, where he himself rested after the act of creation and instituted the Sabbath as a practical need for all his creatures (Gen. 2:1–3). In taking time to rest himself and for his disciples, Jesus was honoring that principle, and so we need to follow his example similarly.

Days off

Thus, Jesus not only takes time to rest himself; he also cares for his disciples by making sure that they do the same. When they returned from being sent out on their first mission practice (Mark 6:7–13), they were excited and "gathered around Jesus, and told him all that they had done and taught." Jesus's response, however, is quite clear: "'Come away to a deserted place all by yourselves and rest a while.' For many were coming and going, and they had no leisure even to eat. And they went away in the boat to a deserted place by themselves" (6:30–32). It is interesting that while Jesus went to the "deserted place" to pray and recharge his batteries, his concern for the disciples is very practical—to rest and to eat.

We have already noted how family mealtimes in clergy households can get constantly interrupted. The same is even more true of the celebrated "pastor's day off." Ministry is not a Monday to Friday, 9 to 5, clocking-on and clocking-off kind of life. Clergy live among the people they serve, almost as a visual example of Jesus's incarnation, taking flesh to "dwell among us" (John 1:14). Also, it will involve visiting people and holding meetings when they are *not* at work, which inevitably means evenings and weekends. Therefore, in order to observe the Sabbath principle, clergy usually take a day off during the week—but it is very hard to protect it.

When I was a young assistant curate, one problem was that my wife was out at work. If I stayed in the house on my own, I swear I could hear a strange pleading noise emanating from my study where a half-written sermon for Sunday desperately needed finishing, not to mention my "part-time" research for my doctoral thesis on the genre of the gospels. And if I resisted the seductive calling of my desk, the doorbell would go: "I know it's your day off, but it's only me and I knew you wouldn't mind, but I need to ask you about the flowers for next Sunday . . ." In the end, I took up golf, since that at least got me out of the house and away from everyone—and the way I played, it certainly quickly became "a deserted place"! A bit later, after we had a baby, well-meaning parishioners would drop in with little presents and toys, which was lovely—except we were never alone. So we joined the National Trust, and ended up spending days off leaving the curate's house to push the pram around much more stately homes or gardens. You have to find creative ways of "coming apart"—or you will literally "come apart," at the seams!

Holidays

In addition to the weekly Sabbath day, Jews also kept an annual cycle of feasts and "holy days," from which we get our modern holidays. However, the annual "holy days" of Christmas and Easter are "your busy time of year, Vicar," rather than holidays for the clergy. And so, after all the endless round of carol services and yet more mince pies, or Lent groups and vigil services, it is vital to book a week off to try to get away and simply recover. After he appointed me as a university chaplain, the Bishop of Exeter required me to come and see him at the end of term. Knowing how busy he was, I expected a brief chat. Instead, it turned into a probing, long interview about all that had gone on in my first months, undergirded by a real episcopal and pastoral care for me. After my grilling in the spotlight, at the end I casually inquired whether he was getting a break after Christmas. "My dear boy," he boomed as he showed me out, "I consider it a sin *not* to!" In this way, he set an example for his clergy that proper breaks are as vital in sustaining ministry as the regular Sabbath "day off."

Of course, it is one thing to stress the importance of taking holidays—but quite another to be able to afford it on a clergy stipend, especially if it has to support a young family as well. One benefit of serving my curacy in a relatively affluent parish was that a couple of people insisted that we should make use of their "little place in the country," while another discovery was a network of holiday homes owned by clergy preparing for their eventual retirement which could be rented at a discount by fellow ministers. And don't forget the charitable funds administered by groups like the Friends of the Clergy and Sons of the Clergy which can also sometimes help a clerical cash-flow crisis.

Traveling with others

These suggestions about taking time apart to pray, eat, rest, and recuperate may seem basic and obvious, but actually they can be far from easy in practice. Another vital dimension in surviving the pressures of ministry is making sure that you do not travel the way of the cross on your own. Living in the goldfish bowl of a clergy house is hard enough for those who have a spouse, partner, or family—but it is even more difficult for those who are living alone. We were therefore always glad that several single friends with whom I had trained at theological college used to come and stay when they had some time off; even if it was still a clergy house, at least it was in a different deanery or diocese, and it gave us the chance to compare notes and have a good catch-up, often over a nice meal or a glass of wine.

You have to have people who love you, support you, pray for you, and accompany you on this way of the cross. Even Jesus couldn't do it on his own, which is why he called disciples to join him; what is more, he taught them in a group together and sent them out in pairs (Mark 6:7). During my ministerial training at Saint John's Nottingham, we were encouraged to form what were called "triads," which have nothing to do with smuggling Chinese drugs, but were groups of three people for mutual support and prayer together. Having been friends and classmates at college, we met every six or nine months to get away for at least twenty-four hours to a retreat center, or someone's holiday home, or even one winter my churchwarden's barge frozen in a marina, which was certainly "a deserted place." We would share what was happening, laugh or cry together, play golf and go to the pub—and spend some time in prayer. Being at similar stages in both our ministry and our personal lives, we often found we were having the same experiences: we had our first major rows with our training incumbent minister about the same time, and then we were having babies, or moving jobs and so on down the years. We would also set targets for each other for the next six months, writing down things for the others to pray for—and to hold us to account. I would never have got my PhD written without my friends' praying and nagging me about it! Sadly one member of our group is no longer in the ministry, having had to take early retirement on health grounds, but two of us are still praying together after over thirty years, as are a surprising number of the triads from those college days.

More recently, it has been interesting to discover that Church of England bishops are encouraged to form similar cell groups with others who are consecrated at the same time. This means that Anglo-Catholics and evangelicals, liberals and traditionalists who may well have trained in very contrasting ways and serve in different dioceses have ended up in groups together just because of when they became bishops. I have had the privilege of being invited to go away as a consultant with a couple of bishops' cells to try to help them with their own continuing studies about the Bible as they share together what it means for them to exercise episcopal oversight. Their willingness to learn and to be honest with each other about the difficulties, pains, and conflicts of ministry is impressive—and a good example for the rest of us!

Therefore, if you are just beginning to consider ministry, are currently in training or already serving out on the front lines, and you are not in some sort of cell group or don't have a partnership like that, it might be a good idea to think about it, and try to set one up. After all, if it was good enough for Jesus and his disciples, or for our bishops today, it might just be helpful for you when the going gets tough to know that someone else knows what it is like, and is praying for you.

Conclusion

After all the excitement of teaching and preaching illustrated in Matthew's gospel and the privilege of sharing the burden of pastoral ministry exemplified by Jesus in Luke's gospel, we have been studying what is often the neglected gospel of Mark. In many ways, that is hardly surprising: lions do not make congenial house pets, and Mark's narrative is not exactly comfortable. On the other hand, I hope that reading it against its probable historical background of persecution at Rome and the destruction of Jerusalem in the 60s has brought out the extraordinary rich resource Mark offers us today, especially to those who are suffering. His entire narrative, carefully composed in three parts, follows Jesus to Jerusalem on the way of the cross, despite all the opposition and incomprehension he meets from family and friends, not to mention the authorities.

And yet, we have also noted that the selection criteria and competencies do not explicitly look for evidence of pain and suffering, while you have to search carefully for the pattern of Jesus's Passion and death underlying the ordination liturgies. On the other hand, I have suggested that pain and suffering are an inevitable experience when walking the way of the cross in any form of ministry. Feeling "the power drain out" of you is exhausting and the daily round can sometimes be overwhelming. Furthermore, sharing the love of God involves participating in the ultimate cosmic struggle against evil and all that opposes the divine intention, however you understand it, sometimes to the extent that we can even feel abandoned and forsaken by God himself. Yet at those points, we are entering into the experience of Jesus's own Passion on the cross—and those who follow him can expect nothing less. Therefore, I have concluded with some practical suggestions about the importance of regular time for prayer, rest, and recuperation, as well as ensuring that you do not walk the way of the cross alone. Even if they seem somewhat trite or obvious, actually they are all vital under the pressures of ministry, so take some time to prepare for this aspect of the cost of mission and ministry now.

For prayer and further reflection

In the light of Mark's portrait of the cost of following the way of the cross, get out your diary and find a day in the not-too-distant future when you can get away on your own to a quiet place or local retreat center. It's a good idea to spend some time reading Mark's gospel as a continuous account—it should only take an hour or so. And then try to get outside and walk the way of the cross, ending up if possible in a garden where there is a representation of the crucifixion. Sit at the feet of Jesus and talk to him about your experience—and listen to see what he has to reply. As before, write down your thoughts and reflections in your journal, and talk to your spiritual and vocational advisers—and once again, you may find the comments on www.facebook.com/FourMinistriesOneJesus to be helpful; why not post a brief account of your retreat day, walking the way of the cross?

PART IV

John

Praying the Divine Life

Figure 4. Saint John, *Lindisfarne Gospels*, Folio 209b

1. John's portrait of Jesus and the life of God

We followed an unusual gospel sequence, jumping straight from Matthew's account of Jesus's teaching and preaching to Luke's portrait of his pastoral care, since these two aspects of mission and ministry belong so closely together. Third, we studied Mark's dark and challenging narrative of the way of the cross, and what it can teach us about the painful and suffering context in which much ministry takes place. In each case, we ended up back with the importance of prayer for sustaining the mission and ministry upon which God is sending us—so it is right that we come now to the Fourth Gospel, with its emphasis on how prayer enables us to share in the very life of God.

Although this is our last study, we are back again to T. S. Eliot's arriving "where we started"—since for many of us our spiritual pilgrimage began with John. Certainly, I was given a newspaper version of this gospel when I was an eager young Christian—and I taped it to my bedroom wall, underlining all the promises which I interpreted straight from Jesus to me personally: "I will not leave you orphaned; I will come to you" (John 14:18). Decades later, while teaching a university course entitled "Johannine Theology and the Problem of the Fourth Gospel," I was still puzzling over those same phrases. John's gospel has been described as something in which "a child can paddle and an elephant swim deep." It is an extraordinary book, which can still speak to fresh-faced converts, yet keep the theologians arguing and the mystics praying for centuries!

It tells the same basic narrative of Jesus's mission and ministry as the other three, yet it has different stories and teachings, all composed in a distinctive style with a relatively small vocabulary, repeating the same few words frequently, like "light," "life," "truth," and—significantly—"Father" and "Son." Somebody has thought about, taught and preached, meditated upon and prayed over this material, through decades of deep reflection, repeating these phrases over, and over, and over again. Our three previous studies each finished with the importance of prayer in sustaining ministry today, so it is fitting that this final study should examine how we share in the divine life.

The image of Saint John in the *Lindisfarne Gospels* (Folio 209b; see fig. 4) depicts the writer seated with his parchment scroll, staring out at us. The other three evangelists are portrayed hard at work writing their gospels, while John appears to have completed his already, and wants to know what we make of it. Above him an eagle with a fierce beak, the *imago aequilae*, clutches the book in sharp talons. Some Celtic manuscripts illustrate John with a more reassuring bird, or the "wild goose" which was also a symbol of the Holy Spirit. All these images seem appropriate, for this gospel can be both comforting and challenging, and ultimately draws us into the life of God.

If Aslan is not "a tame lion" in the *Chronicles of Narnia*, C. S. Lewis also includes Farsight the Eagle, who can discern things far away from flying up high. When I originally wrote *Four Gospels, One Jesus?* my publishers were positive about the Aslan-lion connection, but less convinced about my use of the eagles from Lewis's friend J. R. R. Tolkien. They thought that these reflected the rock music of my youth and that people wouldn't get the references to *The Lord of the Rings*! Subsequently, of course, Peter Jackson's computer-generated movie images of Gwaihir the Windlord and other eagles have given us beautiful images of Tolkien's extraordinary creatures, terrifyingly fierce in battle, yet tenderly gentle when rescuing the heroes from danger.

These images are all true of eagles in the Old Testament. These majestic birds, swooping over the desert on thermals with a flick of the tail, apparently devote much more of their brain to vision than humans, so Job speaks of how they can see, like Farsight, from a great height (Job 39:27–29). The terrifying power of the eagle diving down out of the blue sky on to a flock is often used as an image of God's judgment (e.g., Deut. 28:49; Jer. 48:40; 49:22). On the other hand, God reassures Moses and the Israelites that "I bore you on eagles' wings and brought you to myself," while Isaiah promises that "those who wait for the LORD shall renew their strength, they shall mount up with wings like eagles, they shall run and not be weary, they shall walk and not faint" (Exod. 19:4; Isa. 40:31). So the traditional choice of an eagle to symbolize Saint John is significant, for all these elements, high-flying, far-seeing, fierce in conflict, yet tenderly caring, are reflected in John's account of Jesus's mission and ministry and what we can learn from it for our work and life of prayer today.

The Prologue

The ninth-century spiritual writer John Scotus Eriugena wrote a homily on John's Prologue, *The Voice of the Eagle*; its opening words, "The spiritual bird, fast-flying, God-seeing," reflect John's magnificent curtain-raiser. Where do we start in understanding where Jesus came from? Mark's gospel begins with Jesus fully grown, being baptized, Matthew tackles Jesus's ancestry and the wise men, while Luke introduces Jesus's cousin, the forerunner, and describes his birth. John, however, goes right back to the cosmic context: "In the beginning was the Word, and the Word was with God, and the Word was God. He was in the beginning with God" (John 1:1–2). Jesus's origins are not human; not only was he with God at the beginning, everything else has its origin in him: "All things came into being through him, and without him not one thing came into being. What has come into being in him was life, and the life was the light of all people. The light shines in the darkness, and the darkness did not overcome it" (1:3–5).

This Prologue not only introduces some of John's keywords like "light" and "darkness," "life" and "death," but it also sums up the whole story: "He was in the world, and the world came into being through him; yet the world did not know him. He came to what was his own, and his own did not accept him. But to all who received him, who believed in his name, he gave power to become children of God, who were born, not of blood or of the will of the flesh or of the will of man, but of God. And the Word became flesh and lived among us, and we have seen his glory, the glory as of a father's only son, full of grace and truth" (1:10–14). When the Apollo 11 lunar module touched down, the first words on the moon were, "The Eagle has landed." The Prologue's climax makes it perfectly clear: "no one has ever seen God. It is God the only Son, who is close to the Father's heart, who has made him known" (1:18).

Like an eagle, Jesus nests "up high," sharing the very life of God, yet he swoops down, with hints of judgment for those who will not receive him, to gather under his wings the children of God, and bring them back to the Father's heart. This divine mission lies at the center of all Christian ministry, and if we let ourselves be carried on the eagle's wings, we share not only in this mission, but even the very life of God himself. If you are active in any form of ministry, people will see you as a representative, for good or for ill. You may bring them closer to God, or they may vent their anger and frustration about God on you. The rest of John's story plays this out in Jesus's life and ministry, and ultimately in his death and resurrection.

The Book of Signs with talons bared for conflict

After the Prologue, the first half of John depicting Jesus's acts of divine and healing power is sometimes called the Book of Signs, since John does not call them "miracles," but prefers *semeia*, or "signs." Turning water into wine at a wedding is "the first of his signs, in Cana of Galilee, and revealed his glory; and his disciples believed in him" (John 2:1-14). Other signs include healings of an official's son, a paralyzed man, and a man born blind, as well as the multiplication of loaves and fishes and walking on the water (4:46-54; 5:1-9; 6:1-21; 9:1-41). These are not just amazing miracles for John, but *signs* which reveal Jesus's *sign*ificance, connected to discourses about his claims to be "the bread of life" or the "light of the world" (6:25-58; 8:12-58). John the Baptist did no signs, but directed people to Jesus, and many came to believe in him through his signs (10:41-42). Finally, by raising Lazarus from the dead, Jesus demonstrated the truth of his extraordinary statement, "I am the resurrection and the life" (11:1-44). There is a significant implication for our ministry here, that it is never "ours"; everything we do and say is a "sign" of something greater, pointing to Jesus and bringing the life of God into a situation.

However, signposts point two ways, marking a fork in the road. While Jesus's signs and teachings brought many to believe in him, they were also the focus for growing opposition which led to fierce debates, especially about his "I am" claims. Thus Jesus's healing of the paralyzed man upset the authorities because it was on the Sabbath (5:9-18), while feeding the five thousand and claiming to be "the bread of life" led to a sharp dispute about Jesus's identity in the light of Moses and the Israelites eating manna in the wilderness (6:25-58). Healing the blind man on the Sabbath provoked an even sharper clash, with Jewish leaders interviewing not only the man but also his elderly parents (9:13-41).

Finally, Jesus's raising of Lazarus caused the emergency meeting of the council where Caiaphas the high priest determined that "it is better for you to have one man die for the people than to have the whole nation destroyed," so they planned to put Jesus to death (11:46-53). A high-flying fish-eagle can see below the surface of the water, dive down quickly, and pull a fish out in its sharp talons. So too John often sees through several levels down from the surface to the deeper meaning. Caiaphas seems to be saying cynically that it would be politically better to kill Jesus than risk the Romans getting involved in the disturbances he was stirring up—but John interprets it as a real prophecy from God through the high priest that "Jesus was about to die for the nation" (11:51).

John's portrayal of "the Jews"

Mark demonstrated how ministry stirs up the cosmic struggle with evil, manifesting itself through religious authorities as well as directly. So too John shows that Jesus's signs lead to forks in the road, and his claims provoke growing conflict with those he calls simply "the Jews," which has contributed to millennia of anti-Semitism. Jesus's response to certain of "the Jews" that "you are from your father the devil" (John 8:44) was even used by the Nazis as justification for the Holocaust. The irony is that not only are Jesus and all his disciples Jewish, but all who accept his signs, believe his claims, and receive him are also all "Jews." The Fourth Gospel is the most Jewish in so many ways, constructed against the sequence of feasts like Passover and Tabernacles, centered around visits to the temple, full of symbols for the law like bread, water, vines, and referring to all the great heroes like Abraham, Isaac, Jacob, and Moses, alluding to so many Jewish customs, and quoting the prophets. So we need to understand how such a Jewish gospel has been seen as "anti-Semitic."

We suggested that Mark was written during the backdrop of the Jewish revolt leading to the destruction of Jerusalem in AD 70. John, however, was probably composed a couple of decades later, reflecting the increasing division after the demolition of the temple between those Jews who accepted Jesus as Messiah and shared him with Gentiles in the early church, and other Jews who found their identity in studying the Torah in the synagogue. Unfortunately, the breakup of a family is never easy, and civil wars are often the most bitter—and this is the situation underlying John's depiction of some Jews who accept Jesus, and others who reject him. He made this clear in his opening summary in the Prologue: "he came to what was his own, and his own did not accept him. But to all who received him, who believed in his name, he gave power to become children of God" (1:11–12).

Unfortunately for us reading this gospel two thousand years later, especially after the Holocaust, it all "sounds" very different from its first-century context, especially when read aloud in church. It is crucial that in our ministry today we are sensitive to this, particularly in our preaching and teaching. Think carefully about your words: instead of characterizing Jesus's opponents repeatedly as "the Jews," use more accurate phrases in your sermons like "the religious authorities," the "synagogue leaders," and so on to avoid sounding anti-Semitic.

Similarly, the Pharisees are often attacked from pulpits for being legalistic or "nit-picking," drawing on Matthew's list of "woes" calling them "blind guides" and "hypocrites" (Matt. 23). Doubtless some Pharisees were legalistic—but so are many Christians today! Meanwhile, John also depicts people like Nicodemus, "a Pharisee . . . a leader of the Jews . . . a teacher of Israel," who first comes to Jesus under the cover of darkness, and yet who later speaks up for Jesus against his colleagues' prejudice about Galilee; eventually he brings expensive ointments to help another leading Jew, Joseph of Arimathea, bravely request Jesus's body from Pilate and bury him (3:1–10; 7:50–52; 19:38–40). In fact, in their concern to bring holiness into daily life, the Pharisees come closest to our concerns: don't forget that Paul trained under one of their greatest rabbis, Gamaliel, who spoke up for early Christians in the council (Acts 5:34–39). Therefore be careful in your choice of words in preaching and teaching, and let us all strive to manifest God's grace and love for everyone in our words and deeds.

Sharing the divine life of God—the Farewell Discourses

If the eagle's beak and talons are fierce in conflict, then living under "the shadow of your wings" is to find a place of refuge (see Pss. 17:8; 36:7; 57:1; 63:7; 91:1–4). John begins his account of the Passion by emphasizing that Jesus knows that "his hour" has come; the high-flying eagle must return to the heights of heaven whence he came—but the way leads through the cross. He gathers his disciples together for one last supper, where he cleanses them, feeds them, and explains what will happen. Picking up "his own" from the Prologue, John explains that "having loved his own who were in the world, he loved them to the end" (13:1; see 1:11–12).

Like an eagle with fledglings, Jesus washes them and feeds them: the foot washing is not just a symbol for Jesus's ministry, but also an example for his disciples, which they will understand not "now . . . but later" (13:3–17). In fact, they are confused about everything, and do not comprehend his warnings of betrayal and going away (13:22, 33); one after another Peter, Thomas, Philip, and the other Judas ask where he is going and what he means, but his promise that they will see him again only brings more confusion (16:17–19). When finally they claim to understand, Jesus makes a last attempt to give them peace and courage by warning that they are about to be scattered (16:29–33), before turning to pray for them (ch. 17).

These Farewell Discourses go round and round meditating upon how Jesus is in the Father, and the Father is in Jesus, yet through the

Spirit, both the Father and the Son will "dwell" or "abide" in the believer who "abides" in them (14:10–11, 15–17, 20, 23, 26), which is a primary concern of this study. To clarify things, Jesus uses the image of the vine, which, as we saw previously, often represents Israel or the people of God in the Old Testament. However, Jesus is the "true vine," and the Father is "the vinedresser" who cares for it and makes it bear fruit. The disciples are that fruit if they remain or "abide" in or on the vine, that is, in Jesus's love (15:1–11). The verb "abide" or "remain," *menō*, appears frequently here, connected with the "dwelling places" or "abodes," *monai*, which are in his Father's house (14:2). The heart of John's meditation is the utter conviction that Jesus abides in the Father, the Father abides in Jesus, and they both abide in us through the Spirit, and we in them. This extraordinary insight is something which is more to be lived than explained or understood.

Central to all of this is the gift and promise of the Holy Spirit, whom Jesus describes as "another *paraclete*" (14:16). Greek has two words for "another," and the one used here means "another of the same sort" or "the same again," like when you want a repeat of a drink which you have just enjoyed, as opposed to "something completely different." Meanwhile, the word *paraclete* is often translated as "comforter," "counselor," or "advocate": it means someone "called alongside" to help, assist, or strengthen. Thus the Holy Spirit will be "alongside them," just as Jesus was, "the same again," no different from his physical presence. Therefore the Spirit will teach them everything and remind them of all Jesus has said in the past and guide them into all truth in the future (14:26; 16:13–14).

This is best illustrated by Andrei Rublev's famous icon of the Trinity based upon the appearance of three strangers to Abraham (Gen. 18), who form a circle with the table side facing us left empty. The extraordinary thing, say both Jesus in John and Rublev, is that we are invited to join the circle, to enter into the very life going on within God. Theologians call this *perichōrēsis*, the whirling, exciting dance of love at the heart of the universe—and we are meant to be part of it!

Finally we come to "Jesus's high-priestly prayer." First, Jesus prays for himself to be glorified and to return to the presence of God in the glory which he shared before the creation, echoing the Prologue (17:1–5; see 1:1). Second, Jesus prays for his disciples, whom God gave to him, but whom he is now about to leave, that they will be protected and made holy (17:6–19). Third, Jesus prays over their heads, as it were, for us and all his followers that we may share in the life of God: "as you, Father, are in me and I am in you, may they also be in us." He prays that, at the End of everything, his followers "may be with me where I am, to see my glory" (17:20–24). At the start of the prayer, Jesus explains the nature of "eternal life, that they may know you, the only true God, and Jesus Christ whom you have sent" (17:3); now at the end, he clarifies where eternal life will be lived, with him in the glory of the Father (17:24).

And so John's story of Jesus has come full circle, from the heights of heaven with God "at the beginning," to taking flesh to dwell among human beings and care for people as "his own," so that he can return to the Father's house to prepare a dwelling place for us. The high-flying eagle has landed, gathered together its offspring, and is now ready to ascend back to the heights—except that the way to glory is through suffering and death.

The "hour of glory"—the Passion

Since John's account reflects years of meditation, he often uses words with various levels of meaning. Jesus shared in God's glory "in the beginning" and knows that the "hour" has now come to return to that glory with his Father (13:1; 17:1–5). But "the hour . . . to be glorified" involves falling into the earth and dying, just like a grain of wheat, to bear much fruit (12:23–24). While Mark's roaring, rushing lion becomes silent and passive, in John, Jesus remains in control throughout: he goes to a garden, but not for agonized prayer; when Judas and the soldiers arrive, Jesus announces his identity, "I am"—a typical mix of Johannine levels of meaning, surrendering himself to arrest while claiming the divine name (18:1–8). Throughout his trials with the high priest and Pilate, Jesus remains calmly in control, answering questions, emphasizing that his kingdom is not "of this world," and telling Pilate that he would have no power unless given "from above"—referring not only to the emperor, but also ultimately to God's will (18:19–24, 36; 19:11).

At the crucifixion, there is no sign of Mark's darkness and desolation, Matthew's theophany, or Luke's care for the women and soldiers, and no penitent thief. Instead, Jesus is the King of the Jews, who rules even from the cross (19:19–22). He is concerned for his mother and arranges for his closest friend to look after her, says he is thirsty "in order to fulfill the scripture," and dies with a cry of triumph, "it is accomplished!," even "consummated" as the Latin Vulgate puts it (19:26–30).

"Risen with healing in his wings"—the resurrection

Thus the high-flying, all-seeing, all-knowing eagle has been constantly in control throughout, even on the cross, and now he is risen "with healing in his wings" (see Mal. 3:20/4:2). Jesus appears where and when he chooses—to comfort Mary in her grief, reassure Thomas with his doubts, and restore Peter after his betrayal (20:11–18, 24–29; 21:15–17). Jesus's last words to Peter are the same as his first call, "follow me" (21:19, 22; cp. 1:43). From the heights of the Prologue to the depths of taking human flesh here on earth and back again to nest in the Father's bosom, the eagle has flown full circle, as the divine returns to the divine. But it has caught its fish by the Sea of Galilee and carries it back home. So Jesus invites Peter and the disciples to "follow me," for he wants them—together with you and me—to share the divine life of the Spirit with him in the glory of the Father, where he was "before the foundation of the world" and where we will "abide" and dwell forever, so that "where I am, there you may be also" (17:5, 24; 14:3).

One last time

By now, you have considered the various selection criteria and competencies, together with some ordination liturgies from the different church traditions as reprinted in the appendices or your own church's texts and websites, three times, and you may have marked with contrasting pens the references to teaching and preaching, pastoral care, and suffering the way of the cross. Take a little while now to go through them one last time, looking for references to how we might share in the divine life of God through prayer and spirituality. If you have already marked some phrases with previous colors, this does not matter: choose a distinctive color, or underline them, since this dimension of prayer and the divine life actually undergirds every aspect of mission and ministry. And then take some time once more to pray and reflect upon it all, perhaps write in your journal, or discuss it with a spiritual director, mentor, or vocational guide—and thank God for sending Jesus to find us and bring us back home to share in his divine life through the Spirit.

2. Prayer and the divine life in selection for ministry

I noted earlier that there are currently three advisers at a Bishops' Advisory Panel for ordained ministry in the Church of England. While all these areas of mission and ministry concern all three of them, the *Educational Adviser* concentrates on the criteria about faith, mission, and evangelism and quality of mind when looking for evidence about a call to preaching and teaching, while the *Pastoral Adviser* looks at the areas of personality and character, relationships, and service, leadership, and collaboration to discern the vocation to pastoral care. Third, we noted that while there are few specific criteria or competencies about suffering and the way of the cross, there are various suggestions or requirements which can be very relevant. This final area of prayer and sharing in the divine life of God is a particular concern of the *Vocational Adviser*, who considers the areas of vocation, faith, and spirituality, especially the understanding of ordained ministry within the Church of England. Whatever the selection and authorization processes of your particular church denomination, I am sure that they too will include a central stress on your spiritual life, as well as your sense of vocation and calling, and your understanding of both the church and its ministry within your tradition. Once again, we will illustrate this with some quotations from Anglican, Lutheran, Methodist, and Disciples of Christ resources (as listed in appendix 2), which you can supplement with others from your church.

The call to ministry—individual or corporate?

The first and most important criterion in all the church documents which I have seen is crucial: it is about how we discern whether someone has a call to share in God's mission as part of the recognized ministry of the church—which also means discerning whether this is as a lay person, perhaps with a formal licensing, or as an ordained minister, however that is understood in a particular church, denomination, or ecclesial community or tradition. Thus the Anglican Communion requires candidates to be "able to speak to their sense of vocation to ministry and mission, referring both to their own conviction and to the extent to which others—particularly the local church community—have confirmed it" (TEAC A). This combination of an individual's own sense of calling and the corporate recognition of the wider church is also reflected in the opening sentence of the United Methodist Church's Book of Discipline, paragraph 304: "those whom the Church ordains shall be conscious of God's call to ordained ministry, and their call shall be acknowledged and authenticated by the Church"—and it is similarly true in most statements across many denominations.

We have seen how John's portrait of Jesus reveals a clear "sense of vocation" about what God wants him to do. In fact, Jesus refers to God his Father as "the one who sent me" over twenty times in John's gospel (see, for example, 4:34; 5:30; 6:38; 9:4; 12:44; 14:24; 16:5). Finally, in the particular gospel passage which I was honored to read aloud at my ordination as a deacon, the risen Jesus passes his calling on to the frightened disciples in the upper room: "Peace be with you. As the Father has sent me, so I send you" (John 20:21). It is extraordinary and humbling to realize that Jesus does not just want us to share in the divine life with God the Father, but even to participate in his own vocation and mission.

This is why this criterion says that the calling must be a "sense" or "conviction" of which the individual is personally "conscious," but it is also never a private revelation: it must also be "confirmed," "acknowledged and authenticated" by others. While we may be tempted to talk at times about "my" call, actually any call I may have is for the sake of others, just as we have noted several times that it can never be "my" ministry because any ministry I have is to serve others. Yes, of course, it is important that the individual needs to have some sense of God calling them, which may just grow from a little "niggle" over many years or it may come apparently out of the blue in a sudden and profound experience—though often God only has to shout at us if we have not been listening for the "still, small voice." It is people who are heading determinedly in the wrong direction, like Saint Paul, who have to be knocked off their horse and turned around. Even in such circumstances, it usually then becomes obvious with hindsight how God has been calling earlier, even if we haven't noticed or been listening.

This is why most churches want to examine how it has been confirmed by others and to look for specific and concrete evidence of this—and they have many different systems and processes to "discern" or even "test" such a personal sense of calling. Thus the Anglican Communion requires that "a process of vocational discernment involving individual, parish, diocese and bishop is in place" and that "candidates and bishops, through diocesan processes, engage in an interactive discernment to ensure the corporate nature of selection of candidates" (TEAC A and K)—and this mixture of the individual, local, regional, or even national levels is common across many churches, particularly those with a more developed hierarchy or organization at the more Catholic end, while others of a more evangelical or Protestant tradition will stress both the individual person and the local congregation.

But it begins much earlier than that—and the views of those who know you well, including your strengths and weaknesses, your successes and failures, and yet who still believe you should "think about being a minister" are absolutely vital. At the beginning of Jesus's ministry, John's gospel shows how his cousin, John the Baptist, declared that Jesus was "the Lamb of God . . . the one who baptizes with the Holy Spirit . . . the Son of God" (1:29–34). What is more, the Baptist directs his own disciples toward Jesus, while one of them, Andrew, brings his brother, Simon Peter, to Jesus, and Philip goes to find Nathanael, despite Nathanael's cynicism about what good can come from a place like Nazareth (1:35–51)! Take some time to think about those who have been encouraging you in your vocation—and maybe ask others who know you "warts and all" what they feel about the idea. Write down their reactions, and discuss them with your spiritual director or vocational adviser.

Calling within a community of faith

Thus a call to come and share in the life and mission of God with Jesus can never be an individual affair, especially if it leads to some form of ministry which has to take place within a particular context or community. Even someone like Nicodemus who originally came to Jesus alone by night was a member of the Council where he spoke up against the prejudices of others and went on to help another colleague, Joseph of Arimathea, to bury Jesus (3:1–2; 7:50–52; 19:39–42). The Samaritan woman may meet Jesus at the well on her own in the heat of the day, perhaps to avoid the watchful eyes of others, and argues with him out of her own tradition about where and how God should be worshiped, but she ends up going and talking about him to all her community (4:6–7, 19–22, 29, 39–42).

Therefore most churches want to be reassured that any specific candidate for ministry shares their particular understanding of it, as well as their corporate tradition, and is willing to work within it. Thus the Anglican criteria require that candidates show "an awareness of Anglican-Episcopal tradition and practice of the local church and are willing to work within them" and that "candidates are aware of the difference between lay discipleship, commissioned ministry and ordination, and believe themselves to be called to ordination" (TEAC A and B). Furthermore, section K on "The Anglican Way" requires that "candidates are committed to the worship, mission and ministry of the local church"—though it is also good to see the parenthesis "(not uncritically)"! Similarly, Methodist candidates must "be accountable to The United Methodist Church, accept its Doctrinal Standards and Discipline and authority, accept the supervision of those appointed to this ministry, and be prepared to live in the covenant of its ordained ministers" (UMC 304.*j*). The Evangelical Lutheran Church in America spells out in a little more detail what their understanding of mission and ministry means: "People who have discerned a call to rostered ministry will demonstrate a commitment to Christ and build upon the characteristics of a missional leader as understood through a Lutheran confessional lens" (ELCA 2), as well as the outline of their tradition: "while not claiming to possess exclusive theological wisdom in the one, holy, catholic and apostolic church, Lutherans proclaim the good news of Jesus Christ through a clear focus on God's grace received through faith along with discipleship and participation in God's mission that is a lived response to that grace" (ELCA 2.1.2).

In these increasingly ecumenical days, it is all the more important to be clear about the nature and role of ordained ministry as your particular church and tradition understands it—and to be prepared to work within it. It is not uncommon when I am discerning or examining a potential vocation or interviewing a candidate for ministry in the Church of England that they have been influenced or encouraged by those from other denominations—a generous Roman Catholic priest or an inspiring evangelical preacher—and I am always delighted to hear such stories. But it is vital for Church of England clergy to understand the "distinctiveness" of the Anglican tradition, which prides itself on being both Catholic and Reformed, and to be comfortable ministering within that breadth. Unfortunately, some of our clergy find themselves increasingly unhappy in the Church of England and want to be right at what we call "the top of the candle" or conversely so "low" that they would never use a candle in church! In such situations, the kindest thing is to help them respond to God's calling by moving to a different, more congenial, denomination, even though this process can also be painful—just as many Catholic priests and Free Church ministers find themselves seeking ministry within the Anglican tradition.

Furthermore, many denominations, including perhaps especially the Church of England, contain various traditions, such as catholics and evangelicals, or liberals and conservatives, who can either work together well and complement each other, or spend their time in internal conflict and sniping at their brothers and sisters. Like the Samaritan woman, such people often have strong ideas about where, when, and how we should worship and join in the divine life of God (John 4:19–24)! Therefore it is a good idea to think about your understanding of your own tradition, as well as to have a generous awareness of the diversity of traditions and practice within your church; are you commited to learning from, and working sensitively and flexibly, with others with different ideas and practices? You only have to think about all the various individuals Jesus meets and calls in John's gospel to realize that his disciples would have needed to work sensitively and flexibly with each other! Are you aware of the traditions and churchmanship which have influenced your own spiritual growth, or those of your local church? In addition, it is also a good idea occasionally to go and worship somewhere completely different, perhaps a church very close by in the same street but light-years away in its traditions—and, if things seem strange, ask them about why they do what they do and what it means to them. You never know, you might learn something, or find new ways of sharing in God's divine life.

Spirituality

Supremely, however, John's portrait of Jesus's life of prayer and his call for us to "abide" in the divine glory shared between the Father and the Son in the Holy Spirit is directly relevant to the various criteria and competencies about faith and spirituality. Thus Anglican and Episcopal candidates "should show evidence of a commitment to a spiritual discipline, involving individual and corporate prayer and worship, such as to sustain and energise them in every aspect of their lives" and be "reading the Bible and praying systematically" (TEAC C). A particular aspect of Methodist tradition going right back to John Wesley himself can be discerned in the requirement that candidates "nurture and cultivate spiritual disciplines and patterns of holiness" (UMC 304.*b*). Similarly, Lutherans must practice "the use of spiritual disciplines (e.g., prayer, biblical and theological reflection, and spiritual direction)" (ELCA 2.1.1.3.a) and live a disciplined spiritual life (2.1.2.2.f). The Disciples of Christ remind us that the word "discipline," which can be interpreted negatively or harshly, is actually closely linked to "disciple," with both words coming from the Latin root *disc-*, "to learn," in requiring as its first personal qualification for ministry, "faith in Jesus Christ, commitment to a life of Christian discipleship and nurturing spiritual practices" (DoC A.2.a).

Such discipleship and spiritual discipline also can never be rigidly fixed forever, but must develop and grow over time, "nurtured and cultivated" (to use UMC's words, 304.*b*), if it is to "sustain and energise them in every aspect of their lives" (TEAC C). Thus vocation advisers should seek evidence how your call has changed you, especially in your relationship with God and with others, and your perceptions of the world. Finally, we have seen not only in John, but in all the gospels, how Jesus had a constant rhythm between withdrawing for prayer alone and his public ministry. So too, evidence will be sought about how a candidate for ministry links together their spirituality with their relationships in both the church and the wider world.

Of course, all of this is true for everyone who wants to follow Jesus and to share in the life of God, to be with him in the glory he had "before the foundation of the world." It is not for some sort of "super-spiritual elite." However, for anyone who is contemplating any kind of ministry, lay or ordained, it is particularly important that their spiritual practice should be able to support, "sustain and energise every aspect of their daily life" and future ministry (TEAC C), since without that they will soon run out of the words to say, or the energy to go on caring and pastoring. A clown who has lost their sense of humor is a very sad sight, but that is nothing compared with the terrible situation of a priest who has lost contact with the divine life of God—and unfortunately it is by no means as rare as you might think or hope. So we will return to how we can sustain all of this at the end of this study, as we have done in all three previously—but first we need to consider the various different ordination liturgies and the role of prayer in the ministry.

3. *Prayer and sharing the life of God in the ordination services*

As we might expect, there are many references to prayer, the spiritual life, and the relationship of God the Father, Jesus the Son, and the Holy Spirit within the divine life of the Godhead spread throughout all the different liturgies and ordination services, which you will probably have noted from your careful reading; so we will try briefly to discuss some of them here.

The gathering, welcome, or call to worship

In the Anglican and Episcopal tradition, the service begins with the bishop greeting the people with "Blessed be God, Father, Son and Holy Spirit," eliciting the response from everyone present, "and blessed be God's kingdom, now and for ever. Amen" (TEC). Similarly, in the UCC, the Moderator or other Association Representative greets everyone as follows: "Grace to you and peace from God, who is and who was and who is to come, and from Jesus Christ the faithful witness and the sovereign of the rulers on earth. The *N* Association of the *N* Conference of the United Church of Christ greets you in the name of Jesus Christ, the head of the church," to which the people reply, "To God, who by the power at work within us is able to do far more abundantly than all that we ask or think, be glory in the church and in Christ Jesus to all generations, for ever and ever, Amen" (UCC). So we have an immediate affirmation of the divine life within the persons of the Holy Trinity—and our place in the church within that life. As the means of our entry into this extraordinary way of life, the Methodist Church includes a reaffirmation of our baptismal vows at this point, while the PCUSA has it early in the ordination liturgy itself. In many ordination services, the ministry of the Word is likely to follow soon, for which various different readings are suggested, which, together with the sermon (perhaps from the director of the ordination retreat if that happened), are likely to reinforce the importance of prayer in remaining in the divine life of God.

The presentation of the candidates

Methodist candidates are presented by Members of the Board of Ordained Ministry "with our prayers and support," to which the bishop responds, "We rejoice in the Spirit's work in our lives and the lives of these who come to serve and lead among us," causing the whole congregation also to affirm "our prayers and support." In the Episcopal Church, the presentation of the candidates leads into the invocation of the Trinity:

> God the Father,
> *Have mercy on us.*
> God the Son,
> *Have mercy on us.*
> God the Holy Spirit,
> *Have mercy on us.*
> Holy Trinity, one God,
> *Have mercy on us.* (TEC)

Thus we are immediately aware of the importance of prayer if we are all to share the divine life of the Trinity, and even more so for those offering themselves for ministry.

The declarations or statement of ministry

Alongside all the activities connected with teaching and preaching, as well as the pastoral ministry, which are listed in the introductory statement or declarations, the "job description" for ministers, there are various reminders of the nature of the church and its participation in the life of God. Thus, a Roman Catholic bishop concludes his statement by addressing the candidates: "finally, dear sons, exercising for your part the office of Christ, Head and Shepherd, while united with the Bishop and subject to him, strive to bring the faithful together into one family, so that you may lead them to God the Father through Christ in the Holy Spirit" (RC), reminding us of John's vision of the whole church being caught up in the divine life of God, the Holy Trinity. Similarly, an Episcopal bishop begins by reminding candidates for the priesthood that "the Church is the family of God, the body of Christ, and the temple of the Holy Spirit"; he or she concludes by instructing them, "in all that you do, you are to nourish Christ's people from the riches of his grace, and strengthen them to glorify God in this life and in the life to come" (TEC). In order for the new ministers to be able to do this, they need to make their vows and promises.

Questions, vows, and promises

Several churches stress the link between our public ministry and our private life with God. Thus the UCC Association Representative asks ordinands, "Do you promise to be diligent in your private prayers and in reading the scriptures, as well as in the public duties of your office?" (UCC, and see similar question in AME). A sample Baptist ordination service asks similarly, "Will you promise to be diligent in prayer, in the reading of the Scriptures and in such studies and devotions as will increase your knowledge and love of God and his Kingdom?" (ABC). Meanwhile, the Episcopal bishop not only brings together public and private prayers, but shows how both take us into the life of the Trinity: "Will you persevere in prayer, both in public and in private, asking God's grace, both for yourself and for others, offering all your labors to God, through the mediation of Jesus Christ, and in the sanctification of the Holy Spirit?" (TEC). Finally, the DoC Regional Minister quotes the secret of Paul's life and ministry: "Paul the apostle testified, 'It is no longer I who live but Christ who lives in me.' Will you, *Name*, endeavour to be diligent in your practice of the Christian life: reading the Bible, continuing steadfastly in prayer, deepening in spiritual disciplines, and taking up your cross daily to follow Christ?" Thus we can see in the liturgical words of the vows and promise the same connection between prayer and the Holy Spirit in sharing the divine life of God as we discovered in Jesus's Farewell Discourses in John's gospel. Therefore, it would be right to pause at this point, and turn these reflections into prayer yourself, to ask God for the grace to be able to share the life of his Spirit in Jesus Christ if you are to embark on any ministry in God's name.

The invocation of the Holy Spirit and prayers

It is no wonder, therefore, that in the Church of England ordination liturgy, the bishop solemnly charges the ordinands that "you cannot bear the weight of this calling in your own strength, but only by the grace and power of God. Pray therefore that your heart may daily be enlarged." Therefore the bishop bids them to "pray earnestly for the gift of the Holy Spirit," and promptly leaves his or her seat or throne to kneel with them to invoke the Spirit in singing together the *Veni Creator Spiritus*. This ancient canticle, which picks up all the Johannine themes of living the divine life with the Father, Son, and Holy Spirit, is also listed to be sung at this point in the ordination services of the UCC, AME, and TEC, while others have a rubric suggesting that "a hymn invoking the Holy Spirit is sung" (DoC; see also ELCA; UMC).

> **Come, Holy Ghost, our souls inspire,**
> **and lighten with celestial fire . . .**
>
> **Teach us to know the Father, Son,**
> **and thee, of both, to be but one;**
> **that through the ages all along**
> **this may be our endless song:**
>
> **Praise to thy eternal merit,**
> **Father, Son and Holy Spirit. Amen.**

This may follow on from or lead straight into other prayers, perhaps including the Litany, which begins "In the power of the Spirit and in union with Christ, let us pray to the Father" and ends with "we commit ourselves, one another, and our whole life to Christ our God; to you, O Lord," so once again we see the relationship between all three persons of the Trinity inviting us to share in the divine life.

The ordination or laying on of hands; the welcome

The invocation of the Holy Spirit continues as the ordination service reaches its climax with the laying on of hands, a symbolic or sacramental act (depending upon your theological understanding!) designed to fill the ordinand with the Holy Spirit for their new ministry. In the United Methodist Church, this provides an opportunity for antiphonal prayers to the Spirit between the bishop and all the congregation:

Bishop: Holy Spirit, move among us! Come, Holy Spirit!
People: Come, Holy Spirit!
Bishop: Come upon these, your servants.
People: Come upon these, your servants.

[The bishop lays hands on the head of each of the candidates for ordination as elder. Others may place hands on the candidate's back or shoulder. The bishop says:]

Bishop: Come upon *Full Name* . . .

[The bishop proceeds to each candidate in order. After the bishop has named and placed hands on all, the bishop continues:]

Bishop: Come upon them each and all, Holy Spirit.
People: Come upon them each and all, Holy Spirit.
Bishop: Fill them with every good and perfect gift for the office and
work of an elder.
People: Fill them Holy Spirit!
Bishop: In the name of God, Father, Son and Holy Spirit,
People: All glory and praise are yours, now and forever!
Bishop: As you have placed yourselves into the hands of God
**People: And as we have prayed for the Holy Spirit to empower
you for your ministry among us . . .**   (UMC)

While this may be the most extended example, similar prayers to the Spirit over each ordinand are common in all churches: "Eternal God, through your Son, Jesus Christ, pour out your Holy Spirit upon *name* and fill *her/him* with the gifts of grace" (ELCA); "now bless and sanctify by your Holy Spirit your servant, *name*. . . . Bestow on *name* . . . the power of your Holy Spirit" (UCC); "The Lord pour upon you the Holy Ghost for the office and work of an elder in the Church of God" (AME); "Therefore, Father, through Jesus Christ your Son, give your Holy Spirit to *N*.; fill *him* with grace and power" (TEC); "Gracious God, pour out your Spirit upon your servant N." (PCUSA). Another way in which the

Holy Spirit's power is sought and deemed to be conveyed in a number of churches is in the use of oil to anoint each of the candidates (see, for example, PCUSA and the Roman Catholic Church, where the newly ordained priests are anointed on the palms of their hands). This congruence between all the different denominations makes it abundantly clear that prayer and the gift of the Holy Spirit are essential for any kind of ministry if we are to participate in the divine life of God the Holy Trinity for the sake of his church.

The newly ordained may then be welcomed with texts like, "may Christ dwell in your hearts through faith, that you may be rooted and grounded in love," while the bishop or senior minister can introduce the Peace by declaring that God has "given us the Spirit to dwell in our hearts." Again, both phrases echo Jesus's stress on "dwelling" in the divine life in John's Farewell Discourses—and it is entirely right that this provides the opportunity for the newly ordained to greet all their families, friends, and parishioners with whom they also share the divine life in the Spirit.

The commissioning and sending out

If the ordination takes place within a communion service, then whichever Eucharistic Prayer is used, the bishop or senior minister will be praying for God to send the Holy Spirit on both the bread and the wine, as well as upon all of God's people who will receive the divine life through sharing in this holy communion. The same point is made in the Prayer after Communion, "Eternal God, heavenly Father, you have graciously accepted us as living members of your Son our Savior Jesus Christ, and you have fed us with spiritual food in the Sacrament of his Body and Blood" (TEC). There are of course many ways across the various church traditions to understand the mystery of what happens at and through sharing holy communion, but they all agree about the importance and centrality of participating in it regularly—and we shall return to this in more detail in the next section.

Finally, as what has probably been a long service draws to its conclusion, both the newly ordained ministers and all God's people need to be sent out to share this divine life of the Holy Trinity with God's world—and therefore the final words are likely to be Trinitarian in form. A sample Baptist ordination service concludes with a commissioning for all:

Leader: As the disciples heard Jesus call out, "Come, follow me . . ."
People: We have gathered here by the guidance of God, by the beckoning of Christ, by the power of the Holy Spirit, to celebrate God's call to us as God's people. (ABC)

Both Presbyterians and Methodists use Paul's words in 2 Corinthians 13:13: "The grace of Jesus Christ, and the love of God, and the communion of the Holy Spirit be with you all always" (UMC; PCUSA). Finally, the words provided for the blessing and sending out in the Church of England's ordination liturgy are full of these Johannine themes, as the bishop refers to the "glory" of the Father, the place of Christ, "who has ascended to the heights," just like an eagle, and calls the Spirit the *paraclete*, or "comforter," before concluding, of course, with the blessing of the Trinity to "remain" or "abide" with us always:

> May the Father, whose glory fills the heavens,
> cleanse you by his holiness
> and send you to proclaim his word.
> **Amen.**
> May Christ, who has ascended to the heights,
> pour upon you the riches of his grace.
> **Amen.**
> May the Holy Spirit, the comforter,
> equip you and strengthen you in your ministry.
> **Amen.**
> And the blessing of God almighty,
> the Father, the Son, and the Holy Spirit,
> be upon you and remain with you always.
> **Amen.**

In the Episcopal Church, one of the newly ordained deacons gives the dismissal, "Let us go forth into the world, rejoicing in the power of the Spirit" to which everyone responds, "**Thanks be to God!**" (TEC).

Therefore, this last close study of the liturgical texts used in the various churches' different ordination services has nonetheless revealed how these Johannine themes of the mutual indwelling of the Father and the Son in the Holy Spirit run like a golden thread through all that is said and done on these happy and joyful occasions. Furthermore, it is through prayer that we are all invited to take our place at the open side of the table in Rublev's icon, to share in the holy communion and to join in the divine *perichōrēsis*, the exciting dance of love at the very heart of the universe.

But it is one thing to read about this, and quite another to live it out in our lives day by day. So once again, now might be a good time to put this book aside for a little while, and to reflect and meditate on all these extraordinary words, to write about them in your journal if that helps you—but above all, to talk to God about it all, and listen to what he has to say in response.

4. Prayer and sharing the life of God in your ministry

In each of the three previous studies, we have already noted the importance of taking time apart, going aside for quiet reflection, prayer, and study to be able to sustain the ministries of teaching and preaching, and of pastoral care and walking the way of the cross. It is significant that the other three gospel writers each draw attention to Jesus's habit of withdrawing regularly, to be alone and to pray to his Father (e.g., Matt. 4:1; 14:13; Mark 6:31; Luke 5:16; 6:12; 9:28–29; 11:1). John, however, does not specifically highlight this custom, although there are hints of it: he depicts Jesus attempting to withdraw into the wilderness before feeding the multitude, and escaping there afterwards (John 6:1–3, 15). Equally, Jesus does go up to Jerusalem to a festival "in secret" before teaching publicly in the temple (7:10, 14). Similarly, he stays another two days hiding away after hearing about Lazarus's illness and death before returning to Bethany and the public exposure of his grief (11:6, 14, 21, 32).

These hints recognize that Jesus needs time alone before and after ministry in public, although John's focus is more on the latter. Interestingly, while John notes that after the Farewell Discourses at the Last Supper, Jesus took his disciples into the garden "across the Kidron valley" which they would often frequent, there is no time for agonized private prayer before Judas and the soldiers appear to arrest him (18:1–3). On the other hand, there is plenty of material in John of Jesus's teaching about the life of prayer and how this enables us to share not only in the mission of God his Father, but also in the divine life within the Trinity, so we shall concentrate on several aspects of that in this chapter.

"Overhearing" Jesus talking to his Father

Instead of the other evangelists' rhythm of Jesus withdrawing to pray privately before speaking out in public, John depicts Jesus as always publicly conscious of the presence of God his Father—but still not afraid to address him directly while others are listening. Thus he prays with confidence outside Lazarus's tomb: "Father, I thank you for having heard me. I knew that you always hear me, but I have said this for the sake of the crowd standing here, so that they may believe that you sent me" (11:41–42). Similarly, in the nearest John gets to the agony in Gethsemane, Jesus calls out in the middle of the crowd:

> "Now my soul is troubled. And what should I say—'Father, save me from this hour'? No, it is for this reason that I have come to this hour. Father, glorify your name." Then a voice came from heaven, "I have glorified it, and I will glorify it again." The crowd standing there heard it and said that it was thunder. Others said, "An angel has spoken to him." (12:27–30)

The best example of "overhearing" Jesus's total confidence in his Father is, of course, his final prayer at the Last Supper, where after addressing the Farewell Discourses to his bewildered disciples, Jesus "looked up to heaven and said, 'Father, the hour has come; glorify your Son so that the Son may glorify you'" (17:1). Having promised them earlier that he would ask his Father to give them "another *paraclete*" (14:16), he does not only pray for those frightened disciples present, "but also on behalf of those who will believe in me through their word, that they may all be one. As you, Father, are in me and I am in you, may they also be in us, so that the world may believe that you have sent me" (17:9, 20–21). And so John provides the opportunity even for you and me, and for all the generations down the years, to "listen in," to eavesdrop on Jesus's own prayer for us, not just at the Last Supper two thousand years ago, but as he intercedes for us even now at the right hand of his Father in heaven.

Letting people hear us pray

Praying for our people, for the sometimes lost and confused sheep in our pastoral care—and even more for those in our parishes or institutions who do not realize yet that someone cares enough to pray for them—is a vital part of Christian ministry. Yet, as well as cultivating this habit and practice of praying for people in our private devotions, they need to see—and (over)hear—those who care for them bringing them into the presence of God. Most obviously, this happens in the intercessions in the main services, where clergy and others leading services need to prepare this element carefully and teach others to do it. But it needs to be undergirded by regular and organized daily prayer. When I was a parish priest, we published a monthly prayer diary which included not only the names of all the individuals and families on the electoral roll, but also all the streets and major institutions located within our city center parish, which were read out in the early morning prayers every day in church—and members of the congregation were encouraged to use it also at home.

My predecessor as Dean of King's College London actually used the internal telephone directory for his prayer list. He would take a different page each day, and not only pray for all the names, but ring them up to tell them he was praying and ask them how they were doing! Some colleagues have confessed to me that they thought this was rather bizarre behavior—and yet, many seemed somehow pleased to know that somebody somewhere was at least thinking of them occasionally. Everything like telephone numbers is online these days of course, and with some thirty-five thousand staff and students in our pastoral care today, we cannot pray for them all individually, let alone phone them up. Instead, we publish a daily schedule each term, working our way at morning prayers in our chapels and chaplaincy rooms through the various departments, faculties, and administrative offices—and it is not unusual to find a representative slipping into the back of chapel to hear their department prayed for out loud, or get the occasional email asking us to pray for something forthcoming like a quality inspection, admitting that even if they are atheists, they are glad of any help and support being offered!

Identity, dependence, and mission

John does not just let us listen in on Jesus's prayers to his Father; he gives us a glimpse into the inner workings of the divine Trinity, as we see how much Jesus's entire sense of himself, his identity, and his mission and purpose are intimately bound up with his understanding of his relationship with God. Jesus spends an extraordinary amount of time talking about both

God as his Father and also himself as his Son. His claims could sound like megalomania, compounded by inconsistency. On the one hand, Jesus can assert his complete identity with God—"the Father and I are one"—such that some of the Jewish leaders try to stone him for blasphemy (10:30–31). Yet on the other, Jesus is also explicit that he is totally dependent on God: "I can do nothing on my own" but only what he sees and hears the Father saying and doing (5:19, 30). Such phrases tumble over each other, reflecting the years of meditation by the evangelist about the relationship of Jesus with God; his identity as the Son is based on his awareness of his Father, while his confidence is undergirded by his total dependence on him for everything.

As well as his identity, this relationship with God also provides his sense of purpose and mission. When the disciples find Jesus hungry and thirsty in the middle of the day at Jacob's well in Samaria, he informs them that "my food is to do the will of him who sent me and to complete his work" (4:34). This phrase "him who sent me" is first used by John the Baptist (1:33), but Jesus adopts it as his classic description both for God and for his task here on earth, using it over twenty-five times through the gospel; for example, he announces to the crowd in Jerusalem, "Whoever believes in me believes not in me but in him who sent me. And whoever sees me sees him who sent me" (12:44–45). Throughout the Farewell Discourses, Jesus explains patiently to his confused disciples that it is God who has sent him, and who will send them "another *paraclete*," namely, the Holy Spirit (14:24–26; 15:26).

"As the Father has sent me, so I send you"

Finally, the risen Jesus appears to these same frightened disciples, hiding in the upper room, gives them his peace, *shalom*, and passes his mission on to them: "Peace be with you. As the Father has sent me, so I send you" (20:21). When I was preparing to read that gospel passage at my ordination as a deacon, I memorized it in order to do my best on that day. Yet it is only over the years since that I have really begun to understand what it means for Jesus to share his mission from God with us, that he "sends" us in the same way that his Father sent him. I described previously how both my training vicar and I were initially unsure about why our bishop wanted to "send" me to that parish; later, during the more difficult times, it was important to go on trusting in this sense of calling, a "vocation" from

God not just to ministry in the abstract, but here, now, to this place and in this time. As so often, it is only looking back now that I can discern how correct the bishop's insight was and how God blessed me through those years—and, I hope, others through that ministry.

Similarly, it was only through prayer and conversation with others that I came to see the invitation to move to King's College London, which arrived unexpectedly at an inconvenient time for both my family and my then ministry, as a definite calling. Paradoxically, it was only for a temporary five-year contract: here too, the reasons for this call became clearer only later, and the sense of this vocation has strengthened over the years, while various other possible opportunities have never been accompanied by a clear indication of God's call away from King's. This combination of particpating in Jesus's mission within a community is also stressed by the Roman Catholic Church; Pope John Paul II described seminary formation as "a continuation in the Church of the apostolic community gathered about Jesus, listening to his word, proceeding towards the Easter experience, awaiting the gift of the Spirit for the mission" (quoted in the *Program of Priestly Formation*, p. 4).

John's portrayal of Jesus's sense of identity, purpose, and mission, all grounded in his Father's will, provides a significant guide for us today. It is important to know who we are within the love of God, and what his purposes for us are, if we are to share in the divine mission of love to the world: "as the Father sent me, so I send you" (20:21).

Participating in the life of God

We have seen how the Farewell Discourses go round and round, repeating the idea that Jesus is in the Father, and the Father is in Jesus, and also that through the Spirit, both the Father and the Son will "dwell" or "abide" in the believer who "abides" in them (14:10–11, 16–17, 20, 23, 26; 15:9). This is our ultimate destiny, as Jesus prays finally that all of us will be with him forever in the glory of the Father's presence (17:20–26). Therefore, nothing can be more important than learning to share in the very life of God in our daily lives here on earth, and teaching and helping others to experience and enter into the divine dance of love at the heart of the universe.

And yet, perhaps nothing is more opposed to learning to participate in the divine life than the busy diaries of most clergy. This is despite the fact that, usually, ordination training is organized around a regular rhythm of

daily services, with theological colleges traditionally following a monas-
tery-like pattern of daily morning prayer in chapel, perhaps with meditation and silence and a daily eucharist, with other services through the day,
at evening and even sometimes during the night. My college considered
itself quite "modern" and informal, but we were still expected to be in
prayer groups at 7 a.m. every morning, even if the students leading sometimes tried to invent more wacky ways to pray, rather than just "follow the
old liturgy"! Ordination training is properly viewed as "ministerial formation," rather than just "theological education" (vitally important though
that is), as future ministers are "formed," or shaped, a process which can
sometimes feel like being "conformed," though the ultimate goal is to be
"transformed" in the life of God through the Holy Spirit (see Rom. 12:1). It
is meant to "form" a way of life, "a spiritual discipline, involving individual
and corporate prayer and worship, such as to sustain and energise them
in every aspect of their lives," as the selection criteria put it (TEAC C).

I admit that it was a bit of a rude awakening as a newly ordained curate
to be expected to be in church early every day for morning prayer with my
vicar and other team members, followed by silent meditation and then
sharing in holy communion—especially after the arrival of a young baby
who tended to keep us up at night! However, I have continued to value the
discipline of daily morning prayers in the university chapels both at Exeter
and at King's College, though I note that they are slightly later in the hope
that some students will attend.

And yet, I would be less than honest if I did not also admit that it is
often a struggle to get into chapel myself every morning. There are just so
many meetings (is "strategy planning" really better done over breakfast?!),
crises to attend to, and events to manage. In universities and hospitals, as
well as in churches and parishes up and down the land, the very people
who are actually paid to pray and spend time with God often seem the
busiest, working all hours of the day and night, most days of the week, and
with little time for themselves or family and friends—let alone the God
they serve. This may be the ultimate irony—and certainly one to which I
have no easy answer. On the other hand, the day when this stops being a
challenge is probably the time to hang up your clerical collar.

There is a popular saying, attributed variously to people like Martin
Luther and John Wesley, that Christians should spend an hour or two each
day in prayer—except when they are busy, in which case it needs to be
twice that! While I confess to not managing that, it remains true that the
times when I have been privileged to share time with Archbishops Des-

mond Tutu and Rowan Williams, I am challenged afresh by their discipline and commitment to begin every day with a set period of silent prayer, meditation, and the eucharist—and it is not as though either of them have led sheltered or nonpressured lives. It is clear that they derive their energy and spiritual authority from this daily discipline, so I usually return to my own daily routine with a renewed appreciation of John's vision of Jesus and the Father abiding in one another and in us through the divine life of the Holy Spirit.

In the end, John's portrait of Jesus reminds us that prayer is not so much an activity to be done as a life to be lived. His constant use of the verb *menō*, to "abide" or "remain," and its noun, *monai*, "abodes" or "dwelling places," in the Farewell Discourses is an invitation to "abide" or "dwell" in the divine life of the Father and the Son in the Spirit. As we have seen, in Rublev's famous icon of the Trinity under the oaks of Mamre, the three characters form a circle facing toward us—and we are invited to join in, to participate in nothing less than the dance of love at the heart of the cosmos.

Sharing in the holy communion

Furthermore, Rublev placed the three divine visitors at three sides of a table upon which is placed a cup, while in some versions Abraham and Sarah are preparing a meal (see Gen. 18). We are not just invited to enter into the circle of love, but there is a space waiting for us at the table, if we would only sit down, and eat, and drink. The sacramental overtones of the eucharist or holy communion are impossible to miss. The Greek word *koinōnia* is often translated as "fellowship" or "participation," but literally it is about sharing something "in common" (*koin-*) which then comes through the Latin *communio* ("together in one") into our English word "communion." Interestingly, in the New Testament, *koinōnia* ranges widely from a "sharing" of basic possessions (Rom. 15:26; Heb. 13:16) and "participation" with others (2 Cor. 6:14; Gal. 2:9), through having "fellowship" with one another and with God in the Holy Spirit (Acts 2:42; 1 Cor. 1:9; 2 Cor. 13:13; Phil. 2:1), to sharing "communion" in the body and blood of Christ (1 Cor. 10:16).

Oddly enough, *koinōnia*, and its related words, are curiously absent from John's gospel, although it is used for participation or "fellowship" with one another and with God in the related epistle (1 John 1:3, 6). And yet, all his emphasis on "abiding" in the divine life and the love of God is a perfect example of "sharing" or participating in the relationship of Jesus and his Father in the Spirit. The idea is there—beautifully expressed and expounded upon throughout the gospel, especially in the Farewell Discourses—if not the actual word. This may cast light on another conundrum in the Fourth Gospel: John's account of the Last Supper includes foot washing as the ultimate example of how Jesus manifests the love of God for his disciples and gives us an example to follow (13:1–15), followed by the Farewell Discourses encouraging his disciples to "remain" or "abide" in that love and divine life, concluding with his high-priestly prayer for them and all the church (13:14–17)—but what is missing completely is the institution of the Lord's Supper or holy communion! There is no mention of eating or drinking, much less cups of wine being drunk or bread being broken, or the command to "do this in remembrance of me."

Yet John is perhaps the most sacramental of all the gospels, describing miracles as "signs" of God's love, and images like bread, water, door, shepherd, vine used as not only symbols, but as expressions of Jesus's identity as the "bread of life" or the "true vine." The traditional definition of a "sacrament" is "the outward and visible sign of an inward and spiritual grace." At ordinations, those of a more sacramental tradition see the laying on of the bishop's hands, perhaps with holy anointing, as the "outward and visible sign" of the "inward and spiritual grace" conveyed by the Holy Spirit to ordain a person as a priest or deacon. Similarly, water is used at baptism, or rings at a wedding—and of course, supremely bread and wine at the eucharist.

Furthermore, John likes to link Jesus's signs with the discourses, so that his claim to be "the light of the world" leads into the healing of the blind man (John 8:12; 9:1–12). Similarly, the feeding of the five thousand is followed by the discourse on the "bread of life" with some of the most sacramental language in the New Testament, and the clearest expression that "those who eat my flesh and drink my blood have eternal life" (6:1–12, 25–59). To make things even clearer, "the bread that I will give for the life of the world" is identified as "my flesh," while "my blood is true drink" (6:51, 55). The language is so explicit (the Greek word used for "eat" is *trōgō*, literally to "chew"!) that it is hardly surprising that some of his disciples decided that "this teaching is difficult," refused to accept it, and stopped following Jesus (6:60–66). The undertones are almost cannibalistic, so this language can only be a sacramental way to refer to holy communion—but which John never mentions!

However, we have already seen that while John never uses the actual word *koinōnia* in the gospel, he still provides the best expression of our "participation" in the life of God through the Farewell Discourses. Equally, although John uses "glory" over forty times (more than the other three gospels put together), he does not include any account of Jesus's actual transfiguration, being "glorified" on a mountaintop with Moses and Elijah. While the Word has become flesh and "we have beheld his glory," in the end for John the true path to glory lies through being crucified (1:14; 12:23, 28; 21:19). Jesus's "glory" pervades everything, and cannot be restricted to a single mountaintop experience, no matter how glorious. John suggests that participation in the life of God is about "abiding" in his love, and the sacramental "sharing" in his "communion" or "fellowship" is equally found through all the signs and symbols of living life in all its fullness.

On the other hand, Christian experience down the generations and across the world and all cultures is that regular participation in holy communion is vital for maintaining the spiritual life, however the sacrament is understood. The various selection criteria and competencies about spirituality link it with prayer and Bible study, and this was made clear in my own training at theological college and in the parish. It undergirds the spiritual discipline of all those I respect most. That first time when I met Archbishop Tutu and his small team off an overnight plane early one morning at Heathrow, he wanted to stop and celebrate the eucharist immediately while we were still going through immigration and customs. However, given the tense negotiations between Nelson Mandela and F. W. de Klerk going on at the time, security was understandably strict, so the police bundled us into armored cars to Reading Station. Delays meant that it was several hours before I could obtain a small bottle of red wine and a piece of bread on the train from the dining carriage waiter—even if he did helpfully offer to "cut it up for the Archbishop, and butter it first"! As we celebrated the eucharist and prayed for South Africa, speeding across Salisbury Plain at 125 mph, Jesus had to catch up with us to become present in the breaking of the bread and the sharing of the common cup in the carriage and the local area, South Africa, and across the whole world.

I little realized that day that participating in Archbishop Tutu's daily eucharistic discipline would become a regular feature of our various contacts ever since, but his habit reminds us of the importance of the holy communion for all those in any form of ministry. For some, trained and formed in a more catholic tradition, like Desmond Tutu, it is *so* important that every day must begin with the eucharist; others, especially those from a more protestant or evangelical background, also view it as crucially important (the adverb is significant with its implications of the cross) but with the opposite consequence that they prefer to save it for special occasions. We may disagree on the timing and frequency, and probably on the theological understanding—but all recognize the vital necessity of following the Lord's command, "Do this in remembrance of me."

And while John may not include that command or institution, the "bread of life" discourse warns us that "unless you eat the flesh of the Son of Man and drink his blood, you have no life in you" (6:53). His sacramental approach to the whole of life also encourages us to go out from the communion table with our eyes opened to look for the signs and symbols of the presence of Jesus in everything we say and do, and everyone we meet. Having been fed with the body and blood of our Lord Jesus Christ, we are sent out as "a living sacrifice . . . in the power of your Spirit to live and work to your praise and glory," as the Church of England's post-communion prayer puts it so beautifully.

Thus John's portrayal of Jesus's relationship with God his Father in the Holy Spirit does not just encourage us to participate in the divine life and dance of love; he sends us out to share in the same mission from God: "as the Father sent me, so I send you"—and through regular prayer and sharing in the communion, we are equipped and empowered for that mission and ministry among all those we meet every day.

5. Sustaining the divine life of prayer in ministry

We have seen that John's gospel often seems paradoxical: he refers to "glory" more than any other New Testament writer, yet does not describe the event of the transfiguration; he never uses any of the words for communion and fellowship, *koin-*, yet he constantly invites us to participate in the divine life shared by Jesus and the Father in the Spirit; and lastly, he has no command or institution of the Lord's Supper, yet this is the most sacramental of all the gospels, including explicit eucharistic language in his "bread of life" discourse. Something similar seems to happen with his treatment of people and the church: biblical scholars think that John's particular style and theology reflect years of teaching, prayer, and meditation within a close-knit community, and yet now this "gospel for the church" is loved across all denominations and traditions.

And yet, John hardly mentions the leading disciples or apostles who lead the church in the other gospels. His few references to "the Twelve" are hardly positive: Jesus asks them if they want to leave him, while the one highlighted as "one of the twelve" is Judas Iscariot (John 6:67–71). The only other mention of "the Twelve" points out that Thomas, "one of the twelve, was not with them when Jesus came" to give them his peace and share his mission on the first Easter evening (20:24). Some of the disciples do get mentioned, such as Andrew and Philip (1:40–46; 6:5–8; 12:21–22; 14:8), but most do not appear. Peter does have a leadership role, from his initial call and naming by Jesus, through professing his commitment to follow Jesus, to his appearances at the foot washing in the Last Supper, Jesus's arrest and trial where he denies him, and his restoration at the resurrection (1:42–44; 6:68; 13:6–9; 18:10–11, 15–27; 20:2–10; 21:2–22). However, he often seems overshadowed by the mysterious "disciple whom Jesus loved," who seems connected with the author or "authority" behind the gospel (13:23; 18:15; 19:26; 20:2; 21:7, 20–24).

"You are all individuals"

Actually, John's gospel features some of the most memorable and well-loved individuals who hardly occur elsewhere or even not at all. There is Nathanael, with his cynical comment under the fig tree, "Can anything good come out of Nazareth?" (1:45–51). Or Nicodemus, coming to question Jesus alone by night, yet later not only defending him against his fellow leaders, but even summoning the courage to help Joseph bury Jesus's body (3:1–10; 7:50–52; 19:39–42). Similarly, the Samaritan woman also argues with Jesus alone, in the heat of the day at Jacob's well, yet ends up going to tell all her community about him (4:7–42). Then there are the paralyzed man by the pool and the man born blind, both of whom reward Jesus for healing them by telling the authorities (5:2–15; 9:1–38)! Thousands of paintings have been inspired by the poor woman dragged before Jesus by the guardians of morality (who have let the man escape, who must also have been caught with her in the "very act of committing adultery"!), except that Jesus himself does not condemn her (8:3–11). Finally, John's account of Martha, Mary, and Lazarus is full of beautiful touches showing how Jesus knows each of them individually, and yet loves them as they are and meets their various needs differently (11:1–44).

In *Monty Python's Life of Brian*, a film full of theological insight into religious communities, Brian tries to tell the crowd that they are "all individuals," only for them to parrot back in unison, "Yes! We are all individuals"—except, of course, for one lone voice who hesitantly confesses, "I'm not"! Religious leaders are rightly castigated for forcing people into a herd mentality or using authoritarian methods to compel conformity. We have seen that preparation for ministry is more about "formation" than education, and theological training helps ordinands to be "formed" within a particular tradition which can help maintain the spiritual discipline necessary to survive in Christian ministry. The daily commitment to silent prayer and the eucharist of people like Desmond Tutu and Rowan Williams reflects their early training, which has stood them in good stead over many years of fruitful leadership. However, John's portrait of Jesus's love, care, and understanding for particular individuals at the heart of this most ecclesial gospel may provide a salutary corrective.

The three previous parts of this book have already concluded with "coming apart" to pray, to study and learn, to rest and recuperate if we are to survive and flourish in ministry. Lastly, John's portrayal of Jesus's participation in the life of God through prayer and the Holy Spirit brings all of this together. However, John's collection of fascinating individuals, each loved and cared for by Jesus, reminds us that nothing here is "off the peg," or "one size fits all." The loving God who created the rainbow is a lot more interesting than Henry Ford, who reputedly said of his first mass-produced cars, "You can have any color you like—as long as it is black"!

"Know yourself"

Carved into the ancient wall of Apollo's temple in the oracle at Delphi was the gnomic maxim, *gnōthi seauton*, "know thyself." The spiritual significance of this pithy aphorism is not, however, confined to ancient Greek literature, but is vital here—with one crucial difference. John's portrait of Jesus's care for various individuals means that the discovery of self-knowledge is never something you have to undertake alone. John says at the outset that Jesus "knew all people and needed no one to testify about anyone; for he himself knew what was in everyone" (2:24–25). The invitation to participate in the divine life shared by the Father and the Son in the Spirit is from God, who created each of us as a unique person, and who longs to see us—and all his children—come to full maturity in Christ.

Yes, the various spiritual traditions in which ministers and clergy are "formed" can provide a helpful template at the start—and may become the fruitful basis for a lifelong spiritual discipline. But sometimes it feels like being "conformed," squeezed into a mold which does not enable you to grow. Instead of a wellspring of life, it produces rules and restrictions—what one of my theological teachers called "ought-age and must-ery"! Probably nothing makes Christians feel guilty or ashamed more than being asked about their prayer and spirituality. And yet the selection criteria emphasize that candidates' spiritual practice should be able to "sustain and energise them in every aspect of their lives" (TEAC C). So, please treat all that follows here as suggestions for sustaining your ministry: try them out, experiment, discuss them with others, and pray about them to the God who made you and loves you in the light of Jesus's knowledge of "all people" and "what is in everyone" (John 2:25). Find out what works for you. You will also find that appendix 4 contains various suggestions for further reading, websites, and other resources which will help you develop your understanding of yourself, ministry, and spirituality.

Ways of learning to pray

I was taught to "say my prayers" by my grandmother, who also kindled an early passion for story by reading Bunyan's *Pilgrim's Progress* to me, which I grew to love. From a local church primary school, I was fortunate to get a scholarship at Bristol Cathedral School where days began with an Anglican "hymn sandwich" in the cathedral with Bible reading, prayers, and the headmaster's notices. Interestingly, most of my days working through four decades as a schoolteacher, an ordinand, a curate in a London parish, a university chaplain, and now Dean of King's have begun with some sort of morning service with hymns, Bible passages, and prayers! So perhaps I have been "formed" in a tradition more than I realize?

However, I have also looked for other patterns: my Christian Union at Oxford was suspicious of liturgical "words on a page," schooling me in an evangelical "daily quiet time," struggling to read the Greek New Testament every day between breakfast and lectures. Conversely, borne along on the charismatic winds of the Spirit through theological college, for many people written texts were "out": making it up as we went along was new and exciting—which explains why I exasperated my poor training vicar who was trying to take me through matins, silent meditation, and daily eucharist in our south London parish! Yet all of these different experiences have taught me the abiding importance of a daily rhythm—and of praying with others. Why not stop and reflect on all the different ways you have learned to pray over the years: what stays with you now?

Those experiences also suggested that real spiritual giants are all introverts, who could go into their room and be silent—and actually concentrate, not letting their right hand know what their left hand was doing, and spending hours in silence alone before God (see Matt. 6:3, 6; Ps. 46:10). No wonder I found people like Desmond Tutu and Rowan Williams an inspiration and a challenge simultaneously! Is my attempt, as an extraverted "people-person," to emulate such spiritual practices always doomed to failure? More recently, I have begun to benefit instead from walking to work listening on earphones to online guided prayer resources from websites like www.pray-as-you-go.org/ or www.sacredspace.ie/. So let me encourage you to try out new methods too.

Beads, music, candles, and other aids to worship

During my Cathedral School education, I rebelled by studying biblical prophecy with an Adventist archaeologist, but when Jesus didn't come quickly back on the clouds, I took instruction about becoming a Roman Catholic, though the incense inflamed my asthma! My Protestant suspicions against beads and candles were exacerbated by later undergraduate evangelical prejudices. So I was surprised after ordination to find that I increasingly needed to light a candle before prayer—let alone before turning on my computer to write. Later still, a Greek Orthodox colleague showed me how to illuminate, or "turn on," an icon by lighting a candle before it, and finding myself drawn into its depths. Now, lighting candles in the university chapel, or my local church or just at home, seems a natural way to seek illumination from God, letting my desires or concerns for something or someone rise slowly on the smoke, sometimes even assisted by incense!

Some years ago, I was able to help an international student who had fled the horrors of the former Yugoslavia breaking up by coming to study in London. When she graduated, she thanked me with the gift of a rosary, urging me to use it to pray. I was taken aback by an anti-Papist reaction stirring somewhere deep in my being, yet I was also moved by her gesture and wanted to honor it and remember her with it. After studying prayers traditionally associated with rosaries, I started fiddling with it in time with my breathing during contemplation. To my surprise, while I'll never be completely comfortable with traditional Marian devotion, I found that I couldn't pray without it, and having something to finger helped my concentration. Over the years, I have gone through several sets of beads, variously arranged in three, four, or seven groups, while my current rosary made by a friend from black-stained African horn has been rubbed white through constant use: I'm never without it.

Although I was not a chorister in Bristol Cathedral, choral singing has been on the sound track of my life ever since. On the other hand, as a guitarist I strummed along to repetitive choruses at university, and joined various folk and rock bands. Musicians in my training parish patiently bashed out the clergy sung responses at Evensong on the piano for me to learn, and even managed to teach me to sing the bass lines in staples like the Bach *Passions*, Handel's *Messiah*, and Vivaldi's *Gloria*. Now I look forward to the weekly Book of Common Prayer Choral Evensong sung in King's College Chapel by our wonderful choir, and I've even ended up on BBC Radio 3 recently trying to link Schoenberg to world peace. On the other hand, when we first moved to London the bishop told me to help with whatever the local parish incumbent needed. When he came to take a confirmation, the bishop was taken aback to see me behind the altar with a bass guitar over my cassock—but it was what the vicar wanted!

So don't be afraid to experiment with different traditions and aids to prayer and worship, whether choral or chorus, or what looks like idolatrous tat or the most sublime art. The biblical accounts of worship in the temple at Jerusalem sound like a cacophony, especially added to the smell of blood and burning sacrifices, while Psalm 150 tells us to use everything blow-able or bang-able to praise the Lord. Most things have helped somebody at some point, while offending others—so what might you find helpful and beneficial in your spiritual life?

Keeping a spiritual journal

As an extravert concerned for details, facts, and figures, silent contemplation does not come naturally to me, but, as a writer, I have found keeping a spiritual journal has been essential. I often don't know what I think until I hear myself talking about something, so my chaplains and colleagues sometimes help me think by talking things through. Similarly, writing things down in my journal enables me to reflect on what has been happening to me personally, to see whether God has been trying to do or say something on the winds of the Spirit which blow where they will (John 3:8).

A journal is not like a diary, recording what I had for breakfast, nor something I write every day—although over the years it has been interesting to see where the long gaps have occurred. I started it during my ordination training, using a Church Desk Diary which included the daily readings and prayers. But I found the framework too restrictive, with successive pages of blank space reproaching me for lack of entries, while other days just did not have enough space when something significant was happening. So I soon moved to a simple notebook, in which I would write down thoughts, or sermon ideas which had impressed me, or notes on books I was reading. Sometimes it is a way of thinking things through on paper; just putting pen to paper and seeing what emerges as I let it flow can be quite revealing. At other times, I have kept notes of counseling sessions or some psychotherapy training I was doing, as well as extensive accounts of periods on retreat. Over more than three decades, I have used it to prepare for conversations with my spiritual advisers and to reflect upon these afterwards. It helps to pull things together, or trying to discern any kind of thread running through the disparate things going on—or even the possibility that the Spirit is moving in a certain direction!

I often encourage my students who are thinking about their future or contemplating a call to some form of ministry to try keeping such a journal in order to discern what is happening, and what, if anything, God might be wanting to say to them. That is why I have regularly suggested that you might jot down your reactions to the selection criteria or ordination liturgies in the appendices, or try out other suggestions I have been making. If you have not tried it, why not find a notebook, get out your pen (I find a real ink pen helps it to flow in a way that a keyboard never will)—and try it now?

A rule of life

Throughout the above paragraphs, I have been suggesting that John's depiction of Jesus's loving concern for various individuals in his gospel encourages us to reflect on our differences. But we are not just different from one another, but also different from who and where we used to be, and—please God—who and where we will be in his good future. So participating in the divine life through a spiritual discipline also needs to take *time* into account, the actual here and now of minutes and hours, days and years. The great spiritual traditions and monastic communities like the Benedictines had a "Rule of Life," including a daily rhythm of prayer, services at set hours like dawn, mid-morning, noon, afternoon, evening prayers, and even during the night. This came from the traditional Jewish hours of prayer which were observed by the first disciples (e.g., Acts 3:1) and finds a parallel in the five daily prayer times for observant Muslims, as well as the canonical practice of Anglican clergy in praying the morning and evening offices.

Anyone considering a vocation to ordination or engaged in any form of ministry would be wise to develop a daily rhythm. It might be as basic as a Bible reading in the morning and some time to reflect on the events of the day before going to sleep—perhaps something between childhood bedtime prayers and the Jesuit *examen*, a daily examination before God. But as well as each day, think about other elements to be undertaken weekly, monthly, yearly, or even over longer periods. This is also an opportunity to consider your eucharistic practice: would you benefit from the discipline of a daily mass, or participating in a weekly communion? It certainly ought to be more often than the 1662 Book of Common Prayer's Communions at Christmas and Easter!

Quiet days and retreats

In previous chapters we noted that time to "come apart" is vital for sustaining ourselves in ministry, opportunities to study for teaching and preaching with Matthew, or developing the pastoral ministry seen in Luke, or just time for ourselves, our families, and friends to recuperate from the kinds of pressures depicted in Mark. This, too, needs planning in your "rule of life"; perhaps set aside a couple of hours each week to read, think, and plan for the next sermon, visiting a library, or to develop new skills. Such are the pressures on clergy diaries that unless this is put in well in advance, it is unlikely to happen as the phone rings again and someone comes to the door, or yet another meeting calls.

Ministers also often find that they benefit from a quiet day or two, even going away overnight, at a local retreat center once a month or every couple of months, just to reflect and pray about what has been happening. However, many of us need even longer to slow down and open up to the winds of the Spirit. Scheduling a week or ten-day retreat will require not just advance planning, but a little research and booking the right place or person. Once again, the fact that we are all different is important here—and you will need to try things out to discover what is particularly helpful for you. Some people like doing creative things with their hands, art or pottery, while others just prefer silence; some want to be in groups, with some input or talks, while others need to be left alone; some want to share in frequent and regular services in beautiful chapels, while yet others need to get away from everything and go for a long walk across deserted hills. Over the last decade or two, I have found that I benefit from being away alone in a silent retreat center in Devon which specializes in support for clergy and those in ministry for several days every year or so (it takes me that long just to slow down!)—while every few years I need to take a more formal Individually Guided Retreat for eight or ten days. Try to find out what helps you—and how often you need to plan for it in advance and get it into the diary ahead of time. See appendix 4 for more details.

Personality "types" and profiles

By now, you could be forgiven for feeling bewildered by all these choices: yes, God has created us all different as individuals—but so many options can be confusing. What about a "set meal" or "fixed menu" with fewer choices? Realizing that I am an extravert—someone "orientated outwards" but not necessarily a jolly extravert—has been quite liberating, helping me to recognize that some traditional spiritual practices are more for introverts, so it is no wonder that I have struggled with them. One way of getting to "know yourself" better can be through personality profiles and "types" like the Myers-Briggs Type Indicator (MBTI) or the Enneagram. The MBTI was developed by a mother and her daughter (Myers and Briggs) based on Jungian psychological theories along four spectrums (extraversion-introversion, feeling-thinking, intuition-sensing, judging-perceiving) leading to sixteen (4 x 4) possible profiles. The Enneagram may have roots in ancient mysticism, but it groups individuals into "nine" (*ennea* in Greek) types, which relate to one another and to the wider world in different ways. Of course, some keen devotees of such approaches use them almost like astrological star signs, and this can become an easy cop-out: I cannot relate to you because you are an X, or you cannot ask me to do this because I am a Y, and so forth.

However, getting to know yourself better, and what you find helpful and easy, and what involves harder work or makes you tired or grumpy, can be a real help in discerning which spiritual practices and disciplines you may find beneficial. There are simple online tests available, and many retreat houses and conference centers run short courses to help you discover the sorts of things which will come more "naturally" to you, and which you will have to work at. Appendix 4 provides suggestions for further reading and resources in this area.

Spiritual traditions and the Orders

Interestingly, the great spiritual traditions arising from the ancient and medieval monastic Orders also suit some personality types better than others. Thus Benedictines follow the Rule of Saint Benedict, with a clear and organized timetable for all the various services, meals, work, and study, while Carmelite tradition is more suited for contemplatives. Dominicans were founded as an Order of Preachers, to communicate the gospel in the vernacular, while Franciscans have become synonymous with respect for the natural world. At a Benedictine abbey, you will probably spend a lot of time in chapel, reciting psalms, while a Jesuit retreat provides space for imaginative, though carefully directed, private reflection on certain scriptural passages, following the *Spiritual Exercises* of Saint Ignatius. Some people have even tried to link MBTI types or Enneagram profiles directly with certain Orders: while this is too simplistic, clearly some personality types will find themselves at home in particular traditions and practices, so it is worth exploring which might suit your own personality, habits, or tendencies.

Traditionally, such Orders require total commitment as a monk or nun, from being a postulant to first promises as a novice, before undertaking lifelong vows—and some readers of this book may find themselves being called to that vocation. However, while numbers offering for such a demanding permanent lifestyle have been falling, several Orders have experienced a significant rise in people wanting to be associated with them and to follow their spiritual traditions in ordinary life. In fact, alongside "first" and "second" Orders of monks and nuns, Saint Francis himself started a third, or "tertiary," Order for men and women, single and married, lay and ordained, who take vows and keep Franciscan spiritual traditions in their daily lives. Similarly, the Benedictines have "oblates" for those who wish to be associated with them, and other Orders have similar groups.

The great thing about such monastic traditions is that they can offer a "package deal" or "fixed menu" rather than the bewildering individual choices of all the different spiritual possibilities. If you become a tertiary or oblate, you will be expected to follow a Franciscan or Benedictine Rule of Life, with its particular traditions, habits, and forms of prayer, as well as go to one of their centers regularly for retreat. Even if you do not formally sign up to a lay order or associate group, knowing the sort of spiritual tradition in which you feel most comfortable can be very helpful.

I spent my final year of ordination training on placement under a local clergyman, part of whose ministry also provided spiritual support to various people. As the Big Day approached and the Bishop's hands loomed ever closer, I nervously asked Gordon if he would "take me on" and he kindly agreed to a "temporary" trial—which eventually lasted well over a decade. He was himself a tertiary, wearing a simple Franciscan wooden cross and observing Franciscan daily prayer, as well as going off to a friary for regular retreats and to receive spiritual direction from a wise elderly Brother.

However, we quickly realized that this Franciscan tradition did not particularly suit my personality type or spiritual journey, so he sent me to a couple of Individually Guided Ignatian Retreats at Saint Beuno's, the Jesuit Centre in north Wales where Gerard Manley Hopkins wrote much of his poetry. Being silent for ten days seemed a great opportunity to catch up on several books, until I realized to my horror that reading was not allowed; even with the Bible, we were to concentrate only on the two or three passages set each day by our personal director, spending the time in prayer and meditative conversations with Christ. I got such severe withdrawal symptoms that one day I ended up in the library, fingering the books, obediently not actually reading them—but inhaling the distinctive aroma of beautiful old volumes! Despite my "cold turkey," this retreat was a life-changing experience, and something I have repeated every few years ever since. I cannot do it more often, not just because of diary pressures, but because it usually takes several years to work through what happens each time and process what God seems to be saying. Then I can go back for another ten days—or sometime, hopefully, the thirty-day silent retreat; not bad for an extravert!

Spiritual accompaniment or direction

Throughout this final chapter on participating in the divine life in your ministry through prayer and spirituality, we have emphasized "knowing yourself," since we are all known and loved individually by God. And yet, John's portrait of Jesus's love for individuals being paradoxically in such an ecclesial gospel suggests that we get to know ourselves best through others, as part of a community. Significantly, scholarly reconstructions of John's gospel suggest that it developed over many years, drawing on the prayer, meditation, spirituality, and theological reflection originating with John the Apostle, perhaps involving another John, the Elder, and thence passed on to others. The practice of an older, wiser, more experienced person acting as a spiritual guide for others, especially those at an earlier stage, is deeply ingrained in the Christian tradition, as well as in contemporary literature—just think of characters like Gandalf with Bilbo and Frodo, or Dumbledore looking after Harry Potter!

Each of the previous studies ended by suggesting help and training: a teacher for some further learning (Matthew), a supervisor or therapist to develop pastoral skills (Luke), and a cell group to share the journey, especially during difficult times (Mark). Those are all important, but the one essential person for anyone involved in ministry is a spiritual adviser—which is how I want to end this study of ministry in John's gospel. Unfortunately, the phrase "spiritual director" conjures up all sorts of images from medieval frescoes to characters like Obi-Wan Kenobi or Yoda in the *Star Wars* films. And in these egalitarian days, "direction" sounds very authoritarian; surely we should not be so infantile, but rather work things out for ourselves, like adults?

However, we have also discovered the importance of "knowing yourself" and how God has made us all different and loves us as individuals. We have seen how various personality types pray in different ways, or find the different monastic Orders or ecclesial traditions more, or less, congenial to their spiritual development. After about fourteen years working with my original spiritual director, during which time he had sent me on a couple of Ignatian retreats, Gordon suggested that, as a Franciscan tertiary, he had probably helped me as far along my path as he could. It was time for me explore the Jesuits and find someone trained in more Ignatian methods to take me further. In the couple of decades since then, I have been grateful for the wisdom and insight received first from an older, widely respected Anglican monastic priest, and then a Roman Catholic nun in her "retirement"; now, I see a lay man, a little younger than myself, who enjoys gently twisting my tail with his lack of ecclesiastical concerns!

So, like so much of what we have seen, spiritual direction is never a case of "one size fits all," nor will one person or tradition suit you for ever and ever, amen. In fact, proper training to undertake such ministry takes several years, and a skillful director will be conversant with many different traditions, orders, habits, and practices from which he or she will seek to find the right thing for you at this particular time and place. Many large towns and most dioceses have a Centre for Spirituality, or retreat houses where you can seek advice about finding the right person to help you. Another possibility is to explore a lay association, such as becoming a tertiary or oblate, since the Order will want to encourage you to work with a director of their tradition.

In addition, I believe that it is particularly vital to have someone to accompany you on any journey exploring some form of ministry. In the first place, an experienced guide can help you to discern the way God may be calling you, especially in the early stages, and to sort out mere pipe dreams and wish fulfillment from a real calling. But even more important, we need someone to help us avoid the snares and the temptations. Bitter experience shows that we are a danger to ourselves and to others if we think we can simply go off doing this on our own. Actually, you have no right to go around messing in other people's heads and lives, unless somebody has permission to look into yours. It's like going rock climbing on a slippery cliff face without someone holding on to the other end of a rope around your waist. A major temptation for all in ministry is to think we are "God's representative here on earth"—and to a certain extent that is true, since we bring people to God and God to people. On the other hand, once we start believing our own publicity, the human capacity for self-delusion is incredible. A good spiritual director is like having someone hold up a mirror before us, where we can see who we really are and where we are actually heading. And if there are occasions when we do lose it, or even crash and burn, it is good to have someone who cares enough to help pick up the pieces.

Thus there are many different ways of finding some form of spiritual direction, ranging from seeing the same person locally every few weeks for an hour or so, to going away to stay in a retreat house or monastery for a day or two a couple of times a year. You might want to work with a director who is a man or a woman, lay or ordained, or a lifelong member of a religious Order, who is younger or older than you, from the same church or a completely different ecclesial tradition—or you might not know what you want or where to begin (in which case look at the resources listed in the appendices). But whatever you choose or whichever way you start, the important thing is to do something and find someone who will walk with you on your pilgrimage, to accompany you along the way, to pray for you and perhaps with you—because the one thing that I am sure of is that we were never meant to travel this path on our own!

Conclusion

In this fourth study, we have seen how the eagle symbol for John reflects its high-flying, all-seeing portrait of Jesus's mission, swooping down from the heights of heaven to share our human existence before returning to the glory of the Father through the suffering on the cross. Jesus's miracles are "signs" of his identity and mission, sent by his Father, yet they are also the cause of increasing division between those who accept him and those who do not. Finally, on the night before he suffered and died, Jesus gathered his disciples together, like a mother eagle nurturing her fledglings under her wings, to explain what was going to happen and to reassure them. These "Farewell Discourses" are an extended meditation on how Jesus shares in the divine life with his Father through the Spirit—and they invite us to participate in that same fellowship of love at the heart of the universe.

Therefore it is right that the criteria and selection processes for ordained ministry also seek a clear sense of identity and mission in candidates, a realization that they are being called by Jesus and sent by the Father in the power of the Spirit to serve the church and the world. This is also reflected in the ordination services in which new ministers are blessed and prayed for, and invited to participate in this divine life and love shared between the persons of the Holy Trinity. In both the selection processes and the ordination liturgies, it is rightly emphasized that this can only happen through a life of prayer, stressing the importance of a spiritual discipline to sustain and energize Christian ministry. If we are to share this divine life and love, it must be at the heart of all that we say and do in ministry, as it provides both our sense of identity and also our purpose and mission: "As the Father sent me, so I send you" (John 20:21). Thus it must find practical expression in daily prayer and intercession for those in our care, as well as regular participation in the holy communion.

Finally, we have discussed the various spiritual habits and practices which can help to sustain and undergird both our relationship with God and our ministry. God has made us all individuals with different needs and personalities—and yet the wisdom and experience of the church down the centuries provide extraordinary resources from art and music, visual, aural, and tactile aids to prayer and worship if we will only try some of them. Other practices like keeping a spiritual journal and undertaking regular retreats can be included within a rhythm or "rule of life," helped by an awareness of the great spiritual and monastic traditions of the church. However, we concluded that the most important resource for maintaining a spiritual life under the pressures of ministry is to be involved in spiritual direction, whatever form that might best take for you—so this is probably the best place to start if you do not have this already.

For prayer and further reflection

Spend a little time reflecting on these questions and instructions from the ordination liturgies—and respond by praying for the gift of the life-giving Holy Spirit to assist you to participate in the divine life and love.

- Do you promise to be diligent in your private prayers and in reading the scriptures, as well as in the public duties of your office? (UCC, and see similar question in AME)
- Will you persevere in prayer, both in public and in private, asking God's grace, both for yourself and for others, offering all your labors to God, through the mediation of Jesus Christ, and in the sanctification of the Holy Spirit? (TEC)
- You cannot bear the weight of this calling in your own strength, but only by the grace and power of God. Pray, therefore, that your heart may daily be enlarged and your understanding of the Scriptures enlightened. (CofE)
- Pray earnestly for the gift of the Holy Spirit.
- **Amen.**

Bringing Mission and Ministry Together in the Risen Jesus

Figure 5. Four gospels, one Jesus, Westminster Abbey Psalter, *c.* 1200

This book, like the ordination addresses originally given on retreat at Launde Abbey, has used the traditional symbols of the four gospels to look at four aspects of mission and ministry: teaching and preaching through Matthew's portrait of Jesus the teacher, pastoral care and concern through Luke's image of the burden-bearing ox, suffering the way of the cross following Mark's lion to Jerusalem, and participating in the very life of God through John's insight into the relationship of Jesus and his Father in prayer and spirituality. Yet they are not four separate ministries, and certainly not four missions, any more than the gospels give us four Jesuses. They are all part of the *one* mission and the *one* ministry of the *one* Jesus, even if interpreted through the four portraits of the four evangelists with their different emphases in their respective gospels. It is like a beautiful jewel through which light is refracted differently from various directions, or an intricate sculpture which can be appreciated by walking around and looking at it from each side.

Something similar happens in many ancient depictions of Jesus seated in majesty, with the four living creatures arranged around him, each holding their scroll representing or even quoting from their gospel. Like that beautiful jewel, the symbols reflect the light of these four aspects of ministry on to the one Jesus, who gives us his blessing. At the start of this conclusion, we have included one example for you to consider in prayer and meditation, taken from a twelfth-century Westminster Psalter (see fig. 5). However, there are many versions of this idea, not just across Celtic manuscripts and medieval prayer books, but throughout all the different church traditions, set in frescoes on domed roofs or depicted in stained-glass windows. It is all clearly based on the description of the worship of Christ in heaven led by the four living creatures in Revelation 4–6.

A modern version fills the large east window behind the altar in my parish church in north London. In the center, the artist, Francis Spear, has depicted a large, strong, and dignified figure of the risen Christ, surrounded by the four winged symbols, each with a scroll featuring some opening words from their respective gospels. Jesus has his right hand raised in blessing, while his feet, still clearly bearing the wounds of the crucifixion, stand on a green cliff overlooking the five continents with buildings and churches, surrounded by the three mystical rivers of the Bible. It is all illuminated from above by the glory streaming from the hands of God, with the dove of the Holy Spirit communicating between Jesus and the Father, as we are invited both to participate in the divine life and to share in God's mission to the world below. As Jesus says in the gospel passage which I read at my ordination, "Peace be with you. As the Father has sent me, so I send you" (John 20:21).

It is very significant that it is the crucified yet risen Jesus on that first Easter evening who not only gives his frightened disciples his peace, but commissions them to go out into the world, just as he was sent by the Father. In our study of Matthew's portrait, we concentrated on Jesus's preaching and teaching ministry during his earthly life. On the other hand, we also saw how Luke's picture of Jesus's pastoral ministry reached its climax in his account of the Passion and crucifixion, where at the end Jesus was concerned not about himself, but for the poor weeping women and children, the ordinary carpenters and soldiers carrying out his execution, and assuring the penitent thief that he would be in paradise with him even as he died, committing his spirit to his heavenly Father. Third, this suffering on the way of the cross dominates the whole of Mark's account of Jesus's ministry on the way to Jerusalem right through to its bleak climax in the dark desolation of abandonment, even by God. In contrast, John's narrative depicts the crucifixion as the way Jesus is ultimately glorified, and the divine eagle rises again with healing in its wings to comfort and restore his disciples like Mary, Thomas, and Peter, before sending them all out: "As the Father has sent me, so I send you" (John 20:21).

It has been both interesting and instructive to study these four aspects of mission and ministry in turn through each gospel's portrait of Jesus, but this does not mean that they are separate from each other. Admittedly, we have probably all met some individuals who are particularly gifted with a teaching and preaching ministry, but who can be pastorally quite insensitive at times! Or in contrast, there are those who are clearly called to pastoral ministry but who do not feel that they have the gift of standing up in public to speak.

This dichotomy may be particularly true for lay ministers. The office of lay reader in the Church of England was originally instituted primarily for public spoken ministry, preaching and taking the services of the Word, Morning and Evening Prayer. It is often combined with a full-time job, which may also involve speaking, such as my being a schoolteacher while I was also exercising a reader ministry. In preparing this international edition, I have been struck by how many denominations also have a range of different "offices" or "orders," some of which are ordained, while others are considered lay—but which still feature within these ordination services. When I was a parish curate, we had two well-respected older ladies who gave several days a week to help our team with pastoral care. One had been a highly qualified doctor and hospital consultant, who specialized in bereavement counseling in her retirement, doing follow-up visits after our funerals—but who would never get up and speak in church. The other was a former headmistress who was actually licensed as a lay reader, but who preferred to concentrate on pastoral work, especially among young families, like a surrogate grandmother. In recent years, funerals and other aspects of pastoral ministry have been opened up to the ministry of readers, while many English dioceses now have a licensed office with various titles like Pastoral Auxiliaries; sometimes described as "readers who don't read," in fact they have been trained differently and provide huge amounts of pastoral ministry within parish teams. If you are called to one of these two contrasting groups of lay ministers, you may have found the different emphases of our first two chapters particularly helpful or less relevant according to your vocation and ministry. However, of course, all those involved in any form of lay ministry will also need to follow the way of the cross, and learn to pray and share in the divine life as much as any ordained person, so hopefully you will have benefited from the last two studies on Mark and John.

However, for those who are ordained, especially those in full-time stipendiary ministry, I would argue that all four aspects of mission and ministry need to be present together, even if not necessarily in the same proportion or all at the same time. There is a tendency in some quarters to draw a contrast between "pastoral ministry" and "mission." However, having these four portraits of Jesus's one mission within the canon of scripture reminds us that they can never be different or separate. For Jesus—and his followers, then and now—teaching and preaching about the love of God must always be earthed by putting it into practice in loving pastoral care of all God's people, whether they "go to church" or not. And this is all done on the way of the cross, undergirded by prayer and a spiritual discipline which enables us to share in the life of God—so the emphases of all four gospels are needed.

It is true that some clergy will have a strong preaching ministry, while others may be very pastoral but be the first to admit that preaching is not their forte—but they will still need to undertake both aspects regularly. This reminds us of the importance of ministry teams today; in recent years, we have been moving away from some more traditional patterns of "one-man bands" (and they were, of course, often only men!). In part, this has been driven by financial and practical concerns as parishes have been amalgamated and clergy spread more thinly—but it is also an important development in stressing the mission and ministry of the whole church, and the need for teamwork between the ordained and lay people.

It is also likely that different periods of your ministry, or different contexts, may bring one or other aspect to the fore. Maintaining all four in a constantly equal balance is not easy—and probably not what is needed all the time. There are bound to be times or places when preaching and teaching may need to be emphasized, while elsewhere other occasions may bring pastoral care to the fore. None of us want to suffer, but we may have to go through longer periods of pressure or suffering in ministry, while at other times we meet with great success or happiness. And of course, we will spend our whole lives developing our spiritual pattern, learning to pray, and to respond to the invitation to share in the divine life and enter the dance of love at the heart of the cosmos.

However, in the last chapter, we indicated that as individuals created by our loving God, different people will respond spiritually in different ways at different times, particularly as we learn to grow in self-knowledge and understand more of the riches of the church's spiritual traditions. Therefore, as we seek to respond to God's vocation and calling to share in the one ministry and mission of the church, we will find the balance between these four aspects varying from time to time and place to place. But the impulse of the early church fathers to include all four gospels within one codex and the single canon of scripture suggests that if any one form of this fourfold ministry is missing over a prolonged period, then this needs attention and addressing.

Each study on each gospel in turn has tried finally to provide some basic and practical suggestions about how to sustain each particular aspect over years or even decades of public ministry. The image of a camel filling up at an oasis and plodding for years across the desert may be trivial, but sadly something similar is all too real a possibility, given the pressures on so many clergy these days. We know that for some it becomes too much; overwork, stress, and ill health can take their toll, while others have to face crises of faith. I find it sobering to realize that some of those alongside whom I trained or with whom I was ordained are no longer in active ministry.

So we all need support systems and regular disciplines if we are to survive, let alone blossom and flourish. Matthew's portrait reminds us that regular space for prayerful reading of the scriptures backed up by biblical and theological study is essential to maintain our preaching and teaching. Luke's depiction of Jesus's pastoral concern, especially for the poor and marginalized, challenges us to learn new skills and develop professional networks to improve our ministry to those in our care. Mark's narrative of the way of the cross reminds us of the importance of sustaining close relationships with our families and friends, including things like cell groups, especially for the times of suffering and hardship which will inevitably occur. Finally and above all, John's invitation to us to join in the very life of God encourages us to greater self-knowledge so that we can nurture our inner beings through all the many and varied spiritual disciplines provided by the church's traditions and history, accompanied by some form of spiritual adviser or director on this journey of mission and ministry.

Lastly, the window in my local church rightly has the crucified, risen, and glorified Jesus at the center, but, like many ancient and medieval representations of the one Jesus surrounded by the four gospel creatures, the artist also included at the top of the window the Greek letters alpha and omega. For he is indeed the beginning and the end, the origin and the ultimate goal (see Rev. 1:8; 21:6; 22:13). Our mission and ministry is never "ours," but it comes from the One who was with God at the beginning and involved in the very act of creation, yet who became present and dwelled among us in the incarnation, humbling himself even to die for us on the cross, and who is now reigning in glory and interceding for us at the right hand of the Father, pouring upon us the gift of his Holy Spirit as he sends us out in the same mission of love to the world. That same Jesus of Nazareth who walked this earth and inspired these four different portraits of his life and ministry is the one Christ enthroned in glorious majesty surrounded by the four living creatures who lead the worship of heaven, inviting us—and all creation—into those everlasting praises.

For prayer and final reflection

- "I give thanks to my God always for you because of the grace of God that has been given you in Christ Jesus, for in every way you have been enriched in him, in speech and knowledge of every kind. . . . He will also strengthen you to the end, so that you may be blameless on the day of our Lord Jesus Christ. God is faithful; by him you were called into the fellowship of his Son, Jesus Christ our Lord" (1 Cor. 1:4–9).
- "I am confident of this, that the one who began a good work among you will bring it to completion by the day of Jesus Christ" (Phil. 1:6).

You are warmly invited to leave any final comments and questions (in general terms, of course!) on the Facebook page for this book: www.facebook.com/FourMinistriesOneJesus.

Some Bible studies about various calls within the scriptures

In the Bible there are many examples of people being called in different ways, which reminds us that God knows and loves us all individually. Read some of the following passages and use them to reflect upon your own sense of call and the different ways in which God called people in biblical times. Are any of them like your own experience? Make some notes as you go, paying attention to aspects of the stories which resonate with you and inspire you, and those which challenge—or even scare—you. And then discuss your reactions with your vocational adviser or spiritual director. Or post something about it on Facebook: www.facebook.com /FourMinistriesOneJesus.

The call of Abraham: Genesis 12
The call of Moses: Exodus 3
The call of Samuel: 1 Samuel 3:1–10
The call of Saul: 1 Samuel 9; 10
The call of David: 1 Samuel 16:4–13
The call of Isaiah: Isaiah 6:1–8
The call of Jeremiah: Jeremiah 1:4–9
The call of Mary: Luke 1:26–38
The call of Peter: Luke 5:1–11
The call of the first disciples: John 1:35–46
The call of Mary Magdalene: John 20:1–18
The call of Peter: John 21:15–19
The call of Paul: Acts 9:1–22; 22:1–21; 26:4–29
The call and commissioning of Paul and Barnabas: Acts 13:1–3
The call of Lydia: Acts 16:14–15
The Christian calling: Ephesians 1:3–14; 4:1–16; 1 Peter 1:3–9

Summary of the processes, competencies, and criteria for selection for ordained ministry

Offering for ministry, lay or ordained, in any church of all the different denominations and traditions is not like applying for any other job or career. At the end of the day, the decision to ordain someone or give them the authority, permission, or even a licence to minister, preach, or perform any other form of ministry belongs to others, usually those in authority to represent or speak, not only for a particular church community, but often for its regional, national, or even international identity and institution. In the Church of England and the wider Anglican tradition, derived from its Catholic origins, this authority belongs to the bishops, who rightly guard their prerogative carefully. Technically, I think that there is nothing to stop a bishop ordaining someone whom they have just met over tea if they so wished—but in practice, there are careful processes at the local, diocesan, and national levels which try to ensure parity and continuity across the church. In the Church of England, bishops usually delegate this work to the Diocesan Director of Ordinands (DDO), who will often have a network of Assistant Directors of Ordinands (ADOs) and Vocation Advisers—but you cannot even apply to them; instead, you have to be referred to them by a priest who knows you well and has discussed it all with you. And after you have worked through all the diocesan procedures, the bishop will then "sponsor" a candidate to go to a national selection conference, called a Bishops' Advisory Panel (BAP), who will make the recommendation whether this person should be sent for ministry training or not. Other Anglican churches in South Africa, Australia, or New Zealand, or the Episcopal Church in the USA, tend to work at the diocesan, rather than the national, level—partly because of their large size, and their more federal nature.

As we shall see shortly, most mainline churches also have a similarly detailed process, even if it may not be as long or as complicated as the Church of England's sausage machine! This is because all Christian churches share a basic belief that ministry belongs to all the people of God, given to each unique person beloved of God through their baptism. However, having said that, all the churches recognize that certain people experience some sort of sense of a "calling" from God, while others around them also think that they should be set apart in some way for ministry, with the appropriate training and authorization. An old saying suggests that "God only calls those to be ordained whom he does not trust to remain lay"—and there is some wisdom therein! However, not everybody who thinks that God is calling them to do something should necessarily be immediately ordained. The sad fact is that some people who have heard voices, or dream dreams, or who are just simply convinced that God wants them to do something, have gone on to commit terrible crimes or atrocities in his name, ending up in prison or hospital. Others, who may not be ill like these, may still be confused or deluded in their sense of calling, which might arise from their own personal desires or psychological needs—or having eaten something like too much cheese!

For many people, the sense of a call begins to emerge from a persistent "niggle" or "nudge," a feeling that will not go away, which is reinforced by comments and suggestions from those who know you, both inside and outside the church. Nighttime visits from chorus lines of angels or sudden appearances of hands writing on walls in letters of fire are quite rare in my experience, while it is usually those who are heading in the wrong direction who need knocking off their horses and being turned around, like Saint Paul. So, if you are wondering what God might be calling you to, start by going to have a conversation with your own minister, a local parish priest or pastor, or if you are a student, with a university chaplain or campus minister. They won't think you are crazy, but they will probably want to have several conversations about it with you over a reasonable period of time, just to make sure.

Once they also agree that this sense of calling needs to be taken further, they will refer you to whatever vocation and discernment process is usual within your church or particular Christian tradition. While the actual details and processes of this can vary greatly between different denominations, there are some general assumptions which are similar across most mainline churches, including that: the individual will have a personal sense of calling from God that God wants him or her to do something in ministry, even if they are not sure quite what yet; it will also be apparent to the local church community that this individual already possesses various gifts relevant or necessary for ministry, if only in an initial way, and is already beginning to use or develop them, and that therefore the individual will be supported by their minister or even the whole local community in going forward for further discernment; this local recognition needs to be consistent across a period of several months or even years, before it is then "tested" by the appropriate church authorities, usually delegated to more senior ministers who are trained and experienced in assessing and discerning a call, but often culminating in a regional, diocesan, or even national panel or conference, involving detailed interviews, written tasks, group exercises, even possibly medical or psychological assessments, after which a decision or recommendation is made—usually for the person to enter some form of theological education and ministerial training.

During that period, usually at least two or three years, of possibly residential or part-time training, further discernment will be undertaken constantly before the training institution recommends the candidate back to the church authorities for ordination or some form of accredited ministry, often with them graduating with some form of academic qualification with practical or pastoral application. In all mainline churches, it is accepted that this discernment belongs to the wider church, no matter how strong the individual's sense of their vocation might be—and it is up to the wider church to accredit the person's ministry and to a local church to accept him or her among them as a minister. Furthermore, you often begin with some form of "assistant" ministry, or "curacy" as it is known in some churches, under the watchful eye of a more experienced minister who will assist with further training, particularly with practical ministerial skills with regard to preaching and pastoral care, especially for "occasional offices" for major life events like baptisms, weddings, and funerals.

This might seem like a very long and convoluted process, and it can often take the best part of a decade from your initial sense of call to leading a church as its "incumbent" minister, a parish priest, or senior pastor—but this is not a dissimilar training time from other professions, like medicine or law, which also eventually result in similar positions of great trust and responsibility which will have an impact on many people's lives, for good or ill. So taking some time and care is absolutely right and proper, though it can feel very drawn out and frustrating for the candidate at times, which is why you need to find people who will support, advise, and guide you throughout the process, as I am recommending throughout this book.

And to help and guide all of this discernment process, some churches have produced a set of criteria or "competencies" which outline the gifts and skills required in ministry, as well as the personal qualities and attributes a minister will need to develop. These criteria undergo regular review, updating, and revision, so you should look at the latest summary of them on your own church's or denomination's website. Such criteria will help to guide the development of your sense of calling, and will be used for discernment and assessment at every stage of the process, from the initial conversations to a final report or recommendation. So I always give the list of the Church of England's current criteria to anyone who comes for a first hesitant chat to dip their toes in the water, and suggest that they go away and work through the summaries, line by line, to see which they are on the way to fulfilling—and which ones they would like me to help them develop further. Once I am convinced that they have enough potential under each heading to be taken further, I will then happily refer them to the diocesan process somewhere in London, or perhaps their home diocese if they are a student. The diocesan advisers will then also use these criteria to ascertain if a candidate fulfills each of the areas. When they are confident about this, and the bishop sponsors the candidate for a national panel, then several independent Bishops' Advisers will examine each candidate with regard to particular areas, such as vocational, pastoral, or educational, and then write up the evidence in their final recommendation back to the bishop.

So I usually suggest to those setting out on this journey that they spend a little time working through each of these criteria in turn, thinking about them line by line: which are the ones you feel more confident about, or where would you most like some help? One interesting exercise is to imagine that each line or clause is like a crime—and is there enough evidence to convict you of it, or would you "get off"?! It's a good idea to write down your reactions and reflections about them all in your journal, and take that to a wise priest or spiritual adviser for some further conversation. It is all very exciting—and I wish you joy and fun along the way through the process, as well as every blessing.

To help you with this process, I reproduce here four sets of criteria or competencies, taken from the work of the Theological Education group for the **Anglican** Communion (TEAC), the Candidacy Manual for the Evangelical **Lutheran** Church in America (ELCA—the largest of the Lutheran churches in the USA), the Book of Discipline for the United **Methodist** Church (UMC), and the **Disciples of Christ** (DoC). You will see that there is quite a lot of similarity and overlap between the various lists—so even if you are from a completely different denomination or church, you may find it helpful to work through these criteria, as well as researching to see if your tradition has something similar. It is also well worth spending some time praying over and meditating upon the short lists of criteria for ministry contained within the **New Testament**, such as 1 Timothy 3:1–13 and Titus 1:5–9.

You will also find that these websites and resources also describe the various processes used by the different churches for selection and discernment of potential ministers, and I have also included the processes in other denominations who do not necessarily have lists of criteria and competencies, such as the American **Baptist** Churches, the **Presbyterian** Church, and the **United** Church. It is also interesting and significant that the very full *Program of Priestly Formation* published by the **Roman Catholic** Bishops in the USA provides a detailed account of the processes and areas of formation required for the Catholic priesthood. There is a very helpful web page at the **Yale Divinity School** website with URL links to all the main Protestant denominations' processes and requirements for ministry training, which I have found very useful, see https://divinity.yale.edu/academics/ordination-and-denominational-preparation.

Theological Education for the Anglican Communion Priests and Transitional Deacons Target Group

The main Anglican Communion website has lots of helpful information: http://www.anglicancommunion.org/. For material about theological training, seminaries, and a database of Anglican theologians, see http://www.anglicancommunion.org/mission/theology.aspx. These criteria are taken from their grids of compentencies at http://www.anglicancommunion.org/media/108798/PriestsGrid110406.pdf.

This is a very full and helpful set of criteria, which draws upon and develops those used in the Church of England itself, but which is offered to the whole Anglican Communion, so it may be useful for you, especially if you are a member of an Anglican or Episcopal church in North America, Australia or New Zealand, India, or Africa. However, while the English one is focused on initial selection, this website grid helpfully goes on to give a development of each of these criteria for three other later stages: at the end of training before ordination; after three years of curacy/initial appointment to a local church; and continuing into lifelong ministry. Interestingly, there is also a similar grid for bishops, with developing criteria at the various stages of nomination, election or appointment, at consecration or the end of their first year as a bishop, and throughout the tenure of their office. I must confess that I would like to see those criteria being used back home for bishops in the Church of England!

A: Vocation and discernment

- Candidates are able to speak to their sense of vocation to ministry and mission, referring both to their own conviction and to the extent to which others—particularly the local church community—have confirmed it; this sense of vocation should be obedient, realistic and informed.
- Candidates have an awareness of Anglican-Episcopal tradition and practice of the local church and are willing to work within them.
- Candidates have an understanding of their gifts.
- Candidates have practical experience of lay ministry.
- A process of vocational discernment involving individual, parish, diocese and bishop is in place.

B: Clarity about the nature of ministry

- Candidates have a mature view of ministry as would be expected of the average church member.
- The local church community has openly recognised in each candidate gifts of leadership, respect for all, integrity, loving care and willingness to serve.
- Candidates are aware of the difference between lay discipleship, commissioned ministry and ordination, and believe themselves to be called to ordination.

C: Spirituality and faith

- Candidates should demonstrate personal commitment to Christ and a capacity to communicate the gospel.
- Candidates should show evidence of a commitment to a spiritual discipline, involving individual and corporate prayer and worship, such as to sustain and energise them in every aspect of their lives.
- Candidates are reading the Bible and praying systematically.
- Candidates can talk comfortably of their faith with a wide range of people and demonstrate the love of God in their lives.
- Candidates have an enquiring faith through the discipline of Anglican common prayer.

D: Personality, character and integrity

- Candidates are mature, stable and show that they are able to sustain the demanding role of a minister, and are able to face change and pressure in a flexible and balanced way.
- Candidates are people of proven integrity.
- Candidates have no unresolved personal, spiritual or psychological problems.
- Candidates are keenly aware of ethical issues, particularly those which are faced in their own society.
- Candidates are comfortable with people, individually and in groups.
- Candidates are willing to learn and modify their opinions.

E: Relationships

- Candidates demonstrate self-awareness and self-acceptance as a basis for developing open and healthy professional, personal and pastoral relationships as ministers.
- Candidates respect the will of the Church on matters of sexual morality.
- Candidates are recognised as leaders who have the respect of the congregation and of the wider community.
- Candidates are able to establish good relationships with many types of people.
- Candidates are aware of the demands of human relationships.

F: Leadership and collaboration

- Candidates show potential for leadership in the Church and possibly in the wider community.
- Candidates demonstrate an example of faith and discipleship.
- Candidates collaborate effectively with others.
- Candidates have potential to guide and shape the life of the church community and God's mission in the world.

G: Awareness of context

- Candidates show an awareness of and sensitivity to their own social, and cultural contexts and have the ability to make wise observations about the world around them.
- Candidates have some experience of seeking to meet some of the immediate needs of their community.
- Candidates have some awareness of world issues and of the differing response of the church to diverse contexts.
- Candidates are given the opportunity, if possible, to experience another part of the Anglican Communion during theological studies, through internships.

H: Biblical and theological competence

- Candidates have the necessary intellectual capacity and quality of mind to undertake a course of theological study and preparation and to cope with the intellectual demands of ministry.
- Candidates show an understanding of the Christian faith and a desire to deepen their understanding.
- Candidates have a broad understanding of the scope of the Bible and understand the importance of biblical interpretation.
- Candidates have some appreciation of the value of church history, liturgy, ethics and social action.

I: Practical competence

Preaching, Pastoral care, Liturgy, Training & Education, Ecumenical, Administration
- Candidates show some familiarity with parochial, diocesan and provincial / national church structures.
- Candidates have gifts for and a desire to proclaim the word, communicate the gospel and teach the faith.
- Candidates have a general appreciation of the liturgical tradition.
- Candidates have an approachable and caring attitude.
- Candidates have some experience of basic administration or are willing to learn.

J: Mission and evangelism

- Candidates demonstrate a passion for mission and evangelism that is reflected in thought, prayer and action.
- Candidates understand the key issues and opportunities for Christian mission within the contemporary culture.
- Candidates enable others to develop their callings as witnesses and advocates of the gospel by word and action.

K: The Anglican Way

- Candidates and bishops, through diocesan processes, engage in an interactive discernment to ensure the corporate nature of selection of candidates.
- Candidates are committed to the worship, mission and ministry of the local church (not uncritically).

L: Spouse and family (where applicable)

- Candidates have fully discussed with spouse (and family, as appropriate) the consequences of possible selection, training, ordination and ministry.

The Church of England

Material about exploring a sense of call or vocation can be found on the Church of England website: https://www.churchofengland.org/life-events/vocations, where there are also some helpful ideas about supporting or developing people's sense of calling: https://www.churchofengland.org/more/diocesan-resources/ministry/supporting-candidates-through-selection. The current Summary of Criteria for candidates for ordained ministry can be found at https://www.churchofengland.org/sites/default/files/2017-10/selection_criteria_for_ordained_ministry.pdf.

The Episcopal Church

Main website: https://www.episcopalchurch.org/. See *The Constitution & Canons Together with the Rules of Order for the Government of the Protestant Episcopal Church in the United States of America Otherwise Known as The Episcopal Church*, adopted and revised 2015 (New York: The Episcopal Church, 2016). Available online at https://www.episcopalchurch.org/files/documents/2015_candc.pdf. See especially Article VIII, "Of Requisites for Ordination" (p. 6). And Canons 1-16 of Title III on Ministry (pp. 67–130).

The Anglican Church of Australia

The latest guidelines on the Requirements for Ordination can be found here: https://www.anglican.org.au/data/1074_Minimum_Requirements_for_Ordination_Draft_June_2017.pdf.

The Anglican Church of Southern Africa

Main website: https://anglicanchurchsa.org/.

The Evangelical Lutheran Church in America (ELCA)

The Evangelical Lutheran Church in America (ELCA) is acknowledged as the largest Lutheran church in America, although it must be recognized that there are other Lutheran bodies, such as those linked to the Missouri Synod. For reasons of space in this book, references to the "Lutheran" church or "Lutherans" all refer to ELCA. It publishes a lot of useful material, including a Candidacy Manual, a Summary of Candidacy, a Candidate Plan, and a set of Frequently Asked Questions about Candidacy at http://elca.org/Resources/Candidacy.

The **Candidacy Manual** provides a complete detailed guide to the process of discernment and selection for ministry, endorsement, approval, and assignment, plus examples of interview questions and the various forms and paperwork. We reproduce here the latest available version of the Standards for the Offices of Ministry from the Candidacy Manual, revised May 24, 2017.

2 Standards for the Offices of Ministry

People who have discerned a call to rostered ministry will demonstrate a commitment to Christ and build upon the characteristics of a missional leader as understood through a Lutheran confessional lens.

2.1 Rostered Ministers

Through formation in the candidacy process, candidates will develop an understanding of four basic principles:

2.1.1 We Are Church

The ELCA is a church centered around worship of the triune God: Father, Son, and Holy Spirit. The good news of Jesus Christ conveyed through God's Word and the sacraments liberates God's people and gives them the freedom and courage to wonder, discover and boldly participate in God's mission in the world. In our life together we gather around the presence of the crucified and risen Christ, and we respond to the leadership of the Holy Spirit by engaging in ministry in the world.

Competencies

The list of competencies provided below is a descriptive narrative, not a template or checklist. It attempts to describe the types of skills and characteristics the church seeks for all rostered ministers. Candidacy committees and seminary faculty should use these competency descriptions in a manner that is flexible, adaptive to context and candidate, and attuned to the leading of the Holy Spirit.

1. Rooted in the presence and activity of the triune God: Father, Son and Holy Spirit. A rostered minister nurtures a vibrant faith and relationship with the triune God within a community of faith and leads other Christians to do likewise as they participate in God's mission. This competency can be assessed as a Candidacy Committee inquires about a candidate's ability to:
   a. engage in theological and spiritual discernment that manifests a faith in Father, Son and Holy Spirit,
   b. articulate and live out a clear Christian identity, and
   c. interpret the Scriptures as the norm for understanding God's mission in the world.

2. Actively participates in God's mission as a part of the church. Some key aspects related to this competency are:

   a. an ability to cultivate a compelling vision for ministry,

   b. equipping people to share faith stories,

   c. skills in hospitality that invite people to a life of discipleship, and

   d. an awareness of the interconnectedness of the church beyond the local congregation.

3. Cultivates vision and purpose. This competency includes:

   a. the use of spiritual disciplines (e.g., prayer, biblical and theological reflection, and spiritual direction),

   b. knowledge of societal and cultural trends that can inform the church's vision and sense of purpose,

   c. skills for leading congregations and other groups in discernment of God's mission in the world (including the incorporation of input from a diversity of sources and people), and

   d. courage to lead God's people into that mission as discerned.

4. Leadership skills. Some important indicators of this competency are:

   a. demonstration of adaptive leadership skills that are sensitive to context,

   b. demonstration of skills for leading a community of faith through change while addressing conflicts that might emerge,

   c. capacity to engage people and lead them toward active participation in God's mission in the world,

   d. facility for encouraging collegial decision-making processes,

   e. demonstration of personal holistic stewardship and skill in equipping others, and

   f. grasp of how administrative structures and procedures can serve mission in the life of the church.

2.1.2 We Are Lutheran

While not claiming to possess exclusive theological wisdom in the one, holy, catholic and apostolic church, Lutherans proclaim the good news of Jesus Christ through a clear focus on God's grace received through faith along with discipleship and participation in God's mission that is a lived response to that grace.

Competencies

1. Engages the way of the cross. Empowered by the resurrected Christ, a rostered minister shows people the crucified Christ through word and deed and enables them to envision what God is doing in the world and in their lives. Some indicators of this competency include:

a. willingness to confront and engage suffering in the lives of others and in one's own life, especially among marginalized people,

b. exhibiting qualities of servant leadership,

c. willingness to serve, risk and sacrifice for the sake of God's mission, including an ability to identify and lead in exposing the principalities and powers operative in a given context, and

d. responding to life crises as opportunities for experiencing new life.

2. Proclaims the faith. Clear indicators for this competency are the candidate's ability to:

a. understand the Word as law and gospel,

b. teach Scripture,

c. share the faith with others,

d. provide Christian education for all ages and cultures,

e. articulate theological wisdom, and

f. live a disciplined spiritual life.

2.1.3 We Are Church Together

The ELCA recognizes the interdependence of all expressions of the church—congregations, synods and the churchwide organization—as well as a wider ecclesiastical ecology, which includes seminaries, social ministry agencies, campus ministries, church camps and conference centers, and other affiliated agencies. This church also values the ecumenical interdependence we share with our full communion partners both locally and globally.

Competencies

1. Interprets mission. This competency reflects the ability of a candidate to articulate and interpret in a compelling manner, both theologically and contextually, the wider mission of the ELCA through its interdependent partners and expressions. This competency includes a commitment to the mission of the wider church, including synods and the churchwide organization, as well as related institutions and agencies of the ELCA, and facility in interpreting and motivating support for the ELCA beyond the local congregation.

2. Cultivates Christian community, discipleship, leadership formation and the practice of reconciliation of differences. A rostered minister effectively forms and leads Christian communities that intentionally foster the growth of disciples of Jesus Christ and attend to the formation of leaders in the church. Some indicators of this competency are:

a. gifts for forming partnerships and networks,
b. the practice of reconciliation and mutual empowerment among diverse groups,
c. convening and empowering teams for mission, and
d. a sense of stewardship in cultivating gifts manifest in a community of believers and delegating and sharing tasks tailored to those gifts.

3. Cares for people. A ministry of care encompasses both congregational and community care. Some key aspects of this competency include:

a. visitation,
b. counseling,
c. equipping the baptized to provide ministries of care, both within the congregation and in the wider community,
d. knowledge of community resources for appropriate referrals and participation, and
e. sensitivity to people in major life and cultural transitions.

4. Practices wellness in one's personal life (section 4.1.2). Some factors to consider in this area:

a. a vibrant and resilient faith,
b. a balance of work, play and self-care,
c. a maintenance of clear and healthy boundaries in all relationships,
d. an attention to diet, exercise and mental/physical health, and
e. a nurturing of healthy family relationships.

2.1.4 We Are Church For The Sake Of The World

As baptized people of God, we believe we are freed in Christ to love and serve our neighbor. This church, accordingly, is a catalyst, convener and bridge builder that views both the church and the world as interdependent in a way that fosters mutual learning and growth. We participate in partnerships for the sake of unity among Christians, collaboration and dialogue with other faith communities, and for justice and peace locally and globally.

Competencies

1. Evangelizes. A rostered minister actively believes and carries out Christ's command to go out and share the gospel with neighbors. Some key factors related to this competency are:

a. passion and imagination for sharing the gospel,
b. sensitivity and skill for welcoming the stranger into community,
c. discovering and implementing creative ways to share the gospel with people outside the church,

d. listening to people's stories and assisting them to interpret their experience in light of the gospel,

e. valuing of Christian community as formative for faith, and

f. natural and authentic gift for engaging people, under the guidance of the Holy Spirit, in the depths of their lives.

2. Relates theology with history, context and culture. A rostered minister understands and interprets context and culture through the lens of Christian faith and leads a community to opportunities where the gospel can be understood and shared by people in specific cultural contexts. Some important indicators of this competency include:

a. an ability to engage culture and context theologically, critically and creatively with a sensitivity to historical factors,

b. analysis of community demographics and trends,

c. engagement with complex social and religious issues as a practical theologian in context,

d. sensitivity to cross-cultural, intra-cultural, and counter-cultural dynamics, and

e. skill in addressing cultural differences.

3. Equips and sends disciples into the world. A rostered minister prepares disciples to discern the leading of the Spirit as they share the gospel with neighbors in word and deed. Some important considerations for this competence are:

a. demonstrated capacity to mobilize people of faith with different gifts and perspectives that can enrich the church's witness in the world and lead to acts of mercy and justice,

b. personal embodiment of the Christian faith in one's daily life,

c. demonstrated capacity for cultivating communities of well-being and holistic stewardship as illustrated in the Wholeness Wheel (section 4.1.2),

d. theological sensitivity to the presence and activity of God in the world,

e. recognition of the public vocation of the Christian community in the world, and

f. the ability to interpret that vocation to people of faith.

Because this is a time of unprecedented change and increasing diversity, not all ministry contexts will have the same imagination for mission and ministry. The church, therefore, needs adaptive leaders with demonstrated abilities for appreciating and celebrating different orientations toward mission, fostering positive relationships within a context, and moving together with others toward a common vision for mission. Adaptive leaders are prepared to undertake ministry in a variety of locations and to assist a community in developing a common life that participates more fully in God's mission in the world. The church acknowledges that a rostered minister's adaptive leadership skills, reflecting the cited competencies, will not be fully formed during the candidacy process. A well-prepared missional candidate understands that the candidacy process is the beginning of a lifelong process of learning and formation for leadership.

The United Methodist Church

Main website: http://www.umc.org/. *The Book of Discipline of the United Methodist Church* (Nashville: United Methodist Publishing House) sets out the "qualifications for ordination" in paragraph 304 (pp. 225–26 of the 2016 edition; http://www.umc.org/what-we-believe/para-304-qualifications -for-ordination) as follows:

¶ 304. Qualifications for Ordination

1. Those whom the Church ordains shall be conscious of God's call to ordained ministry, and their call shall be acknowledged and authenticated by the Church. God's call has many manifestations, and the Church cannot structure a single test of authenticity. Nevertheless, the experience of the Church and the needs of its ministry require certain qualities of faith, life, and practice from those who seek ordination as deacons and elders. In order that The United Methodist Church may be assured that those persons who present themselves as candidates for ordained ministry are truly called of God, the Church expects persons seeking ordination to:

   a) Have a personal faith in Christ and be committed to Christ as Savior and Lord.
   b) Nurture and cultivate spiritual disciplines and patterns of holiness.
   c) Teach and model generous Christian giving with a focus on tithing as God's standard of giving
   d) Acknowledge a call by God to give themselves completely to ordained ministry following Jesus's pattern of love and service.
   e) Communicate persuasively the Christian faith in both oral and written form.

f) Make a commitment to lead the whole Church in loving service to humankind.

g) Give evidence of God's gifts for ordained ministry, evidence of God's grace in their lives, and promise of future usefulness in the mission of the Church.

h) Be persons in whom the community can place trust and confidence.

i) Accept that Scripture contains all things necessary for salvation through faith in God through Jesus Christ; be competent in the disciplines of Scripture, theology, church history, and Church polity; possess the skills essential to the practice of ordained ministry; and lead in making disciples for Jesus Christ.

j) Be accountable to The United Methodist Church, accept its Doctrinal Standards and Discipline and authority, accept the supervision of those appointed to this ministry, and be prepared to live in the covenant of its ordained ministers.

2. For the sake of the mission of Jesus Christ in the world and the most effective witness to the Christian gospel, and in consideration of the influence of an ordained minister on the lives of other persons both within and outside the Church, the Church expects those who seek ordination to make a complete dedication of themselves to the highest ideals of the Christian life. To this end, they agree to exercise responsible self-control by personal habits conducive to bodily health, mental and emotional maturity, integrity in all personal relationships, fidelity in marriage and celibacy in singleness, social responsibility, and growth in grace and in the knowledge and love of God.

For the rest of the Book of Discipline, see http://www.umc.org/what-we -believe/is-the-book-of-discipline-available-online. The Baltimore-Washington Conference of the United Methodist Church District Committee on Ordained Ministry produces a very helpful and useful **handbook** which provides a good example of the process and procedures for discernment, plus all the forms and paperwork:http://78455c2ccb400d517780-dac 10a94c714bbb9d8050040bb216432.r90.cf2.rackcdn.com/uploaded /d/0e5330681_1470938323_dcomhandbookforthebwc.pdf.

The Christian Church (Disciples of Christ)

General information about the Christian Church (Disciples of Christ) can be found on their main website at http://disciples.org/gcom/. The Christian Church (Disciples of Christ) sets out its criteria, policies, and processes in its *Theological Foundations and Policies and Criteria for the Ordering of Ministry of the Christian Church (Disciples of Christ)*; see: http://disciples.org/wp-content/uploads/2014/07/TFPCOM-Final.pdf. We reproduce here the section on personal qualifications, taken from the version Amendment 3 (2016, posted online in August 2017), p. 16:

A.2. Personal Qualifications for the Order of Ministry.

The church expects to find within the women and men it receives into the order of ministry:
  a. Faith in Jesus Christ, commitment to a life of Christian discipleship and nurturing spiritual practices;
  b. A sense of call to the ministry affirmed by the church;
  c. An understanding of pastoral identity;
  d. Capacity to engage in theological reflection;
  e. Strong moral character and personal integrity;
  f. Commitment to spiritual, physical and emotional wellness sufficient for healthy ministry;
  g. Care and compassion for all people with appropriate relational skills;
  h. Responsible personal financial management;
  i. Wise and generous stewardship in the use of God's gifts;
  j. Skills and abilities necessary for the rigorous, pastoral tasks of ministry.
See also the further details about educational requirements for training and ordination on pp. 19–21, and also the ministerial Code of Ethics, pp. 42–44; some information on procedures and processes for candidacy can be found on pp. 22–23.

Other Churches' Processes and Procedures

Several of the various mainline churches referenced in this book do not seem to publish easily identifiable information about their ordination criteria or requirements. However, their official websites still contain lots of interesting and helpful material about their understanding of ministry and their processes for selection and ordination.

The African Methodist Episcopal Church

Their official website contains lots of very interesting and helpful information about the AME Church, although specific information about ministry and vocation discernment procedures is not immediately obvious; see https://www.ame-church.com/.

American Baptist Churches

The Baptist tradition and ecclesiology is much more centered on the individual and the local congregation, rather than on national structures or episcopal-type leaders. For more information, see the helpful description on the Yale Divinity School website: https://divinity.yale.edu/academics/denominational-programs/denominational-programs-baptist. However, American Baptist Churches still have detailed processes for discernment, selection, and authorization of potential ministers. See their *Recommended Procedures for Ordination, Commissioning, and Recognition for the Christian Ministry in the American Baptist Churches* (Valley Forge, PA: Ministerial Leadership Commission & The Ministers Council, American Baptist Churches USA, revised November 1997), available at www.abc-usa.org/wp-content/uploads/2012/06/Ordination_Stds.pdf.

The Presbyterian Church of the United States of America

See their main website at http://www.pcusa.org/. Although PCUSA does not have a list of criteria or competencies in the same way as these other churches, it has very helpful pages about preparation for ministry: http://oga.pcusa.org/section/mid-council-ministries/prep4min/. There is also a very useful work, *Advisory Handbook for Preparation for Ministry in the Presbyterian Church (U.S.A.)*, which outlines all their procedures for fostering and discerning vocations, available at http://www.pcusa.org/site_media/media/uploads/prep4min/pdfs/p4mah_2017_rel_2.1.pdf.

The United Church of Christ

See their main website at http://www.ucc.org/. You can find a helpful explanation of their different forms of ministry at http://www.ucc.org/ministers_authorized, and further information about discerning a call at http://www.ucc.org/ministers_considering-ministry, and their handbook for those going through the process at http://d3n8a8pro7vhmx.cloudfront .net/unitedchurchofchrist/legacy_url/1299/mom-2003-20ordained-1 .pdf?1418424766.

The Roman Catholic Church

Like the above churches, the Roman Catholic Church does not publish a simple "checklist" of criteria or compentencies for potential ordinands. However, the United States Conference of Catholic Bishops does publish a very interesting and helpful *Program of Priestly Formation*, 5th ed. (Washington, DC: USCCB, 2006), which has a detailed treatment of the "nature and mission of the ministerial priesthood," as well as extensive descriptions of the various areas of formation needed by candidates for the priesthood, especially human formation (character, self-knowledge, sexuality, and preparation for celibacy), spiritual (prayer, the eucharist, Bible reading, spiritual direction), intellectual (theology and philosophy, moral theology, homiletics, ecumenism), pastoral (preaching, sacraments, pastoral sensitivity), and living in community. There is also an impressive commitment to continuing evaluation and life-long formation and education. The *Program* is also available online at http://www.usccb.org /beliefs-and-teachings/vocations/priesthood/priestly-formation/upload /ProgramforPriestlyFormation.pdf.

Liturgies and services of ordination

In appendix 2, we noted that while the actual criteria, competencies, and procedures in the different churches varied, there was still a remarkable congruence both in the seriousness with which they all take the process of discernment and testing of a vocation, and also in the general shape of the list of criteria and competencies—they are all looking for similar things. Equally, we should expect that the liturgies and words used in the various services to mark ordination or the setting apart of a person for ministry will vary considerably, reflecting the different traditions, churchmanships, theological and ecclesiological understandings of the range of Christian denominations.

And yet, there is still an extraordinary similarity in the overall shape of these services. Most, if not all, Christian churches apparently feel the need to mark the occasion of somebody offering their life to the service of God and his church with a formal ceremony which bears a striking resemblance to a baptism or a wedding, with hymns, readings, prayers, and a sermon, framing a central event in which blunt questions are asked and solemn vows and promises are made, culminating in a symbolic—or sacramental, if you are from a more catholic tradition—act, not the use of water as in baptism or the giving of a ring as in marriage, but the formal laying of the leaders' hands upon the head of each candidate in turn, while invoking the gift of the Holy Spirit. And as with baptism and marriage, some traditions prefer to hold these ceremonies within the context of a communion service or eucharist—before sending out those who have been somehow changed by the ceremony into their new life in the church and the world.

At the original retreat in which these addresses were first given, I gave the candidates for ordination draft printouts of the actual service which would take place a couple of days later with the specific words which would be said or sung or prayed over them, and asked them to highlight in different colors the four themes of preaching and teaching, pastoral care, suffering the way of the cross, and entering into the very life of God through prayer—and then to pray and meditate upon their colored orders of service. They found it such a profound experience that they all insisted on using these scrappy bits of paper with the colorings in and the highlighted scribbles in pen or pencil on their great day in preference to the beautifully printed orders which better reflected the grandeur of the ceremony in the beauty of the cathedral! Therefore in the English edition of this book, I reprinted—with permission—the Church of England's Liturgy for the Ordination of Priests and Deacons in this appendix, and encouraged readers to highlight the text in the way that you may have just done for the criteria and competencies in appendix 2.

In preparing for this revision, I have studied as many examples of ordination services as I could find from the Church of England and the Anglican Communion, with slightly different services being used in the Anglican churches of Southern Africa, Australia, New Zealand, and the Episcopal Church in the USA, comparing them with examples from the Roman Catholic and Orthodox churches, the Presbyterian Church, the United Methodists, the African Methodist Episcopal Church, Lutherans, Baptists, the Disciples of Christ, and various versions of the reformed United or Uniting Churches of Christ—and I have quoted liberally from them in the third chapter of each Part about each particular ministry within the ordination services. With so many different forms of service and versions of liturgies across all these mainline denominations, it is simply not possible to reproduce them all here—and it would be invidious to prefer some over others. Instead, there are some websites and resources to find examples used in your own church tradition provided at the end of this appendix, but first we need to spell out briefly the overall shape of the usual pattern followed in these ordination services.

The gathering, welcome, or call to worship

These services are usually presided over by one or several senior church leaders like an archbishop or bishop, moderator, superintendent, chairman or chairwoman, that is, those who have authority to represent the wider church, usually at a more than local level, perhaps at a regional, diocesan, or even national level. This is because, except for the most independent congregationalist churches, ordination or recognition for ministry is much wider than the local—and brings with it accompanying responsibilities and authority to speak on behalf of the church, or even for God! And so the appropriate senior minister, leader, or bishop—often beautifully arrayed in colorful robes—will welcome everyone to the service, especially if it is in a large church like a cathedral, and invite us all to participate in worship, to praise God and to pray for those to be ordained. This part of the service may also often include the opportunity for confession of sin and absolution, so that we enter into the rest of it as the forgiven people of God.

The presentation of the candidates

Probably nervous, like a bride walking up the aisle, those who are to be ordained will be formally presented to the senior leader or bishop, perhaps with their individual names being read out and details of the church or congregation where they will serve. The bishop or senior minister will usually interrogate the person(s) presenting the candidates about whether they have been properly trained and examined, and their vocations tested and affirmed by the wider church. The candidates themselves may also be asked if they truly believe themselves to be called by God to this ministry.

The declarations or statement of ministry

The bishop or leader will then often deliver a substantial statement, declaring or describing the work or ministry to which these candidates will be ordained. The former Bishop of London used to call this part the "Job Spec"—and it is not hard to see why. There will be a list of tasks or functions which a deacon, priest, elder, or minister will be expected to perform, ranging from preaching and teaching to the pastoral care of those committed to his charge, along with special occasions like baptisms, weddings, and funerals, all in the context of proclaiming the good news of the Christian gospel. It can be all very daunting—especially for those who are about to have these expectations thrust upon them!

Questions, vows, and promises

As a consequence of the declarations, the candidates will now be expected to stand up and be counted. There are likely to be formal questions from the leader or bishop to check that they really do believe and accept the Christian faith as this particular church understands it, and that they are willing to work within it and teach it. They will be asked to make solemn promises, binding for the rest of their lives, about their own way of life and that of their family, a commitment to prayer, Bible reading, and theological study, an acceptance of the discipline of the church and the authority of their senior leaders, and a willingness to serve whatever the cost. As with wedding vows, these promises are pretty much like signing an open check—and we have no idea what it will cost us in due course in the future. It is therefore good that these vows and promises usually conclude with the candidates' families, friends, and congregations being asked to promise to pray for them and support them in their ministry ahead.

The invocation of the Holy Spirit and prayers

But even with this support of our loved ones, this kind of life is not something any human being can take on lightly or easily survive. Therefore the leaders will normally remind the candidates at this point of the foolish pointlessness of trying to perform their ministry solely in their own strength. Sometimes, the bishop or senior minister(s) will leave their seats, *cathedra*, or throne, and come down to kneel alongside the candidates to lead them in prayer to almighty God to provide the strength, courage, and wisdom necessary for Christian ministry. This is often accompanied by singing a version of a very old canticle dating back to the early church invoking the Holy Spirit—the *Veni Creator Spiritus*—"come, Holy Spirit, our souls inspire." This leads naturally into a period of silent prayer, culminating in spoken prayers, perhaps using a litany, or individual prayers for the candidates.

The ordination or laying on of hands

If water is the sign of baptism, and rings for marriage, the symbolic or sacramental act which brings about the reality of ordination is laying on of hands. This goes right back to the days of the earliest church in Antioch: "while they were worshipping the Lord and fasting, the Holy Spirit said, 'Set apart for me Barnabas and Saul for the work to which I have called them.' Then after fasting and praying, they laid their hands on them and sent them off" (Acts 13:2–3; see also Paul's comments about laying hands on Timothy in 1 Tim. 4:14 and 2 Tim. 1:6). Therefore, the individual candidates will come and kneel before the bishop or senior minister(s), who lay their hands on each candidate's head, praying for them by name in turn to receive the Holy Spirit. This may be done by the bishop or leader alone, symbolizing their authority, or by several senior ministers together, symbolizing the corporate nature of leadership—or indeed by all the ministers present, symbolizing the collegiality of ministry, which is never just mine alone.

Giving of the Bible and the welcome

There may be other additional symbolic acts as the candidate is given a copy of the Bible to remind them to preach and teach it, or a chalice and paten to use at communion services, or they may be robed with a stole or some other vestment denoting their office. This part of the service usually ends with some form of welcome, where other ministers present accept the newly ordained into their fellowship, which may lead naturally into the sharing of the Peace—and the chance for the ordinands to greet their families, friends, and new congregational members and receive their congratulations. It can all take quite some time!

The commissioning and sending out

The actual ordinations may be sandwiched in the middle of a larger service, with hymns, readings, and an appropriate sermon beforehand, and followed by a communion service or eucharist in which the newly ordained participate in some way, perhaps assisting with the administration of bread and wine. Eventually, however, the service reaches its final climax as the new ministers are lined up with the bishop or senior leaders and given a final prayer of blessing and commissioning, before being sent out from the church or cathedral into their new ministry in the church and the world.

For more information, see Stephen V. Sprinkle's helpful book *Ordination: Celebrating the Gift of Ministry* (St. Louis: Chalice Press, 2004), which contains interesting discussions about the understandings of ministry and ordination, including reprinting in an appendix examples of ordination liturgies taken from PCUSA, UCC, DoC, and a specific sample of a Baptist ordination with other texts from the ABC (used in my chapter 3's above). For further detail and history, see the very careful treatment of all the various processes and liturgies from basic principles and earliest rites up to the vast array of different services in all the various churches today, in James F. Puglisi's massive work in four volumes: *The Process of Admission to Ordained Ministry: A Comparative Study* (Collegeville, MN: Liturgical Press, 2001). A more accessible discussion of the different understandings of ministry in churches where ministry is recognized and shared between ABC, DoC, ELCA, PCUSA, UCC, and UMC can be found in *God's Ecumenical Ministry, Shared: A Manual for Persons Involved in Ecumenical Shared Ministry*, introduction by Michael Kinnamon (Ecumenical Shared Ministries Roundtable, January 1999)—see especially the explanation of the different terms and forms of ministerial office across these churches, pp. 27–28, and the comparison of different guidelines, authority, procedures, salaries, pensions, benefits, etc., in its appendices.

The various texts quoted in the third chapter of each Part about each particular ministry within the ordination services can mostly be found online, as follows:

Anglican Communion

CofE, Church of England: https://www.churchofengland.org/prayer -and-worship/worship-texts-and-resources/common-worship/ministry /common-worship-ordination-services.

APBA: A Prayer Book for Australia, Ordinal: http://www.melbourne anglican.org.au/mission/theologicaleducation/Documents/The-Ordinal -abridged.pdf.

ANZPB: A New Zealand Prayer Book/ He Karakia Mihinare o Aotearoa (authorised 26 May 1988): http://anglicanprayerbook.nz/, see especially pp. 885–924.

TEC, The Episcopal Church of the United States of America: https:// www.episcopalchurch.org/files/book_of_common_prayer.pdf —see pp. 509–55 .

The Roman Catholic Church

RC: The Roman Pontifical, the main compendium of all Catholic services and liturgies, does not seem to be available freely online, but the liturgy for the Ordination of Priests, as published by the United States Conference of Catholic Bishops, can be found at http://ordination.ceegee.org/rite.pdf.

Other churches and liturgies quoted include:

ABC, American Baptist Churches: www.abc-usa.org/wp-content /uploads/2012/06/Ordination_Stds.pdf. For more information, see also https://ministerscouncil.com/. Sample service quoted from Sprinkle, *Ordination*, pp. 247–56.

AME, African Methodist Episcopal Church; a sample service can be found at http://www.famechurch.org/Annual-Conference/87th-schedule -ORDINATION-SERVICE-web.pdf.

DoC, Disciples of Christ: http://disciples.org/wp-content/uploads /2015/04/Ordination_Service_Guidelines.pdf.

ELCA, Evangelican Lutheran Church of America: http://www.elca .org/Resources/Worship?_ga=2.60431469.1791219526.1517615116-4351915 63.1517615116#Liturgy.

PCUSA, Presbyterian Church of the United States of America: www.pgh presbytery.org/forms/pdfs/com/book_of_occasional_services.pdf. See also https://www.presbyterianmission.org/ministries/worship/pastoral -occasional-services/.

UCC, United Church of Christ: http://d3n8a8pro7vhmx.cloudfront .net/unitedchurchofchrist/legacy_url/245/order-for-ordination-o-min istry-bow.pdf?1418423611.

UMC, United Methodist Church: https://www.umcdiscipleship.org /resources/services-for-ordering-of-ministry-in-the-united-methodist -church-2017-2020.

Further reading, websites, and other resources

For this international edition, we have combined books published in both the UK and the USA, since many are available worldwide through websites like https://www.amazon.com/ and https://www.bookdepository .com/. Websites are of course internationally available, and you are encouraged to check those particularly relating to your own church, denomination, or country. Don't forget that there is also a public Facebook page dedicated to this book where you can find resources, post comments and questions, and join in the discussions. See www.facebook.com /FourMinistriesOneJesus.

A very helpful and comprehensive guide to Christian ministry in all the mainline American Protestant churches can be found in Ian S. Markham and Oran E. Warder, *An Introduction to Ministry: A Primer for Renewed Life and Leadership in Mainline Protestant Congregations* (Malden, MA: Wiley-Blackwell, 2016). Chapter 1 on vocation and calling, and chapter 2 on the importance of proper training, are both extremely relevant to this book and include helpful bibliographies; the rest of the book deals with all the different aspects of ministry from liturgy and worship to theology and preaching, church history, ethics, education, music, evangelism, and church growth, as well as practical application to administration, finance, congregational dynamics, etc., much of which is applicable whatever is your church or wherever you live and minister.

Websites about vocation and selection

There is a lot of helpful material on vocation for lay and ordained ministry, including about the processes and criteria for selection for the Church of England, at https://www.churchofengland.org/life-events/vocations/.

There are of course similar pages on all the websites of the main Christian denominations, as listed in Appendix 3 above.

Bible-reading websites for preaching and teaching

Oremus, which means "let us pray," is a very helpful website which contains a lot of useful resources about the Bible, liturgy, hymns, and prayer: http://www.oremus.org/index.html. It also contains a Bible browser, where you can choose from several translations of the Bible and find passages quickly: http://bible.oremus.org/.

You can also download the Revised Common Lectionary (RCL) into your online diary or calendar from the Oremus Almanac website, which is very convenient as it gives you links to all the readings set for each day of the year: http://almanac.oremus.org/lectionary/2017.html. There are lots of other websites which include resources about the RCL set readings, and ideas and resources connected to them; see, for example, www.textweek .com, which is based in the USA and has lots of helpful links for the RCL to books, commentaries, films, art, and much more, as well as links to sites designed to help you prepare sermons for each Sunday, such as http://www.workingpreacher.org/.

Prayer and spirituality websites

There are any number of online prayer resources, but here are a few to get you started.

The Church of England website is again helpful, providing the texts for daily prayers and readings set for Morning Prayer, Evening Prayer, and Night Prayer for yesterday, today, and the next four weeks at https://www.churchofengland.org/prayer-worship/join-us-in-daily-prayer.aspx.

The two sites from a Jesuit tradition which were mentioned in Part 4, on praying with John's portrait (page 163 above), are:

- www.sacredspace.ie/, which is maintained by the Irish Jesuits and Loyola Press, and gives you daily readings and prayers, with gentle music if you wish;
- www.pray-as-you-go.org/, which is maintained by the British Jesuits, and provides a daily audio podcast, lasting ten to fifteen minutes, with

music, Bible reading with some comments, and guided prayer. The site also contains a large amount of other information about Ignatian spirituality, retreats, and other resources.

The **London Centre for Spiritual Direction**, right in the heart of the City, next to the Bank of England and the temples of mammon, maintains a very useful website, https://www.lcsd.org.uk/, including information about spiritual direction, what it entails, and how to go about finding a director: https://www.lcsd.org.uk/spiritual-direction/.

Retreats and pastoral support for ministers

There are many retreat houses and spirituality centers around the world, including some monasteries and convents, which organize retreats, spiritual direction, and refreshment for those in Christian ministry, so check out those near you. I have been involved with the **Society of Mary and Martha**, a retreat and support center in the Teign Valley on the edge of Dartmoor in Devon, since its early days, having been founded in 1987, and I am honored to have been involved with it since the early days. Visit their website for ideas or suggestions: https://www.sheldon.uk.com/, or contact them at smm@sheldon.uk.com. International readers may also benefit from their more recent initiative, the Sheldon Hub, an online resource and community for all those in active ministry, with videos, blogs, discussion fora, and so forth; you apply to join it at https://www.sheldonhub.org/.

Further reading

We have noted at the end of each part of this book the importance of maintaining a habit of prayer and reflection, together with reading and reflection. The suggestions below are not meant to be exhaustive (though some may be exhausting!), but are based on my experience of guiding callings and vocations both in London and in many seminaries around the world. Please add any new suggestions of books you find helpful, or comments about any of those below, on the Faceook page for this book, www.facebook.com/FourMinistriesOneJesus.

On vocation and calling

Adair, John. *How to Find Your Vocation*. Norwich: Canterbury, 2000; 2nd ed., 2002.

Bradshaw, Paul F. *Rites of Ordination: Their History and Theology*. Collegeville, MN: Liturgical Press, 2013.

Cahalan, Kathleen A. *The Stories We Live: Finding God's Calling All Around Us*. Grand Rapids: Eerdmans, 2017.

Cahalan, Kathleen A., and Bonnie J. Miller-McLemore, eds. *Calling All Years Good: Christian Vocation throughout Life's Seasons*. Grand Rapids: Eerdmans, 2017.

Crafton, Barbara Cawthorne. *Called*. New York: Church Publishing, 2017.

Cutié, Albert. *Talking God: Preaching to Contemporary Congregations*. New York: Morehouse Publishing, 2016.

Dewar, Francis. *Called or Collared?* New ed. London: SPCK, 2000.

Koskela, Douglas M. *Calling and Clarity: Discovering What God Wants for Your Life*. Grand Rapids: Eerdmans, 2015.

Lathrop, Gordon. *The Pastor: A Spirituality*. Minneapolis: Fortress, 2006.

Mellott, David M. *Finding Your Way in Seminary: What to Expect, How to Thrive*. Louisville: Westminster John Knox, 2016.

Portaro, Sam Anthony. *Transforming Vocation*. Louisville: Westminster John Knox, 2015.

Richardson, Charles. *This Is Our Calling*. London: SPCK, 2004.

Smidt, Corwin E. *Pastors and Public Life: The Changing Face of American Protestant Clergy*. New York: Oxford University Press, 2016.

Willimon, William H. *How Odd of God: Chosen for the Curious Vocation of Preaching*. Louisville: Westminster John Knox, 2015.

Witham, Larry. *Who Shall Lead Them? The Future of Ministry in America*. New York: Oxford University Press, 2005.

On Christian ministry

Billings, Alan. *Making God Possible: The Task of Ordained Ministry Present and Future*. London: SPCK, 2010.

Brown, Rosalind. *Being a Deacon Today*. Norwich: Canterbury, 2005; Harrisburg: Morehouse, 2005.

Burns, Bob, Tasha Chapman, and Donald Guthrie. *Resilient Ministry:*

What Pastors Told Us about Surviving and Thriving. Downers Grove: IVP Books, 2013.

Caminer, Matthew. *A Clergy Husband's Survival Guide*. London: SPCK, 2012.

Cocksworth, C., and R. Brown. *On Being a Priest Today*. Norwich: Canterbury, 2002; Cambridge: Cowley, 2004.

Coles, Richard. *Bringing in the Sheaves: Wheat and Chaff from My Years as a Priest*. London: Weidenfeld & Nicholson, 2016.

Coles, Richard. *Fathomless Riches: Or How I Went from Pop to Pulpit*. London: Weidenfeld & Nicholson, 2014.

Croft, Stephen. *Ministry in Three Dimensions*. London: DLT, 1999; rev. ed., 2008.

Ellis, James. *Tell the Truth, Shame the Devil: Stories about the Challenges of Young Pastors*. Macon, GA: Smyth & Helwys, 2015.

Farnham, Suzanne G., and Timothy H. Grayson. *Keeping in Tune with God: Listening Hearts Discernment for Clergy*. Harrisburg, PA: Morehouse, 2011.

Foss, Michael W. *Reviving the Congregation: Pastoral Leadership in a Changing Context*. Minneapolis: Fortress, 2014.

Gula, Richard M. *Just Ministry: Professional Ethics for Pastoral Ministers*. New York: Paulist Press, 2010.

Hoyle, David. *The Pattern of Our Calling: Ministry Yesterday, Today and Tomorrow*. London: SCM, 2016.

Lindner, Cynthia G. *Varieties of Gifts: Multiplicity and the Well-Lived Pastoral Life*. Lanham: Rowman & Littlefield, 2016.

Markham, Ian S., and Oran E. Warder. *An Introduction to Ministry: A Primer for Renewed Life and Leadership in Mainline Protestant Congregations*. Malden, MA: Wiley-Blackwell, 2016.

Mason, George. *Preparing the Pastors We Need: Reclaiming the Congregation's Role in Training Clergy*. Herndon, VA: Alban Institute, 2012.

Olsen, David C. *Saying No to Say Yes: Everyday Boundaries and Pastoral Excellence*. Lanham: Rowman and Littlefield, 2015.

Percy, Emma. *What Clergy Do: Especially When It Looks Like Nothing*. London: SPCK, 2014.

Pritchard, John. *The Life and Work of a Priest*. London: SPCK, 2007.

Ramsey, Michael. *The Christian Priest Today*. Eugene, OR: Wipf and Stock, 2012.

Rowling, Cathy, and Paula Gooder. *Reader Ministry Explored*. London: SPCK, 2011.

Sorensen, Sue, and William H. Willimon. *The Collar: Reading Christian Ministry in Fiction, Television, and Film*. Eugene, OR: Cascade Books, 2014.

Threlfall-Holmes, Miranda. *Being a Chaplain*. London: SPCK, 2011.

Tomkinson, Raymond. *Called to Love: Discernment, Decision Making and Ministry*. London: SCM, 2012.

Ward, Robin. *On Christian Priesthood*. London, New York: Continuum, 2011.

Wheeler, Sondra Ely. *The Minister as Moral Theologian: Ethical Dimensions of Pastoral Leadership*. Grand Rapids: Baker Academic, 2017.

Willimon, William H. *Pastor: The Theology and Practice of Ordained Ministry*. Revised edition. Nashville: Abingdon, 2016.

On particular churches and denominations

ANGLICANISM, THE CHURCH OF ENGLAND AND THE EPISCOPAL CHURCH IN THE USA

Brown, Andrew, and Linda Woodhead. *That Was the Church That Was: How the Church of England Lost the English People*. London: Bloomsbury, 2016.

Chapman, Mark. *Anglicanism: A Very Short Introduction*. Oxford: Oxford University Press, 2006.

Chartres, Caroline, ed. *Why I Am Still an Anglican*. London: Continuum, 2006.

Countryman, Louis William. *Living on the Border of the Holy: Renewing the Priesthood of All*. Harrisburg: Morehouse, 1999.

Cox, R. David. *Priesthood in a New Millennium: Toward an Understanding of Anglican Presbyterate in the Twenty-First Century*. New York: Church Publishing, 2004.

Davie, Martin. *A Guide to the Church of England*. London: Mowbray, 2008.

Furlong, Monica. *The C of E: The State It's In*. London: Hodder & Stoughton, 2000; 2nd ed. 2006.

Hawkins, J. Barney. *Episcopal Etiquette and Ethics: Living the Craft of Priesthood in the Episcopal Church*. New York: Morehouse, 2012.

Humphrey, N. J. A. *Gathering the Next Generation: Essays on the Formation and Ministry of Gen X Priests*. Harrisburg: Morehouse, 2000.

Thompsett, Fredrica Harris, ed. *Looking Forward, Looking Backward: Forty Years of Women's Ordination*. New York: Morehouse, 2014.

Wells, Samuel. *What Anglicans Believe*. Norwich: Canterbury, 2011; US ed.: *What Episcopalians Believe*. New York: Morehouse, 2011.

For an enjoyable account of the history, theology, and spirituality of the Church of England through the twentieth century, read the Starbridge novels of Susan Howatch, based around Salisbury, and the follow-up three volumes set in the Barbican, London, during the turn of the millennium; similarly, the more recent novels by Catherine Fox, drawing on Cambridge and Durham and the imaginary Diocese of Lindchester, provide an up-to-date and very funny account of the current life of the Church of England.

DISCIPLES OF CHRIST

Hunter, Victor L. *Desert Hearts and Healing Fountains: Gaining Pastoral Vocational Clarity*. St. Louis: Chalice, 2003.

Sprinkle, Stephen. *Ordination: Celebrating the Gift of Ministry*. St. Louis: Chalice, 2004.

EVANGELICAL LUTHERAN CHURCH IN AMERICA

Black, Gary. *Exploring the Life and Calling*. Foundations for Learning. Minneapolis: Fortress, 2014.

Evangelical Lutheran Church in America. *Candidacy Manual* (November 2016): http://download.elca.org/ELCA%20Resource%20Repository/Candidacy_Manual_2017.pdf?_ga=2.132503757.2110613236.1518123006-463898216.1517881327.

Evangelical Lutheran Church in America. *Vision and Expectations: Associates in Ministry, Deaconesses and Diaconal Ministers in the Evangelical Lutheran Church in America*. Chicago: Evangelical Lutheran Church in America, 2010. http://download.elca.org/ELCA%20Resource%20Repository/Vision_and_Expectations_for_Rostered_Lay_Ministers.pdf?_ga=2.32378366.1348835913.1535403705-1848542806.1535403705.

Evangelical Lutheran Church in America. *Vision and Expectations: Ordained Ministers in the Evangelical Lutheran Church in America*. Chicago: Evangelical Lutheran Church in America, 2010. http://download.elca.org/ELCA%20Resource%20Repository/Vision_and_Ex

pectations_for_Ordained_Ministers.pdf?_ga=2.225837146.1348835913
.1535403705-1848542806.1535403705.

Goetting, Paul F. *Members Are Ministers: The Vocation of All Believers*. Eugene, OR: Cascade Books, 2012.

Reumann, John Henry Paul. *Ministries Examined: Laity, Clergy, Women, and Bishops in a Time of Change*. Minneapolis: Augsburg, 1987.

United Methodist Church

Lassiat, Meg. *The Christian as Minister: An Exploration into the Meaning of God's Call and the Ways the United Methodist Church Offers to Live Out That Call*. Nashville: General Board of Higher Education and Ministry, 2013.

Lawrence, William B. *Ordained Ministry in the United Methodist Church*. Nashville: General Board of Higher Education and Ministry, 2011.

Lyght, Ernest S., Glory E. Dharmaraj, and Jacob S. Dharmaraj. *Many Faces, One Church: A Manual for Cross-Racial and Cross-Cultural Ministry*. Nashville: Abingdon, 2006.

Pieterse, Hendrik R., Mark Wesley Stamm, Grant Hagiya, Ted Campbell, Benjamin L. Hartley, and Jeffrey Gros. *The Orders of Ministry: Problems and Prospects*. Nashville: General Board of Higher Education and Ministry, 2007.

On prayer and spirituality

Barton, Ruth Haley. *Strengthening the Soul of Your Leadership: Seeking God in the Crucible of Ministry*. 2nd ed. Downers Grove: IVP Books, 2018.

Conkling, Kelly Schneider. *Prayer of the Heart: A Journey through the HeART with Visual Prayer*. Harrisburg: Morehouse, 2006.

Eldredge, John. *Moving Mountains: Praying with Passion, Confidence, and Authority*. Nashville: Nelson Books, an imprint of Thomas Nelson, 2016.

Hughes, Gerard, SJ. *God in All Things*. London: Hodder & Stoughton, 2003.

Hughes, Gerard, SJ. *God of Surprises*. 3rd ed. London: DLT, 2008; Grand Rapids: Eerdmans, 2008.

Hughes, Gerard, SJ. *In Search of a Way*. London: DLT, 1980; New York: Image, 1980.

Martin, James. *In All Seasons, for All Reasons: Praying Throughout the Year.* Collegeville, MN: Liturgical Press, 2017.

Mayne, Michael. *The Enduring Melody.* London: DLT, 2011.

Mayne, Michael. *Prayer.* London: DLT, 2013.

Mayne, Michael. *This Sunrise of Wonder.* London: DLT, 2008.

Mayne, Michael. *A Year Lost and Found.* London: DLT, 2007.

McBeth, Sybil. *Praying in Color: Drawing a New Path to God.* Brewster, MA: Paraclete, 2007.

Pritchard, John. *How Do I Pray?* London: SPCK, 2015; New York: Church Publishing, 2018.

Pritchard, John. *How to Pray.* London: SPCK, 2002, 2011.

Pritchard, John. *Living Faithfully.* London: SPCK, 2013.

Ramon, Brother, SSF. *Deeper into God: A Handbook on Spiritual Retreats.* Basingstoke: Marshall Pickering, 1987; Grand Rapids: Zondervan, 1987.

Ramon, Brother, SSF. *Franciscan Spirituality: Following St. Francis Today.* London: SPCK, 2008.

Ramon, Brother, SSF. *The Heart of Prayer.* London: Marshall Pickering, 1995.

Ramon, Brother, SSF. *Heaven on Earth: A Personal Retreat Guide.* London: Marshall Pickering, 1991.

Ramshaw, Gail. *Praying for the Whole World: A Handbook for Intercessors.* Minneapolis: Augsburg Fortress, 2016.

Rose, Margaret, et al., eds. *Lifting Women's Voices: Prayers to Change the World.* Harrisburg: Morehouse, 2009.

Rowell, Geoffrey, et al., compilers. *Love's Redeeming Work: The Anglican Quest for Holiness.* Oxford: Oxford University Press, 2001.

Wilder, Ginny. *All My Words Have Holes in Them: Simple Daily Meditations.* New York: Church Publishing, 2017.

Williams, Rowan. *Holy Living: The Christian Tradition for Today.* London: Bloomsbury, 2017.

Wright, J. Robert, ed. *Prayer Book Spirituality: A Devotional Companion to the Book of Common Prayer Compiled from Classical Anglican Sources.* New York: Church Hymnal Corporation, 1989.

Introductions to the Bible and theology

Bell, Rob. *Velvet Elvis: Repainting the Christian Faith.* Grand Rapids: Zondervan, 2005.

Billings, J. Todd. *The Word of God for the People of God: An Entryway to the Theological Interpretation of Scripture*. Grand Rapids: Eerdmans, 2010.

Burridge, Richard A. *Four Gospels, One Jesus? A Symbolic Reading*. London: SPCK, 1994, 2005; classic ed., 2013; 3rd ed., Grand Rapids: Eerdmans, 2014.

Ford, David. *Theology: A Very Short Introduction*. Oxford: Oxford University Press, 1999; 2nd ed., 2013.

Green, Joel B. *Practicing Theological Interpretation: Engaging Biblical Texts for Faith and Formation*. Grand Rapids: Baker Academic, 2011.

Green, Joel B., and Tim Meadowcroft, eds. *Ears That Hear: Explorations in Theological Interpretation of the Bible*. Sheffield: Sheffield Phoenix, 2013.

Holcomb, Justin S., ed. *Christian Theologies of Scripture: A Comparative Introduction*. New York: New York University Press, 2006.

Kapic, Kelly M. *Reading Christian Theology in the Protestant Tradition*. New York: Bloomsbury Academic, 2018.

Lathrop, Gordon. *Saving Images: The Presence of the Bible in Christian Liturgy*. Minneapolis: Fortress, 2017.

Markham, Ian S. *Understanding Christian Doctrine*. 2nd ed. Hoboken, NJ: John Wiley and Sons, 2017.

McGrath, Alister. *Theology: The Basics*. Oxford: Blackwell, 2004; Hoboken, NJ: John Wiley and Sons, 2018.

O'Day, Gail R., and David L. Petersen, eds. *Theological Bible Commentary*. Louisville: Westminster John Knox, 2009.

Sonderegger, Katherine. *Systematic Theology*. Minneapolis: Fortress, 2015.

Walton, John H. *Old Testament Theology for Christians: From Ancient Context to Enduring Belief*. Downers Grove: InterVarsity, 2017.

Ward, Keith. *Christianity: A Short Introduction*. London: SPCK, 2000.

Warner, Meg. *Abraham: A Journey through Lent*. London: SPCK, 2016.

Williams, Rowan. *On Christian Theology*. Oxford, Malden, MA: Blackwell, 1999.

On knowing yourself, and pastoral ministry and relationships

Goldsmith, Malcolm, and Martin Wharton. *Knowing Me—Knowing You: Exploring Personality Type and Temperament*. London: SPCK, 1993, 2004.

Jacobs, Michael. *Still, Small Voice*. London: SPCK, 2001.

Jacobs, Michael. *Swift to Hear*. London: SPCK, 2000.

Lamdin, Keith. *Finding Your Leadership Style: A Guide for Ministers.* London: SPCK, 2012.

Oliver, Gordon. *Holy Bible, Human Bible: Questions Pastoral Practice Must Ask.* London: SPCK, 2006; Grand Rapids: Eerdmans, 2006.

Oliver, Gordon. *Ministry without Madness.* London: SPCK, 2012.

Osborne, Graham. *Be a Better Leader: Personality Type and Difference in Ministry.* London: SPCK, 2016.

There are doubtless many more books and resources I could recommend, or things to suggest, but perhaps it is best to leave the last word to the wise old Preacher from Ecclesiastes:

> Of anything beyond these, my child, beware. Of making many books there is no end, and much study is a weariness of the flesh. The end of the matter; all has been heard. Fear God, and keep his commandments; for that is the whole duty of everyone. For God will bring every deed into judgment, including every secret thing, whether good or evil. (Eccl. 12:12–14)

Index

Note: Page numbers in **bold** indicate significant or detailed treatments.